5⁰⁰

No Condemnation

OTHER BOOKS BY THE AUTHOR

Help! I'm a Parent
A Guide to Child Rearing
You Can Be a Better Parent
An Ounce of Prevention
The Power of Positive Parenting
Why Children Misbehave: A Guide to Positive Parenting
You're Someone Special
Parenting With Love and Limits
The Integration of Psychology and Theology:
   An Introduction (co-author)

No Condemnation

S. BRUCE NARRAMORE

Academie
Books

Grand Rapids,
Michigan

Zondervan Publishing House

No Condemnation
Copyright © 1984 by The Zondervan Corporation
Grand Rapids, Michigan

Academie Books are printed by Zondervan
Publishing House, 1415 Lake Drive, S.E.,
Grand Rapids, Michigan 49506

Library of Congress Cataloging in Publication Data

Narramore, S. Bruce.
  No condemnation.

  Bibliography: p.
  1. Guilt—Religious aspects—Christianity.
  2. Conscience—Religious aspects—Christianity.
  I. Title.

BJ1471.5.N37	1983	241'.1	83-14570

ISBN 0-310-30401-6

Edited by Ben Chapman
Designed by Louise Bauer

Printed in the United States of America

86 87 88 89 90 / 10 9 8 7 6 5 4

To my colleagues at Rosemead School of Psychology for their years of personal and professional stimulation.

Contents

Acknowledgments

I would like to express my deep appreciation to the many faculty and students at Biola University who have contributed to this work. For the past several years, doctoral students at the Rosemead School of Psychology at Biola have read and reacted to early drafts of this manuscript. Their discerning questions and thoughtful input have been of immense help in clarifying key issues and concepts.

Special words of thanks go to Dr. John Carter, Dr. Bill Edkins, and Dr. Denise Thomas, colleagues at Rosemead who read all or parts of the manuscript and offered helpful input on psychological and integrative issues. Dr. Bing Hunter of Talbot Theological Seminary, Dr. Curtis Mitchell and Dr. Harry Sturz of the School of Arts, Sciences and Professions at Biola University, and Dr. Ray Andersen of Fuller Theological Seminary have also made valuable contributions with their careful theological readings of the manuscript. Joan Jones went above and beyond the call of duty by not only typing the entire manuscript but by offering insightful suggestions and developing the index. Although none of these individuals can be held responsible for weaknesses that remain, they have all made major contributions to whatever strengths this book has.

The main draft of this manuscript was completed during a sabbatical study leave from Biola University. The University's support in providing the leave and the secretarial assistance for this project are deeply appreciated.

Part 1

The Repression of Guilt

In proclaiming freedom from our spiritual and moral heritage our psychologically sophisticated society has minimized the impact of feelings of guilt. Psychologists and counselors have substituted anxiety for guilt as the cause of maladjustment; consequently, the responsibility has been shifted from the individual to the environment. Christian counselors have been so influenced by this thinking that they also tend to overlook the pervasive presence of guilt as a cause of personal maladjustment. Part 1 attempts to unmask the hidden guilt operating in each of our lives and suggests that guilt feelings play an equally prominent role with anxiety in causing psychological maladjustments. This part also explores the relationship between sin and psychopathology.

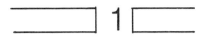

Touched by Guilt

> Hounded by nagging guilt? Get rid of it the modern way, the same way you eliminate underarm wetness, bad breath, or limp curls. Spray it away with "Guilt Away."[1]

That's the idea Mike Corning and Craig Bersma came up with while nursing hangovers during a sailing trip. Trading jokes about guilt, they decided the world needed a modern way to get a handle on it. So they returned home, founded Corn-Berg Laboratories, and are now selling eight-ounce spray bottles of rose water in stores throughout America. One bottle is sitting on the shelf of my study—a gift from a student who knew I was working on this book!

Guilt Away's "invention" reveals an important truth about human nature. In spite of our psychological sophistication and alleged freedom, feelings of guilt continue to be a universal experience. In fact, it is *so* common the inventors of Guilt Away planned to sell a million bottles (at $3.98) in their first year of operation!

THE SEASONING OF LIFE

I had been a practicing psychologist for several years before I realized the vast influence of feelings of guilt. Until that time I saw guilt feelings largely as a problem for depressed and obsessive-compulsive personalities—the so-called guilt neuroses. In depressed persons I had encountered the harsh, self-condemning

---

[1]The Seattle *Times*, "Guilty? Spray Away" (December 27, 1980).

attitudes that drive 21,000 United States citizens to suicide annually. And in obsessive-compulsive persons I had seen the haunting self-doubts, cautious inhibitions, and restricted lifestyles that produced constant pressure. But I had not recognized guilt as the wide-spread problem that it really is.

As I gained clinical experience I began to recognize that more people were troubled by guilt than I had realized. Their guilt was hidden. I found that some people who were never able to "get their act together" and achieve academic, vocational, or marital success were troubled by guilt. Feeling undeserving of success (because of guilt), they repeatedly involved themselves in situations doomed to failure. Some sabotaged their consciously hoped-for success by selecting mates who repeated the neurotic relationship they had with their parents or a previous spouse. Others set up a no-win situation with their employer. The woman who runs through two or three marriages with abusive husbands is a classic example. You would think she would be careful after a bad experience or two but instead she selects a carbon copy of her first spouse. She seems to have a desire to be mistreated and in fact she does. Since she does not believe she is deserving of a loving husband, she searches out men who make her suffer.[2]

As I became more sensitive to the problem of guilt feelings, I found that they weren't limited to pathological personalities. Doesn't close observation reveal that even "healthy" people occasionally experience guilt or at least use it to motivate others? We tell our spouses, "You *never* spend any time with the family!" We question our friends with, "You're not leaving *already* are you?" Or we say to a waiter, *"Oh no!* What do you mean you don't have your special soup? We drove an hour across town just so our guests could try your chowder!" We accuse others hoping to instill

---

[2]A similar dynamic sometimes operates in individuals with physical symptoms. Their pain is a way of punishing themselves for perceived failures and misdeeds. Psychiatrist James Knight writes: "Involved in a hypochondriacal system are depreciation, guilt, unworthiness, and usually satisfaction in self-punishment. Such patients have a strong sense of right and wrong and may seek punishment in handling their guilt. A frequent unconscious mechanism in them is an attempt to provoke the doctor to punish them. The more painful the treatment, the better the therapy works for these patients" (*Conscience and Guilt* [New York: Appleton-Century-Crofts, 1969], pp. 96-97).

feelings of guilt so they will either give us what we want or suffer pangs of conscience.

Sometimes our inability to accept praise or compliments grows out of guilt. Because we feel undeserving, we pass off praise or squirm uncomfortably when a compliment comes our way. As Allison put it,

> Many of us feel embarrassed when we are complimented, when people say nice things about us. We find ourselves strangely ill at ease when something wonderful happens to us, as though we did not deserve it. Guilt tends to rob the self of any sense of well being and does not allow us to enjoy fully our health, wealth, and well being while we have them.[3]

Many parents experience guilt over their children. They condemn themselves for every real or imagined failure, read every book available, attend every seminar that comes through town, and try to be perfect parents. Some are so overwhelmed by their own guilt that they blame their children. "It's *their* fault," they say. "We did the best we could and they can't blame *us* for *their* hangups!" Since no parent is perfect, most of us have at least a few qualms of conscience about our relations with our children.

The recent shift in male/female roles has caught some married women in a dilemma. Working outside the home, they feel guilty for "neglecting" their families, breaking away from their traditional role, or "being selfish." But if these women stay home, they feel a sense of guilt for "failing to develop themselves" or being "just a housewife"!

Adults are not the only sufferers of guilt, however. Children feel guilt too. Parents and teachers have ingenious ways of saying things like, "You're not going out looking like *that*, are you?" "I've told you a thousand times!" or "After all I've done for *you!*" And our children return the favor with accusations like, "*Everybody* else gets to go!" "*Everyone* else gets to stay out that late!" and "You *never* let us do *anything!*" All such statements communicate, "You *should* feel badly (guilty) for not doing as I wish." Even after children grow up and begin their own families, guilt is frequent in family dialogue. Older parents write, "*Why* don't you call (or write,

---

[3]C. Allison, *Guilt, Anger and God* (New York: Seabury, 1972), p. 12.

or visit) more often?" "Aunt Mary is *still* waiting to hear from you." or "We *never* see you any more!"

A friend recently handed me this portion of a letter from her sixty-five year old mother:

> We hope you are feeling better. We figure you must be in the hospital since we can never reach you. Your "old aging" parents are concerned about you and worry when we don't hear from you more often!

Because this woman felt unloved and neglected, she resorted to the only means she knew to gain her daughter's attention—making her feel guilty! Unfortunately this maneuver usually backfires. It creates more resentment than concern. Recipients of these letters tend to write even less frequently or, when they do write, do it more to relieve their guilt feelings than to express their love and interest! Russ, the twenty-three-year-old son of a guilt-inducing minister told me how as an adolescent he would go on a drinking binge, raise a beer to his lips, and say, "Here's one for the deacons' board!" His experience with a guilt-inducing father who put the ministry ahead of his family gave Russ reason to rebel and he did it.

In his very helpful analysis of guilt, Paul Tournier suggests:

> ... a guilty conscience is the seasoning of our daily life. All upbringing is a cultivation of the sense of guilt on an intensive scale. Especially the best education, that by parents who are most anxious about the moral training of their children and their success in life. It consists above all in scolding; and all scolding, even if it is only discreet and silent reprobations, suggests the feeling of guilt. "Are you not ashamed to behave like that?"[4]

Then Tournier goes on to point out how guilt is reflected in our handling of money (We *should* have sufficient but we *should not* have too much!), in illness (I *shouldn't* be sick!), in matters of time (I'm late *again*!), in difficult choices (I *should* write this book but I *should* be with my family), in embarrassment (Look what I've done!), and in unfinished work (I *should* have finished!). Concluding his survey of the extent of guilt, Tournier challenges his colleagues:

[4]Paul Tournier, *Guilt and Grace* (New York: Harper & Row, 1962), p. 10.

> Open your eyes! and ... see among your patients that huge
> crowd of wounded, distressed, crushed men and women laden
> with secret guilts, real or false, definite or vague; even a sort of
> guilt at being alive, which is more common than we think.[5]

Because I have become increasingly sensitive to these subtle
and often hidden expressions of guilt, I would say we need to
open our eyes not only to guilt in our patients and parishoners,
but also to the guilt in our own lives and the lives of our friends
and colleagues. As counselors, pastors, therapists, and physicians
we face guilt when we are not as helpful as we would like to be—
a patient takes his life, a parishoner leaves the church, a marriage
falls apart, or a counselee shows little growth or progress. Although we may attempt to blame these failures on a difficult life
situation, a lack of commitment, an impossible marriage partner,
or therapeutic resistance, don't we still feel a sense of responsibility and a tinge of guilt? We all at least occasionally struggle with
the awareness that we are not all that we want to be, and this
awareness is generally accompanied by feelings of guilt. Truly, guilt
is "the seasoning of our daily life."

A THERAPIST'S DILEMMA

As I was beginning to understand the widespread influence of
guilt I was also challenged to reevaluate my understanding of the
role of guilt and conscience in the Christian life. I grew up believing that guilt feelings were the voice of God designed to lead
us to repentance and constructive Christian living. As a child,
when I committed an obvious sin I felt guilty and assumed this
was divine conviction. In fact, I grew up believing guilt was one
of God's major means of motivating His children to desired behavior.
During my undergraduate study of psychology I began to
realize that guilt was not necessarily a constructive motivation,
and that it could actually be seriously debilitating.[6] I was also in-

---

[5]Ibid., p. 60.

[6]My graduate psychology professors either neglected the topic of guilt entirely or saw it as a highly negative emotion, a kind of masochism resulting from
overly strict religious training. In contrast, my seminary professors tended to
equate feelings of guilt with divine conviction.

troduced to the theory that there are two sources of guilt and that only one of these is divine. I came to believe there was a true guilt that comes from God as a consequence of violating divine standards and a false (neurotic) guilt that comes from one's own misinformed conscience, parental upbringing, or misguided social conditioning.

I began my practice as a Christian psychotherapist with this view of guilt. I assumed some individuals were experiencing feelings of guilt resulting from divine conviction while others were experiencing similar feelings because their parents had been excessively critical, condemning, or judgmental. Since I worked in a Christian psychological clinic, the majority of my clients were professing Christians. Many were troubled with guilt, depression, and inadequate self-esteem. I repeatedly saw the negative, inhibiting effects of guilt. Guilt undercut these people's self-esteem and self-acceptance. It brought harsh, punitive, self-criticisms. It robbed them of enjoyment, and it made much of their Christian experience miserable.

Paradoxically, many of these guilt-troubled people were among the most active and committed Christians in their communities. Their guilt would have made sense if their lives were filled with dishonesty and duplicity or if they cared little about Christian commitment. But just the opposite was true. Many were pastors, missionaries, and active lay workers. They had a good deal of biblical knowledge and were serious about their Christian lives. They desired to live constructively and most of them had not committed any "major" sins. But for some reason they could not throw off the shackles of their self-condemning thoughts. Repeated confessions brought only temporary relief and sometimes even magnified their self-devaluations.

To this psychic battle ground I brought my understanding of true and false guilt. I assumed some of my patients were in need of confession to the Lord or to someone they had offended. Their guilt was a God-given means of motivation. And I assumed others needed to track down the childhood sources of their overly-strict or self-condemning attitudes. Their guilt was neurotic, inhibitory, or false. After a few years of practice, however, I started questioning these assumptions. As I thought back over my counseling experiences, I had to admit that I could not remember any instance where guilt feelings had a truly beneficial influence in a patient's life. I saw instead the anxiety, inhibitions, and withdrawal guilt caused. I saw the rebellion it stirred in some adolescents and young adults who had been reared in religious homes. But I could not find any positive effects. I knew of patients who, after a period of emotional guilt, grew and moved in positive directions. But I wasn't sure whether the growth was because of or in spite of the experience of guilty feelings.

With the growing awareness of the role guilt played in psychological maladjustments I had a desire to begin an intensive study of the whole concept of guilt and conscience—both biblically and psychologically. That study led me to question two assumptions held by many Christians. The first is the belief that many (if not all) guilt feelings either come from God or are somehow ordained by Him. The second is the belief that guilt feelings are a helpful form of motivation. I have now come to believe that not only are guilt feelings destructive, they are diametrically opposed to a scriptural view of motivation and actually reflect our own independent efforts to solve the problem of sin in our lives. They actually pose a barrier to spiritual growth and maturity rather than being an incentive for it! This book is a result of that study.

AN EVANGELICAL VOID

More than twenty years ago Paul Meehl and a group of Lutheran theologians and mental health professionals produced one of the first serious attempts at relating Christian theology to the data and theories of psychology. In *What, Then Is Man?* they stressed the absolute necessity of working out a unified Christian psychological understanding of at least six basic issues if a truly helpful perspective on the relationship of psychology and theology was to be reached.

> We are prepared to state firmly that he who does not come to terms with such theoretical problems as determinism, guilt, original sin, materialist monism, conscience, and conversion cannot even begin to work out a cognitive approachment between Christian theology and the secular sciences of behavior.[7]

[7] P. Meehl, ed., *What, Then Is Man?* (St. Louis: Concordia, 1958), p. 5.

In the two decades since this declaration hundreds of books and articles have been penned on the relationship of psychology and Christianity. Unfortunately, very few have grappled in depth with the issues Meehl and his colleagues so clearly set before us. Nowhere is this more true than in the study of guilt and conscience. In a time when secular psychologists[8] have been pursuing both research and theoretical understandings of guilt the Christian community has been largely silent. We have a few stimulating writings from Catholic[9] and liberal Protestant[10] perspectives. And we have a number of books for laypersons that touch on guilt and self-esteem.[11] But the only relatively in-depth book from an orthodox Protestant perspective is Tournier's *Guilt and Grace*.[12] And while Tournier provides penetrating insights into the phenomenology of guilt and brings the implications of God's grace to bear on the problem, he does not attempt to present a biblical understanding of the nature and functioning of conscience. Nor does he critically review alternative secular viewpoints, develop a careful conceptual analysis of the nature and origin of guilt, or suggest specific therapeutic implications of his conceptualizations.[13] This book is designed to help fill those gaps. It is written primarily for

[8]See, e.g., G. Piers and M. Singer, *Shame and Guilt: A Psychoanalytic and Cultural Study* (New York: Norton, 1971); E. Becker, *The Denial of Death* (New York: Free Press, 1973); L. Kohlberg, "Development of Moral Character and Moral Ideology," *Review of Child Development Research*, vol. 1, pp. 383-427 (New York: Russell Sage Foundation, 1964); H. Lewis, *Shame and Guilt in Neurosis* (New York: International Universities Press, 1971); and D. Mosher, "Sex, Guilt, and Premarital Sexual Experiences of College Students," *Journal of Consulting and Clinical Psychology*, vol. 36 (1), Feb., 1971, pp. 7-32.

[9]E. Nelson, ed., *Conscience: Theological and Psychological Perspectives* (New York: Newman 1973).

[10]C. Allison, *Guilt, Anger and God*; E. Stein, *Guilt: Theory and Therapy* (Philadelphia: Westminster, 1968).

[11]W. Counts and B. Narramore, *Freedom From Guilt* (Santa Ana, Calif.: Harvest House, 1974); W. Justice, *Guilt: The Source and the Solution* (Wheaton: Tyndale, 1981; and M. Wagner, *The Sensation of Being Somebody* (Grand Rapids: Zondervan, 1976).

[12]Paul Tournier, *Guilt and Grace*, 1962.

[13]Tournier's apparent universalism and his failure to distinguish clearly between God's universal love and His forgiveness based upon personal appropriation of Christ's atonement also pose significant theological problems for Evangelicals.

, mental health professionals, pastors and Christian workers, and students of psychology and theology. It is also written for laypersons with a serious interest in feelings of guilt.

Since our understanding of guilt grows out of our understanding of the nature of man and the problems of sin and psychopathology, many of the concepts we will be developing attempt to relate biblical and psychological facts about personal maladjustment. Consequently, although my original intent was simply to address the problem of guilt, I have found it necessary to address some broader questions regarding the nature of psychological maladjustment and its relationship to sin. I have also enlarged my discussion to include several chapters on counseling and an appendix on alternatives to using guilt in parenting and preaching. While these chapters focus especially on guilt they also address the larger problem of what is unique about Christian counseling and psychotherapy.

In some ways, then, this book has turned out to have a much larger scope than I intended. It is not simply a study of guilt. It is also an attempt to formulate some of the key issues involved in relating biblical concepts of sin and sanctification to the psychological concepts of maladjustment and psychotherapy. In examining the function of guilt I have found it necessary to look at alternative forms of motivation—expecially those positive ones growing out of the dynamic of love. Consequently several major portions of this book address the broad issue of biblical motivation.

My primary goal, however, is to present a biblically-based understanding of guilt and conscience that has relevance for counselors and pastors. A dozen years spent in the training of doctoral level psychologists have convinced me that a clear understanding of guilt and conscience is one of the most basic prerequisites of effective counseling. Three decades of experience in the Christian community have also convinced me that in spite of our intellectual knowledge of the role of confession and forgiveness in the Christian life, many Christians are experiencing no more freedom from guilt than non-Christians. Consequently guilt remains a live issue in the Christian community and one that needs a great deal of clarification if we are to receive the full fruits of the freedom promised us through Christ.

IS GUILT FROM GOD?

As I studied the dynamics of guilt and conscience I soon realized how many problems in the Christian life relate to guilt. The discouraged, defeated Christian, the perpetual altar-goer who never feels secure in his Christian life, the religious legalist who rigidly orders his own life and finds it easier to condemn others than to love them, and the rebellious adolescent from a highly religious home have all been touched by guilt. So, too, have many who have lost the vitality they once had in their Christian faith and who have seen that love replaced by religious ritual and orthodoxy devoid of personal meaning. In fact, I became convinced that the guilt feelings experienced by some Christians are actually compounded by a misunderstanding of the biblical role of guilt and conscience in the Christian life.

Instead of realizing that the processes we know as guilt and conscience were distorted by the Fall, we tend to accept them as divine conviction. Consequently we heap unneeded condemnation on ourselves and other sensitive people and impose a burden that interferes with the freedom we could have in Christ. In the following pages I will attempt to point out this very common yet serious abuse of guilt and conscience and offer a biblical alternative.

Since an understanding of guilt and conscience is central to a proper theological understanding of humanity, I hope that students of theology and laypersons will also find these pages interesting. To that end, I have purposely kept psychological jargon to a minimum. The only technical language included is in the discussion of psychoanalytic views of guilt in chapter seven. Readers with limited interest in psychological views may want to skip chapters seven, eight, and nine and move directly to the discussion of guilt and conscience from the biblical point of view in chapters ten through seventeen.

AN OVERVIEW OF THE BOOK

To present a comprehensive understanding of guilt, I will begin part 1 by describing the emotion we know as guilt and showing the subtle forms of its appearance. Then I will discuss guilt as it relates to anxiety, the Fall, and psychological maladjustment.

Part 2 summarizes the essential features of three commonly held psychological perspectives on guilt and conscience. This section focuses on the views of Sigmund Freud, Erich Fromm, and Hobart Mowrer. Part 3 explains the biblical view of guilt and suggests an alternative to some common Christian misconceptions about guilt and conscience. Part 4 is a biblical study of conscience and integrates the biblical understanding of guilt and conscience with a dynamic view of personality development and psychopathology. Part 5 discusses the therapy of guilt.[14]

[14]I have neither attempted to present an apologetic for the Christian faith nor to develop the foundations for each biblical concept or doctrine discussed. Since I am writing primarily for those interested in relating Scripture to a psychological understanding of guilt and personal adjustment, I have assumed a basic familiarity with the Bible. Readers interested in an apologetic may find these volumes helpful: B. Ramm, *The Christian View of Science and Scripture* (Grand Rapids: Eerdmans, 1954); E. Carnell, *An Introduction to Christian Apologetics* (Grand Rapids: Eerdmans, 1948). Those interested in a survey of basic Christian beliefs may find helpful background for the application and integration of biblical doctrine and psychological understanding in: John Stott, *Basic Christianity* (Grand Rapids: Eerdmans, 1971).

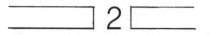

Guilt and Self-esteem

We will begin our study by describing the essential features, or components, of the emotion of guilt. At this point we will be dealing strictly with psychological guilt—the feeling, or emotion, of guilt. In later chapters we will turn our attention to the relationship of these guilt feelings to both the objective condition of guilt, or sin, and *godly sorrow,* a biblical alternative to guilt feelings.

THE NATURE OF GUILT

In spite of the many different views of professional psychologists and counselors one thread of agreement runs through almost every discussion of guilt feelings. This agreement is on the feelings that one experiences in connection with guilt and the thoughts that underlie or accompany these feelings.

Nearly every author describes guilt as a painful inner feeling involving some sort of self-punishment, rejection, or disesteem. Charles Brenner, an orthodox psychoanalyst, speaks of *"penalties and punishments," "feelings of inferiority or lowered self-esteem,"* and *"disapproval."*[1] Jay Adams, a proponent of nouthetic counseling, speaks of *"the misery of alienation,"* the "depressing *shame* of a guilt conscience," and *"painful* inner sensations."[2] From widely divergent theoretical perspectives, both of these authors allude to self-punishment, self-rejection, and disesteem (shame or inferiority) as key ingredients of guilt. In agreement with these and

[1]Charles Brenner, *An Elementary Textbook of Psychoanalysis* (Garden City: Anchor Press, 1965), pp. 134-35.

[2]Jay Adams, *Competent to Counsel* (Nutley, N. J.: Presbyterian and Reformed, 1972), pp. 212-13.

other authors,[3] I would define guilt as *a complex cognitive-emotional reaction we experience over the disparity between who we are (or how we act) and who (or how) we think we ought to be. This reaction may involve self-punishment, self-rejection, and a sense of shame, disesteem, or inferiority.* Here are some ways clients have described their experience of psychological guilt.

Self-Inflicted Punishment

> "My mind has a tendency to kick itself several times."
> "I feel like if somebody finds out, I'll be punished and they will scream what I've done to everyone."
> "I feel like I deserve to die."

Shame or a Loss of Self-Esteem

> "I feel like a raunchy person."
> "I feel stupid, low, and remorseful."
> "I feel rotten inside; worthless."

Feelings of Isolation and Rejection

> "I find it hard to like myself."
> "I feel that nobody could love me—especially God."
> "I feel depressed and separated from others."

Since we vary greatly in our emotional lives, some of us experience guilt essentially as self-punishment, others as shame, and still others as self-rejection or isolation.[4] Based on our differing developmental experiences, some of us have few problems with self-punishment but are terribly bothered by a sense of shame

---

[3]David Ausubel, an ego psychologist, writes in *Ego Development and the Personality Disorders: A Developmental Approach to Psychopathology* (New York: Grune & Stratton, 1965), p. 421, "Guilt makes punishment inevitable, since in addition to the anxiety which it evokes by threatening *self-esteem*, the intense reactions of self-condemnation and reproach, *shame*, self-disgust and remorse are generally more punishing and inescapable than external punitive agents" (italics mine).

[4]Although I know of no research in this area, my clinical experience suggests that men are more likely to experience guilt as self-inflicted punishment while women are more likely to experience guilt as self-inflicted rejection or a sense of alienation. This appears to match the tendency for men to fear punishment and women to fear a loss of love.

and a loss of self-esteem.[5] Others are not troubled by shame but engage in repeated self-inflicted psychic punishments. Although these ingredients of guilt are closely related, they are significantly different. The self-punitive element of guilt is typically triggered by violation of prohibition, whereas feelings of shame and disesteem arise more from the failure to live up to one's goals or expectations. Rebellion against a parent's standards, for example, may trigger self-punitive guilt feelings while the failure to fulfill the parent's expectations gives rise to feelings of shame or disesteem.

Judas is a biblical example of extreme self-punishment. After Jesus was betrayed and delivered to Pilate, Judas tried to resolve his guilt by returning the thirty pieces of silver. When that failed, he threw the money into the sanctuary and went off and hanged himself.[6] The action prompting Judas's guilt-laden response was not a failure to live up to an ideal but rather an aggressive act, a violation of another person. Consequently his experience was not so much shame and alienation as it was self-condemnation and punishment.

This distinction between self-punishment and inferiority (disesteem) helps explain why some people find freedom from guilt through confession while others engage in a perpetual cycle of sin, guilt, and confession with little relief. When the problem is fear of punishment or self-inflicted punishment, confession tends to lessen the need for punishment. We know we will not be punished since we have already confessed. And since we no longer fear external punishment we feel less need to punish ourselves. But if the problem is a feeling of inadequacy, inferiority, and disesteem, confession may magnify our sense of inferiority. In light of the other's apparent strength and goodness we look even worse! This is why some Christians find that confession reinforces their feelings of inadequacy and failure rather than providing reassurance of forgiveness.

When we look at biblical guidelines for resolving guilt we will

---

[5]Oriental cultures rely heavily on shame motivation in child rearing, and shame tends to be a more prominent feature of their experience of guilt than the fear of punishment.

[6]Matt. 27:5.

see that different biblical doctrines relate more to one aspect of guilt feelings than another. Justification and propitiation, for example, relate directly to the fear of punishment and self-inflicted punishment. The doctrines of sonship and union with Christ relate to the feelings of alienation or rejection. And the doctrines of creation and sanctification speak to our sense of self-esteem.

INFERIORITY, SHAME, AND GUILT

Some writers separate what I am here calling a loss of self-esteem from guilt proper and label it shame.[7] Although I agree that there is a significant difference between self-inflicted punishment for the transgression of a fixed standard, and shame for the failure to live up to an inner expectation, it seems to me that since both of these experiences come from self-judgment (conscience), they can be treated as different aspects of one process.[8] When Adam and Eve sinned they experienced both shame and fear of punishment as a result of their condition of guilt. This close connection between shame and guilt is also reflected by authors such as Ausubel and Kirk, who conclude that "the core ingredient of guilt is the feeling of shame."[9] For our purposes, then, I will consider the lowering of self-esteem or the sense of shame as one aspect of the broader emotion of guilt even though there are some differences between the experience of self-punitive guilt and the guilt of shame or inferiority.

[7]G. Piers and M. Singer, for example, write: "The following seem to me properties of shame which clearly differentiate it from guilt: 1) Shame arises out of a tension between the ego and the ego ideal, not between ego and superego as in guilt. 2) Whereas guilt is generated whenever a boundary (set by the superego) is touched or transgressed, shame occurs when a goal (presented by the ego ideal) is not being reached. It thus indicates a real 'shortcoming.' Guilt anxiety accompanies transgression, shame, failure. 3) The unconscious, irrational threat implied in shame anxiety is abandonment, and not mutilation (castration) as in guilt. 4) The Law of Talion does not obtain in the development of shame, as it generally does in guilt" (*Shame and Guilt: A Psychoanalytic and a Cultural Study* [New York: Norton, 1971], pp. 23-24).

[8]An excellent discussion of guilt and shame and the importance of recognizing shame in the therapeutic process is found in H. Lewis, *Shame and Guilt in Neurosis* (New York: International Universities Press, 1971).

[9]D. Ausubel, *Ego Psychology and Mental Disorder*, K. Kirk, ed. (New York: Grune & Stratton, 1977), p. 183.

Some of my students and colleagues have asked if it is not more appropriate to see self-esteem and feelings of inferiority as more basic and fundamental than viewing them as components of guilt. They suggest that guilt and inferiority (problems of self-esteem) are separate processes, and that we exaggerate the importance of guilt if we view inadequate self-esteem, or inferiority, as a part of the broader experience.

Although I am aware that we usually think of guilt and self-esteem somewhat separately and that we may even assume that problems of self-esteem are more basic than problems of guilt, I believe that both the biblical and psychological understandings of personality lead to the opposite conclusion. The loss of self-esteem is a part of the experience of guilt, a result of it, or at least a parallel process growing out of the function of conscience. Sidney Jourard, for example, writes:

> Self-esteem is the name given to the complex cognitive-affective response *which accompanies behavior in accordance with the conscience.*
>
> When a person behaves in opposition to his conscience he experiences guilt. ... When he behaves in conformity with his conscience, he experiences a heightening of the feelings of self-esteem....[10]

Psychoanalyst Brenner writes:

> *the commonest cause of painful and apparently unwanted feelings of inferiority is a disapproval by the superego. For practical purposes such feelings of inferiority are the same as feelings of guilt.*[11]

And Paul Tournier says:

> I do not think that a clear line of demarcation can be drawn between them. *All inferiority is experienced as guilt.*[12]

---

[10]S. Jourard, *Personal Adjustment* (New York: Macmillan, 1963), p. 255.

[11]C. Brenner, *An Elementary Textbook of Psychoanalysis* (Garden City: Anchor, 1974), p. 120. Brenner goes on to say, "This is obviously a point of considerable clinical importance, since it tells us that a patient who has considerable feelings of inferiority or lowered self-esteem is probably unconsciously accusing himself of some misdeed, regardless of what reason he may consciously give to account for his feelings of inferiority."

[12]Paul Tournier, *Guilt and Grace* (New York: Harper & Row, 1962), p. 24.

No matter what theoretical perspective we use to analyze self-esteem, we end up tracing its source to the person's success, or lack of it, in living up to his or her standards or ideals. Self-esteem, in other words, results from self-evaluation, precisely the origin of guilt feelings. In the only careful study designed to clarify whether guilt and inferiority are two different emotional states, Harold Geis performed two experiments comparing guilt and inferiority. In both experiments the hypothesis that guilt and inferiority feelings are independent states was rejected. In concluding that guilt and inferiority feelings are operationally similar he wrote:

> Persons experiencing guilt feelings and persons experiencing inferiority feelings share the general tendency to depreciate themselves. . . . This kind of behavior is a function of a definition or concept of oneself as being of low worth or worthless if one behaves in a certain kind of negatively valued way (e.g., wrong or incompetently) or exhibits a certain kind of negatively valued characteristic (e.g., wrongness or incompetence).[13]

I am of the opinion that one reason psychologists prefer to see self-esteem as a separate process from guilt is that they can thus remove problems of self-esteem from the moral realm. If self-concept problems are not part of a process of guilt, we can minimize issues of responsibility and the relationship of our sinful state or moral condition to the origin and resolution of problems of self-esteem. If, on the other hand, self-esteem is a function of conscience, we cannot isolate the treatment of self-esteem from issues of sin, morality, and guilt! As Geis put it: "To the extent that this then is valid, the practitioner should recognize that this kind of clinical problem is philosophical and moral in nature, as well as psychological."[14]

This concludes our brief overview of the content of psychological guilt. From now on when I refer to subjective or psychological guilt or guilt feelings, I will have in mind an affective state (either conscious or unconscious) that includes these feelings of self-rejection, self-punishment, and a loss of self-esteem. I insert the words conscious or unconscious because, as we will see in

---

[13]Harold Geis, *Guilt Feelings and Inferiority Feelings: An Experimental Comparison* (Ann Arbor: University Microfilms, 1965), p. 84.
[14]Ibid. p. 88.

the next chapter, guilt feelings often operate outside of our awareness.

FEAR, GUILT, AND GODLY SORROW

Before leaving our discussion of the nature of guilt, I would like to suggest a distinction between guilt feelings and two closely related psychological experiences. The first of these is *fear* and the second is what I have chosen to call constructive, or *godly sorrow*.

When Adam and Eve sinned they immediately experienced guilt feelings or psychological guilt. They covered themselves to hide their nakedness and began blaming each other. But guilt was not their only experience. They were also afraid of God's judgment and tried to hide from Him. The threat of God's wrath was (and is) an *external* threat that is not the same as self-inflicted punishment, rejection, or disesteem. Adam and Eve *were* in danger of punishment from God. The emotion accompanying this awareness is best labeled anxiety or fear. This anxiety is related to guilt but it is also different.

Just as we can distinguish between Adam and Eve's fear of God's judgment and their feelings of guilt, we can also distinguish between fear and guilt feelings in our own experience. If the source of threat is external, then our response is best labeled anxiety or fear. If we are about to be run down by a car (external threat), for example, we experience anxiety or fear. On the other hand, if we believe we *should* be hit by a car because we are sinful, we are experiencing guilt feelings. We are inflicting psychological pain on ourselves in the absence of (or in addition to) an external threat.

Sometimes fear and guilt are experienced simultaneously. Fearing (perhaps realistically) retaliation from an external source, we may also punish ourselves. This would be true, for example, if we ran off with another person's spouse and felt guilt (internal attack) but also heard the abandoned spouse was planning to run us down with an automobile (external attack)! Sometimes fear and guilt are so closely tied together that it is difficult to tell the difference. If we feel inwardly guilty, we expect others to punish or condemn us. And fearing punishment, we learn to punish ourselves much like a child who spanks his own hand when his mother catches him in the cookie jar!

A third emotion related to guilt feelings and fears of punishment is what I call constructive sorrow. Paul writes of this in 2 Corinthians 7:9-10, where he reminds the Corinthians there is a difference between worldly sorrow that leads to death and godly sorrow that leads to righteousness. Constructive sorrow is a love-motivated emotion closely related to guilt feelings yet radically different. Whereas psychological guilt is a self-punitive process, constructive sorrow is a love-motivated desire to change that is rooted in concern for others. I believe a confusion of psychological guilt and constructive sorrow has often interfered with the church's efforts at promoting wholeness and health in the body of Christ.

Other writers have used "true guilt" (Tournier)[15] or "existential guilt" (Pattison)[16] to describe this experience. But because constructive sorrow is based on dynamics opposite from those of psychological guilt and because there is such a universal tendency to confuse the two, I do not believe it is helpful to label this experience guilt.

We will explore the concept of constructive, or godly, sorrow and the implications of differentiating godly sorrow from guilt in chapter 11. I would, however, like to distinguish guilt feelings from constructive sorrow. When I attempt to demonstrate the universal presence and growth-inhibiting nature of guilt feelings in the next three chapters *I am not referring to a love-motivated remorse, contrition, or godly sorrow that should result from divine conviction. I am referring instead to psychological guilt, or guilt feelings, which we have described as self-inflicted punishment, rejection, or disesteem.* I am also not referring to our objective condition of guilt before God. In fact, one of the main reasons we need to unmask the often hidden and growth-inhibiting functions of guilt feelings is to free individuals to face their condition of guilt so they can experience a healthy, constructive sorrow, which is the foundation of moral maturity.

SUMMARY

In this chapter I have suggested that psychological guilt is comprised of internal self-punishment, rejection, and disesteem. This

---

[15]Tournier, *Guilt and Grace*, 1962.

[16]M. Pattison, "Ego Morality: An Emerging Psychotherapeutic Concept," *Psychoanalytic Review*, 1968, vol. 55, p. 187.

definition shows that problems of self-esteem cannot be separated from guilt and moral concerns. It also shows how guilt feelings can be differentiated from both anxiety and constructive sorrow. With these initial definitions in mind, we will now look at some of the disguised forms guilt feelings take and at the problems guilt creates when it is not recognized and resolved.

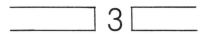

The Repression of Conscience

Our psychologically sophisticated society has a strong tendency to minimize the influence of guilt feelings. Believing we have moved beyond this "primitive" or "immature" motivation, laymen and professionals alike discuss problems of personal adjustment without the slightest reference to guilt or conscience. Many textbooks in psychology do not even mention conscience and most give only a brief mention of the experience of guilt. This lack of attention to guilt and conscience appears to be the result of the increasing secularization of society, the naturalistic explanations of the behavioral sciences, and an overemphasis on personal autonomy and individualism. We are becoming increasingly more hesitant to view societal problems from a religious perspective; we are prone to explain psychological phenomena without reference to spiritual dimensions. We are also prone to say that each person must be free to choose his or her own values—so long as these choices do not infringe upon the rights of others. In the words of a bumper sticker, "If it feels good do it."

These societal trends have not been nearly as successful in removing the phenomenon of guilt from our experience as in eliminating the words from our vocabularies. As Helen Lynd put it:

> Terms associated with guilt have tended to be dropped as inciters to desirable action. Sophisticated parents, teachers, or therapists no longer say that a child is good or bad. But the words good and bad have been replaced by mature and immature, productive and unproductive, socially adjusted and maladjusted. And when these words are used by the teacher,

the counselor, or the therapist they carry the same weight (together they constitute as rigid a code as that of any church or creed). An individual feels the appropriate guilt if he does not attain maturity in the prescribed manner.[1]

Here we have a penetrating insight. Our twentieth-century society with its new morality, psychological explanations, and relativistic standards is actually no more free from guilt than earlier generations. We have simply adopted a kind of cultural defense against guilt, renamed it, and proclaimed our freedom. We now talk about inferiority, self-esteem, and depression. But all of these things are indications of hidden guilt. The only difference is that large numbers of people are now experiencing the subjective elements of guilt without realizing it. Having disguised and renamed the problem, however, we may now be even further from the real solution. In this chapter, I will attempt to unmask this repression of guilt and conscience by demonstrating how most of us routinely use common defense mechanisms to ward off painful awareness of guilt feelings.

DISGUISES OF GUILT

After King David committed adultery with Bathsheba, God sent the prophet Nathan to convict him. Although David had tried to hide his tracks by encouraging Uriah to spend the night with Bathsheba (Uriah would assume he was the father of his wife's child) and eventually by having Uriah killed, he had still not been willing to acknowledge the depth of his sin. Nathan posed the following situation for David and asked the king to pass judgment:

> There were two men in a certain town, one rich and the other poor. The rich man had a very large number of sheep and cattle, but the poor man had nothing except one little ewe lamb he had bought. He raised it, and it grew up with him and his children. It shared his food, drank from his cup and even slept in his arms. It was like a daughter to him. Now a traveler came to the rich man, but the rich man refrained from taking one of his own sheep or cattle to prepare a meal for the traveler who had come to him. Instead, he took the ewe lamb that belonged

[1]Helen Lynd, *On Shame and the Search for Identity* (New York: Harcourt, Brace & World, 1958), p. 18.

to the poor man and prepared it for the one who had come to him.[2]

David responded with "righteous indignation." "As sure as the LORD lives, the man who did this deserves to die! He must pay for that lamb four times over, because he did such a thing and had no pity."[3]

At that point Nathan interrupted and said, "You are the man!" Needless to say David was shocked. He had been sincerely (he thought) passing judgment. He saw the rich man as guilty of a heinous sin and heaped angry condemnation upon him. But the condemnation David so fully dished out to the rich man was apparently an expression of the hidden self-condemnation he harbored in his own heart. David was shifting the focus from his own guilt by using one of the most common mental mechanisms, the defense of projection.

In *projection* we repress our own feelings of guilt, sins, unacceptable wishes and feelings, and attribute them instead to others. Projection operates most clearly in the paranoid personality where there is a complete disavowal of one's own guilt producing wishes and fantasies. Here another person (or persons) is chosen to be the persecutory object. The guilt-laden person puts his or her own unacceptable wishes or self-accusing thoughts into the other person and becomes the victim of the very attitudes he unconsciously disowned.

Another example of projection is found in the angry person who denies his own hostility and imagines others are plotting against him. His own wiley imaginations are projected into the minds of others. A more complex form of projection is sometimes found in paranoid personalities with repressed homosexual wishes. The male paranoid's unconscious reasoning goes something like this:

Step 1: I am attracted to him, but I cannot acknowledge my desire because I fear punishment, condemnation, shame, or rejection.

Step 2: I really do not love him; I hate him. But I still feel guilty because it is not right to hate.

[2] 2 Sam. 12:1-4 (NIV).
[3] 2 Sam. 12:5, 6 (NIV).

Step 3: It is really not me who hates. It is he who hates. He hates me.

Step 4: I must be on guard because he (and others like him) hate me.

Through a neat little psychic process the person has moved from a state of subjective guilt to one of subjective innocence. As a matter of fact, he is not only not guilty, he is now the innocent victim of others' angry attacks!

Marriage counselors daily see this dynamic operating as partners attempt to hide their failures by blaming spouses or finding their own negative attitudes in their mates. Projection is frequently a problem with the jealous spouse who instead of facing his or her own lustful feelings, imputes these desires to the mate and then hesitates to let the mate out of sight. One of my clients, Paul, was a very rigid, compulsive, driven person. He was also insanely suspicious of his wife and any man who came near her. He tried to prevent her from going to the beach and if she did he attempted to coerce her into wearing an extremely modest bathing suit. He bombarded her with warnings of how she might tempt men because "sex is all most of them have on their minds." In a very self-righteous manner he condemned both his wife and other men.

Only after months of therapy did Paul begin to see his own lustful feelings and realize how hard he had to struggle to keep them under control. By projecting his own wishes onto other men he avoided feeling guilty for them. Unfortunately the price Paul paid to deny his guilt was a severely neurotic style of life with conflicts in his marriage. Only when he saw his guilt could Paul start giving up his rigid, obsessive-compulsive actions, and become a more open, trusting, sensitive, and loving person. And when he did, he realized he had been distorting biblical injunctions such as "Flee the evil desires of youth,"[4] in order to reinforce his avoidance of his own sinful wishes. He had interpreted these passages to mean that there was lust in the world (not in himself) and he must therefore run from it, rather than from his own sinful tendencies.

In a similar way, some parents experience great anxiety because they project their own adolescent sexual struggles onto

[4] 2 Tim. 2:22 (NIV).

their teenage sons or daughters and try to relieve their anxiety or guilt by carefully controlling their offspring's experiences with the opposite sex! Rather than facing their own guilt and struggles, such parents externalize the problem by locating it in their children.

Repression is another common way of warding off uncomfortable emotions like guilt. An uncomfortable wish, desire, memory, or emotion is simply pushed from awareness. In combination with other defenses, we strive to keep these unacceptable desires or feelings from coming back. But why do we attempt to press these things from consciousness? Is it not because of either fear or guilt? If we acknowledged these hidden feelings or desires we would fear condemnation from others or ourselves. Consequently, we expend great amounts of energy keeping these things out of our awareness. This process starts early in life. We are taught, for example, "Tell him you're sorry" (even when we are not). "Give her a big hug" (even when we can't stand her). "Don't be a baby" (when we feel like crying). "We don't *hate* our brother, we *love* him" (though at the moment we *do* hate him). Because we know that these feelings will be condemned, we push them from awareness. "Good" children don't feel that way!

In adult life repression can show up as a void of emotion or in difficulty handling one's emotions. We may fail to laugh when others do, or to cry or show other normal affective expressions. Allison speaks of those whose guilt has "incarcerated them from access to their feelings, their bodies and their very vitality."[5] This absence of emotions is a good indicator that something has been pushed from awareness and shut off from the remainder of our personality. Overreactions to apparently inconsequential situations can also reflect the operation of repression. Strong feelings that have been pushed from awareness break through at inappropriate times.

Religious rigidity and legalism may also indicate an earlier repression of thoughts or feelings. In fact, all forms of legalism are built on repression. Struggling to keep potentially guilt-producing thoughts from awareness, the legalistic person maintains a continued focus on external actions, works, and effort. This helps shift

[5]C. Allison, *Guilt, Anger and God* (New York: The Seabury Press, 1972), p. 57.

attention from hidden, but unacceptable attitudes and feelings. Hulme described the process this way:

> The success of legalism depends upon keeping one's motives buried. The emphasis on overt behavior is an emphasis on the *seen* and consequently on the observer. This dependency upon the approval of at least certain others prevents the development of individual consciousness because the security derived thereby depends upon a self-affirmation at the expense of reality. In this manner legalism becomes a neurosis—a method of defense for the ego center.[6]

Jesus, of course, denounced this avoidance of reality when he told the Pharisees that on the outside they appeared righteous, but that inwardly they were full of hypocrisy and lawlessness.[7]

The Pharisees' obsession with cleanliness, order, and details of the law also reflected their use of *reaction formation.* In reaction formation we assume a conscious attitude or action directly opposed to our hidden inner wish or feeling. The Pharisees had convinced themselves they were clean and spiritually alive. But Jesus said they were dead and dirty. Their overt actions were apparently precisely opposite their inner attitudes. Jesus said to them, "You clean the outside of the cup and dish, but inside they are full of greed and self-indulgence. Blind Pharisee! First clean the inside of the cup and dish, and then the outside also will be clean."[8]

In the same way people today can rely on reaction formation to obscure their inner attitudes or wishes. A person with hidden passive desires may take on an aggressive, dominant stance in order to deny his passive wishes. A person with a great deal of inner anger may act extremely nice and loving. And a person with strong sexual desires may go to extremes to keep the opposite sex at a distance to avoid being aware of his or her own sexual wishes. One acquaintance of mine watches television with the remote control in his hand so that he may quickly change the channel at any hint of sexual immodesty. Although there is a lot of "junk"

[6]W. Hulme, *Counseling and Theology* (Philadelphia: Fortress, 1967), p. 137.
[7]Matt. 23:28.
[8]Matt. 23:25-26 (NIV).

on television, his extreme behavior suggests to me some deep inner struggles and guilt over his own sexuality. In his mind, however, he is simply being "pure" and "spiritual."

In every instance of reaction formation, the repression of true wishes and the development of opposing outward attitudes or actions is motivated by feelings of guilt. This was classically illustrated to me when a young mother came to me for therapy because of obsessive fears that her youngest child might open the rear door of their car, fall out, and be killed. She knew she worried excessively but also was convinced the danger was real. She was so concerned that she continually pressured her husband to trade in their four-door car for a two-door model. Consciously, she harbored no ill feelings toward her child. As therapy progressed, however, she told me how upset she had been when she found out she was pregnant. She already had one child in diapers and her husband was in school. Gradually she came to realize that she had resented having this baby and had unconsciously wished something would happen to him. To avoid the guilt of her unconscious wish, she repressed it and consciously took on exactly the opposite attitude. Her overconcern, like much parental overindulgence and overprotection was a reaction to hidden resentment and guilt.

Compulsive activity is another common means of handling guilt. Some people are driven to achieve but are never fully satisfied with what they've done. As students they are nearly always at the top of the class; as housewives, their homes are spotless. At work they spend long hours and are generally successful. But their work and lives reflect a pressured flavor. Rather than being spontaneous and happy, they are driven. They are always busy because things *have* to be done. Feeling immensely responsible, they carry out their duties and are seldom able to relax. Evenings and weekends are filled with meetings or left-over work. Even vacations are difficult. Although they have been saying how hard work has been for months, when summer rolls around they find it difficult to get away. They want to take it easy but also pack up a few things from the office to do in their "spare time." If they sit down and do nothing but relax, they soon start feeling tense or guilty for their inactivity; they must get up and *do* something.

They live under what Karen Horney calls the "tyranny of the should."[9] Paul Tournier asks this about the "workaholic":

> Is it not true, in a sense that men seek refuge from a body of diffused guilts in a frenzy of work rather than face up to them? Does not this overwork ... provide a fine alibi which we can envoke in self-exculpation? Or very often, a kind of expiation by work? And when it is a seeking after gain or social esteem or gratitude from those we serve that draws us into this maelstrom, should we not see in this too, a cloak for guilt? For this quest is the expression of a need to regain self esteem, as an antidote to the loss of it which guilt brings in its train.[10]

While many of us share a few of these characteristics, they are found most prominently in the obsessive-compulsive personality. From early life these people have worked hard to keep their feelings under control. Fearing they might do something wrong or displease their parents they limited their spontaneity. They tried to earn acceptance from their parents and others and they developed a performance-oriented lifestyle. They became their own task masters to make sure that they were always busy with "important" activities. Whenever they started to relax or take it easy, their inner task master reminded them of their responsibility.

While we all know people like this (and many of us suffer from some of the same symptoms), we generally do not relate this perfectionistic lifestyle to hidden guilt. Actually, it is one of the clearest expressions of unconscious guilt. The perfectionist is constantly driven to work to maintain self-esteem and try to feel loved and accepted both by himself and those about him. The underlying motivating fear is that he will not be good enough to avoid rejection and protect his fragile self-image. From early childhood he felt he had to control himself and be the best in order to value himself and be accepted. Now, years later, he has become a slave to his own ideals. He does not want to be guilty of being slothful, sloppy, disorganized, ineffective, or even average. Other people are similarly driven to perfectionism to try to "atone" for long-forgotten

---

[9]Karen Horney, *Neurosis and Human Growth* (New York: W.W. Norton & Co., 1950).

[10]Paul Tournier, *Guilt and Grace* (New York: Harper & Row, 1962), p. 30.

sins. By being good and performing well they hope to ease the lingering accusations of a guilty conscience.

Closely related to this achievement-oriented living is *obsessive thinking*. Most of us have had the experience of leaving the house, closing the front door, starting downtown, and then thinking, "Wait a minute. Did I lock that door?" We know we always lock it but we think, "Maybe I forgot today." We argue with ourselves with no solution. Finally, to settle our inner doubts, we return home and check the door. Sure enough, it was locked all the time! To understand how this common obsessive doubting can be a disguised form of guilt, we might rephrase that inner dialogue:

> "Did I remember to lock the door?"
> "Of course, I did. I always lock it."
> "But maybe I didn't this time."
> "Perhaps I am guilty of forgetting."
> "But I always lock it."
> "Yes," a silent voice replies, "but sometimes you forget. I'm going to keep bugging you until you go and check it."

We are accusing ourselves of failing to do the right thing! We are also threatening painful consequences for disobedience. Someone might enter the door and rob us!

A little of this doubting is normal but for some people it becomes a way of life. Every time they face a decision they are threatened with anxiety. Mentally weighing every pro and con, they are unable to come to a conclusion. They think, "That seems best—but on the other hand . . . !" They can never be certain about a decision because they dare not take a chance on being wrong! Their fear of making a wrong decision is another indication of guilt. Riddled with obsessive doubts, these people find all decision-making and commitment difficult. It is easier not to choose than to risk being wrong!

Other people go ahead and make decisions but then look back with worrisome second thoughts. Continually wondering whether they've made the right decision, they review every decision on their mental "instant replay." Over and over they ponder the correctness of their actions in a vain attempt to assure themselves they have made the right decisions. Unfortunately, this repeated checking usually turns up more and more doubt and perpetuates the vicious cycle.

In Christian circles obsessive doubting can show up in an inability to feel forgiven or in the belief that one has committed the unpardonable sin. Since obsessive persons are rarely able to feel satisfied with their performance, even after confessing their sins they may question the sincerity of their repentance and think, "Maybe I didn't *really* mean it." "How could I possibly be a Christian and have thoughts like *this?*" "God couldn't *completely* forgive someone like me." Behind these thoughts lie guilt's inner accusations: "You are bad," "You'll never be good enough," or "How can *you* expect to feel forgiven?"

Martin Luther was apparently troubled by these doubts, especially before he came to an understanding of the grace of God. He expended great energy meeting the requirements of his religious order, confessing his sins repeatedly, and, on one occasion, for six hours. He was so obsessed with confessing even the minutest sins that once his superior chided him by saying, "If you expect Christ to forgive you, come in (to confession) with something to forgive—patricide, blasphemy, adultery—instead of all these peccadilloes."[11] In fact, Luther's personal struggles with depression and guilt were clearly influential in his eventual understanding of the grace of God.[12] [13]

Another common defense against guilt (and one of the most adaptive) is *sublimation.* In sublimation we work out some socially unacceptable and potentially guilt-producing impulse or feeling in a socially acceptable way. A friend of mine used to play tackle on a major university football team. He was married during that time and things were going quite well. A couple of years after

[11]R. Bainton, *Here I Stand: A Life of Martin Luther* (New York: Mentor Books, 1955), p. 41.

[12]A reading of Bainton's biography of Luther in combination with E. Erickson's, *Young Martin Luther: A Study in Psychoanalysis and History* (New York: W. W. Norton, 1962), provides an excellent description of one man's struggle with guilt and the impact of an understanding of God's grace on that conflict.

[13]The compulsive worker and the obsessive doubter are dynamically related to the defense mechanisms of *isolation* and *intellectualization* — the other common ways of avoiding guilt. In these defenses we split off or isolate our feelings from our thoughts. We may recall events or thoughts but repress our feelings.

graduating, however, he started having problems with anger in his marriage. As we talked about his temper he said it hadn't been a problem as long as he was playing football. With a sense of real enjoyment he said, "There's nothing I enjoyed more than getting out there and knocking heads with someone across the line!" It soon became obvious why he was suddenly having problems with anger in his marriage. Since he no longer had a way of releasing his anger acceptably, his wife was becoming the object of his anger. He no longer had opportunity to sublimate his hostility!

This same defense can also be seen in some spiritual and political activities. Some ultra-conservative, political radio preachers can become outraged, denounce everyone a step or more to their left, and close in prayer, content with their "righteous indignation." But if you listen carefully you hear a constant current of anger and resentment. Some of these people aren't just standing firmly for a position—they are using their cause as a vehicle for expressing underlying hostility.

This angry sublimation isn't limited to any one point on the religious or political spectrum. Under the guise of "love," people on the political left have burned buildings, angrily denounced anyone who differed with them, and engaged in all sorts of character assassination. Although they may have a justified cause, they are using their political activities to express their pent-up rage. Rather than saying "I'm an angry person," they say in so many words, "I am not *wrongly* angry. I am not guilty. I am just fighting for a cause!"

There are some advantages to this defense. Sublimation does discharge anger in more sociably acceptable ways. But it also has its drawbacks. If we kid ourselves into thinking we are simply working for a good cause, we blind ourselves to our real motives and may naïvely pursue some activity we think we are doing for a constructive motive when we are actually working out our own unresolved problems!

THE PRICE OF REPRESSION

All of the defenses we use to avoid guilt have one thing in common. They deny or distort reality and keep us from seeing ourselves realistically. This process causes more problems than it solves. Repressed wishes and feelings go unresolved. Projected feelings erect barriers between ourselves and others. Compulsive work puts us under constant pressure and detracts from family life. Obsessive doubts undermine self-confidence and cause unneeded worry and depression.

In one way or another all of these defenses attack our mental health. They cut us off from aspects of our true selves, alienate us from our own thoughts and feelings, and cause us to live a lie. They also play key roles in the development of the neuroses and other maladjustments. In chapters 4, 5, and 6 we will look at how that happens. Before we do, however, I want to briefly discuss Jesus' attitude toward repression.

JESUS AWAKENS GUILT

Jesus' life contains an intriguing paradox on the matter of guilt. On several occasions He condemned people for their lives and teachings. Yet on others He offered pardon and forgiveness. To the scribes and Pharisees Jesus spoke harsh words of condemnation.[14] Yet to the woman taken in adultery He spoke the assuring words, "Neither do I condemn you . . . Go now and leave your life of sin."[15] This apparent paradox is resolved when we see that Jesus gave each person what was needed. To those who hid their guilt Jesus spoke words of judgment and conviction. He attempted to increase their awareness of their guilt and bring it into focus so that it could be resolved. As the prophet put it, "I will pass judgment on you because you say, 'I have not sinned.' "[16] But to those who faced their guilt Jesus offered forgiveness.

On several occasions Jesus denounced those who repressed or hid their guilt. He cut through their desensitized consciences and revealed the guilt that lay beneath outward acts of conformity, goodness, and even religious orthodoxy. God wants to bring the hidden things to light. "He reveals the deep things of darkness and brings the deep shadows into the light."[17] And at the end of

[14]Matt. 23:1-39 (NIV).
[15]John 8:11 (NIV).
[16]Jer. 2:35 (NIV).
[17]Job 12:22 (NIV).

time He will fully reveal the hidden motives in man's heart. "Wait till the Lord comes. He will bring to light what is hidden in darkness and will expose the motives of men's hearts."[18]

As long as we hide and repress our guilt, "we lie and do not live by the truth."[19] And until we face the truth of the guilt that lies buried beneath our repressions, our projections, our sublimations, and other defenses, we cannot hope to find true release from guilt. As Tournier expressed it, "God blots out *conscious* guilt (feelings), but He brings to consciousness *repressed* guilt (italics mine).[20]

SUMMARY

In this chapter I have attempted to unmask the hidden sinful attitudes and feelings of guilt lying behind the various psychological defense mechanisms. Because we don't like to face our sin and because guilt feelings are so painful we use these mental mechanisms to hide guilt's presence. Unfortunately, this reinforces rather than resolves guilt feelings and interferes with spiritual and emotional growth. Psychologically this repression leads to neurosis. Spiritually it causes legalism and Pharisaism.

The Bible, in fact, discourages repression. It speaks words of conviction to bring repressed guilt to awareness and words of forgiveness to clear the conscience of those who admit their sins. Jesus never had a harsh word for an admitted sinner but he spoke forcefully to those who hid their guilt. In the following chapters I will discuss the means of resolving debilitating guilt feelings. But to do that we must first understand the extent of the problem. No one is entirely free of guilt; everyone at least occasionally hides guilt by using various defense mechanisms.

[18]1 Cor. 4:5 (NIV).
[19]1 John 1:6 (NIV).
[20]Tournier, *Guilt and Grace*, p. 112.

Is Anxiety Enough?

Guilt feelings are more prevalent than we sometimes think, and the accusations of a guilty conscience can motivate repression. To push away the pains of a guilty conscience we resort to projection, reaction formation, and other defenses. These defenses are designed to hide our actual guilt and the guilt feelings associated with it. By blaming others, looking good, or ignoring our own negative attitudes and actions, we declare our innocence and our right to be free from guilty feelings. Unfortunately this repression of guilt disrupts personal adjustment more than is generally recognized. In this and the next two chapters, I am going to suggest that the repression of conscience and feelings of guilt plays a critical role in the development of all personality maladjustments. As a background for that study, we will summarize the traditional psychodynamic theory of the neuroses.

THE TRADITIONAL FORMULATION

Since the time of Freud, psychodynamically oriented psychologists have viewed anxiety as the root cause of psychological maladjustments. According to this view the human organism has a tendency to respond to unpleasant, overwhelming, or threatening situations with anxiety. To ward off unpleasant anxiety we develop a series of defensive maneuvers designed to protect against either internal or external threats. If the perceived threats are too great we begin relying excessively on these defense mechanisms and in the process develop neurotic symptoms. The pathological symptom is viewed as a result of the interaction between a threat to the self and our attempt to defend against it.

Some people involved in traumatic accidents, for example, suffer a hysterical loss of vision or perhaps the use of a limb. They do this because the psychic trauma was too much to handle. In attempting to blot the painful memory from awareness through denial and repression, they are forced to restrain use of their limb or vision lest the usage remind them of the painful event. In similar ways we defend against threatening internal attacks. Strong, angry feelings can also lead to the development of hysterical paralysis. In this case, paralysis makes certain we will not act on our anger. A paralyzed person cannot strike out in rage! Consequently the hysterical symptom helps block feelings of anger from awareness.

Other types of neurotic symptoms are seen as coming into existence the same way. If we are exposed to life situations (either internal or external) that are too much to handle we resort excessively to repression and other mechanisms of defense and consequently develop a variety of psychological maladjustments.

In early life the threats to our well being are largely physical. Inadequate food or covering, loud noises, and actual physical attacks cause anxiety. In classical psychoanalytical thinking, the infant's own biological urges are seen as the first source of anxiety. The infant or young child is afraid of his own wishes, desires, or impulses (namely sexual and aggressive drives) and tries to keep them from awareness.[1] Initially he tries to push them from consciousness because of fear of the reaction of parents and significant others. Later, as we will see, he tries to repress them for his own internal reasons.

Phenomenologically oriented theorists like Carl Rogers emphasize the interaction of environmental influences with the child's inherent wishes and growth tendencies in the development of anxiety. As a result of our interaction with a judging or rejecting environment we develop a self-concept that forces us to deny awareness to certain inner wishes and experiences in order to

[1]R. Greenson summarizes the psychoanalytic view this way: "Psychoanalysis maintains that psychoneuroses are based on the neurotic conflict. . . . A neurotic conflict is an unconscious conflict between an id impulse seeking discharge and an ego defense warding off the impulse's direct discharge or access to consciousness" (*The Theory and Practice of Psychoanalysis* [New York: International Universities Press, 1967], p. 17).

avoid rejection or punishment. Rogers, for example, writes of the enjoyment a young child has in making a bowel movement any time or place he wishes and in hitting or trying to do away with his baby brother. According to Rogers these feelings "are not necessarily inconsistent with the concept of self as a lovable person." He continues:

> But then to our schematic child comes a serious threat to self. He experiences words and actions of his parents in regard to these satisfying behaviors, and the words and actions add up to the feeling "You are bad, the behavior is bad, and you are not loved or lovable when you behave in this way." This constitutes a deep threat to the nascent structure of self. The child's dilemma might be schematized in these terms: *"If I admit to awareness the satisfactions of these behaviors and the values I apprehend in these experiences, then this is inconsistent with my self as being loved or lovable."* [2]

Here we see the interaction of Rogers's belief in the basic "goodness" (or at least neutrality) of the child and his view of psychopathology. He believes that we become neurotic[3] because we repress our own satisfactions and perceptions to gain the love and approval of others. Our parents' judgments, not our own wishes, constitute the threat to our developing self-image. Although this view differs from the stress of psychoanalysts on inherent anxiety-provoking wishes within the young child's psyche,[4] it does have one very important common understanding. *Both psychoanalytically and phenomenologically oriented theorists see the crucial step in the formation of neuroses to be a turning to defense mechanisms to ward off anxiety.* Brenner, for example, says, "Freud asserted that anxiety is the central problem of mental illness, and his assertion is accepted by most of us today.[5] And Maddi, discussing Rogers's view of maladjustment writes:

> Once you have conditions of worth, some of the thoughts, feelings, and actions that you could well engage in would make

[2]Carl Rogers, *Client Centered Therapy* (New York: Houghton Mifflin, 1965), pp. 499-500.

[3]I am here using *neurotic* in a general way to represent all psychopathologies.

[4]It also differs from orthodox Christianity's understanding of the nature of man, which traces the origin of adjustment to humanity's sinful nature.

[5]C. Brenner, *An Elementary Textbook of Psychoanalysis* (New York: International Universities Press, 1966), p. 78.

you feel unworthy or guilty, and hence, a process of defense is activated when the person has some small inkling or cue, in the form of anxiety, that unworthy behavior is about to occur.[6]

The next step in the traditional view of the formation of psychological maladjustments is a shift in the motivation for repression of one's wishes or feelings. Instead of repressing aspects of our "true selves" because of the fear of our own impulses or parents' reaction to our actions or wishes, we begin to repress because of concern about our own internal self-judgments. Theorists from a variety of orientations see children beginning to take in (through some form of internalization or imitation) both their parents' values and their corrective attitudes. Previously external threats of rejection and punishment thus become incorporated into the growing child's personality as part of the conscience.

Up to this point, a safer and more accepting environment brings a positive change in a child's adjustment, because anxiety is triggered only by external situations. As soon as the child is able to evaluate his or her own performance and pass out self-judgments and punishments, however, all of this changes. Now it is the child's own self-rejection and judgment that is feared. In other words, as soon as what we generally know as the *superego*, or conscience begins to function, it becomes a primary source of anxiety. This special form of anxiety, generated by the conscience, or superego, is called guilt. For Freud, this takes place between four and six years of age.

While fears of external rejection, punishment, and disesteem still have some effect, they are now seen as secondary to guilt feelings in the development of neurosis. External threats can be avoided or altered, but internal threats are ever present and nonrelenting.[7]

[6]S. Maddi, *Personality Theories: A Comparative Analysis* (Homewood, Ill.: Dorsey Press, 1972), p. 95.

[7]Our internal threats also influence our perception of external events. The person who enters adulthood with a healthy sense of self-esteem and a minimum of guilt, for example, tends to interact freely with others. When he encounters occasional rejection, failure, or attacks on his self-esteem he takes these events in stride. The person with a strong sense of guilt has an entirely different experience. Being highly critical of himself, he expects others to be critical. He not only accuses himself and evaluates himself as inferior or inadequate; he also projects his self-accusations onto others and assumes they are equally critical, rejecting, or punitive. His external environment is turned into a continuously threatening situation based on his own struggle with inner guilt.

According to this viewpoint, once the conscience or superego has developed, we expend large amounts of energy trying to keep anything that would trigger our internalized fears of punishment or rejection out of awareness. Unfortunately in trying to hide unacceptable portions of our personality, we lose touch with our real selves. We spend so much effort trying to be what we *ought* to be that we lose touch with what we *are*. While it is great to have ideals and be moving toward them, we sometimes attempt this at the expense of an honest acceptance of ourselves. Because we are afraid of displeasing our own internal judge, we so carefully monitor our wishes and behavior that we become rigid, or driven, or we begin to feel sterile, depressed, and empty.

Because we are so invested in actualizing a false self, or ego,[8] and because we are constantly "on guard," we expend so much energy to avoid potentially wrong reactions that we have little energy left for positive, creative, growth-enhancing activities. Guilt, in other words, has forced us to hide our true selves beneath a variety of defenses and has seriously disrupted our potential for growth. Jourard describes this process:

> The person who habitually responds to threat with defense mechanisms eventually becomes alienated from his real self. He consumes energy in defending his self-structure and hence has little left over for constructive work. His relations with people are impaired because he does not have all of his real self accessible to him for interpersonal relationships. Ultimately, he must remain lonely and unknown to others, because he does not dare make himself known to others. In time, the habitual addict to defense mechanisms may display the clinical symptoms of neurosis and psychosis.[9]

The result of this process is psychological maladjustment. Figure 1 summarizes the traditional four-step process that leads to the formation of pathology.

The process begins with some conflict or threat. Next, anxiety grows out of the conflict or threat (and with it a special form of anxiety called guilt). The third stage is reliance on one or more

---

[8]D. Winnicott, *Through Pediatrics to Psychoanalysis* (New York: Basic Books, 1975).

[9]Jourard, *Personality Theories*, pp. 193-94.

Figure 1

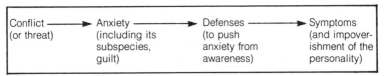

Conflict ⟶ Anxiety ⟶ Defenses ⟶ Symptoms
(or threat)   (including its   (to push   (and impover-
              subspecies,   anxiety from   ishment of the
              guilt)   awareness)   personality)

defense mechanisms to push the threat or conflict and the attendant anxiety or guilt from awareness. The fourth and resulting stage is impoverishment or constriction of the personality and the development of neurotic symptoms.

Although theorists differ on the specific nature and origin of the conflicts that initiate this process, almost all dynamically oriented theorists see this general process as the core issue in the development of neuroses. Some, like Rogers and Jourard, place the responsibility for these conflicts largely on the environment. Others, following Freud, emphasize the presumably inherent anxiety producing nature of the infant's wishes. In all cases, however, the formula for the development of psychopathology follows this four-step process. Some type of threat generates anxiety, which motivates defense and causes symptoms. The threat of guilt from the superego is seen simply as a special form of anxiety, having its origin in the internalization of parental values and corrections.

AN INCOMPLETE EXPLANATION

This formulation has been helpful in shedding light on the problem of psychopathology. It has brought into focus the crucial role of early developmental factors (especially parent-child relationships) in the formation of neuroses. It has helped us understand some of the environmental causes of neuroses and allowed us to formulate therapeutic processes that are directed by a logical, developmental understanding.

This understanding of the origins of psychopathology also has some significant biblical parallels. Scripture consistently relates the bondage of humanity to fear. Adam tells God, "I was afraid because I was naked; so I hid."[10] Paul said, "You did not receive

[10]Gen. 3:10 (NIV).

a spirit that makes you a slave again to fear."[11] And the author of Hebrews said that Christ, by His death, would "free those who all their lives were held in slavery by their fear of death."[12]

In Genesis 3:10, Adam's hiding (defending) is related to fear. And in Romans and Hebrews the solution to this fear is a relationship to a "perfect parent"—one who accepts unconditionally and does not attempt to make us into something we were not created to be. According to Scripture, fear (or anxiety) does lead to attempts to hide or deny our sinfulness and to bondage rather than liberation.

There are a couple of missing ingredients in this psychological formulation, however. One is the lack of an internal cause justifying the fear. In each biblical passage cited above, fear exists in the context of sin, so that there is an internal basis for the anxiety. *Anxiety, in other words, is not portrayed biblically as arising fully out of environmental mistreatment.* A person experiences anxiety and guilt not simply because the environment makes him *feel* guilty but because he *is* guilty.

The other problem with the traditional formulation of the neuroses is that neither psychological analysis nor the biblical exegesis of the Genesis account of Adam and Eve's sin supports the assumption that guilt feelings are simply a subtype, or specialized form, of anxiety. In fact, both suggest precisely the opposite.

The tendency to view guilt as simply another form of anxiety can lead to some serious misunderstandings. To begin with, it obscures the moral and spiritual roots of psychopathology. In fact, one wonders if this is not precisely why secular theorists have labeled these experiences anxiety instead of guilt. When we think of anxiety we tend to think of concern over nonmoral issues. With a stroke of the theorist's pen the nature of humanity's emotional maladies is changed from moral to nonmoral, and the source shifted from the individual to the environment. Guilt feelings, in other words, become simply an internalized expression of the experiences of punishment, rejection, and disesteem we have with others. Along with our values and ideals, they come to be seen as due entirely to the socialization processes.

[11]Rom. 8:15 (NIV).
[12]Heb. 2:15 (NIV).

This shift from the individual to the environment and from guilt to anxiety is accompanied by a shift in terminology from *sin* to *sickness*.[13] In this view, the infant is a morally good—or at least neutral—person. Maslow, for example, says:

> This inner nature, as much as we know of it so far, is definitely not "evil," but is either what we adults in our culture call "good," or else it is neutral.
>
> If this essential core (inner nature) of the person is frustrated, denied or supressed, sickness results....[14]

In other words, we are born essentially good, with a positive growth potential; neuroses result when this positive direction is frustrated or repressed due to the influence of the environment.

Although I am not personally troubled by the current tendency to use medical labels for psychological maladjustments, I am concerned over the tendency to shift all responsibility from the individual to the environment. It is interesting that this tendency is nearly always accompanied by an elevation of anxiety to the central role in pathology and a consequent minimizing of the role of guilt. As I will attempt to demonstrate in the next chapter, *both biblical revelation and clinical experience call for a view of human disfunctioning that places greater stress on the role of guilt and upon personal responsibility.*

SUMMARY

The traditional dynamic theory of the neuroses sees anxiety as the primary cause of excessive use of defense mechanisms and consequently as the source of the neuroses. This view, however, neglects the role of personal sin in the development of maladjustments and shifts responsibility to the environment. Consequently the spiritual roots of psychopathology are obscured. In

[13]My own view of the use of the medical model is essentially pragmatic. To the degree labels serve to communicate useful data I see them as helpful. If, however, they obscure information such as the necessity of personal responsibility, then we should either refine their usage or find better ways of describing problems of adjustment.

[14]A. Maslow, *Toward a Psychology of Being* (Princeton: D. Van Nostrand, 1962), p. 181.

chapter 5 I demonstrate that the Bible contradicts the theory that anxiety is the cause of all adjustment conflicts and guilt is simply a form of anxiety. In chapter 6 I demonstrate that the phenomenological analysis of anxiety and guilt also contradicts this theory. After doing this, I will propose a biblical alternative to traditional psychodynamic theories of neurosis.

5

Anxiety, Guilt, and Eden

Created in the image of God and living in the idyllic Garden of Eden, Adam and Eve were in perfect harmony with themselves, one another, and God. Although they were naked, they were not ashamed.[1] They knew no disunity or conflict; they were inwardly whole and peaceful. If Adam and Eve had taken time to reflect upon their self-esteem before the Fall they probably would have thought things like "We are whole, happy, and fulfilled individuals because we know our identity in relation to our creator. We are what we were created to be and we feel comfortable in our position." They would have felt no burden to prove their worth, to avoid guilt, or to build their own identity because their emotional harmony was a gracious gift rather than something earned.

COMPETITORS WITH GOD

Into this setting came the serpent saying:

> "... has God said, 'You shall not eat from any tree of the garden'?" And the woman said to the serpent, "From the fruit of the trees of the garden we may eat; but from the fruit of the tree which is in the middle of the garden, God has said, 'You shall not eat from it or touch it, lest you die.'" And the serpent said to the woman, "You surely shall not die! For God knows that in the day you eat from it your eyes will be opened, and you shall be like God, knowing good and evil."[2]

[1]Gen. 2:25.
[2]Gen. 3:1-5.

Satan paints God as a restrictive parent by saying, "Has God said You shall not eat from any tree of the garden?" when God actually prohibited eating of only one tree. Eve corrects that distortion but exaggerates the extent of God's prohibition. She adds to it, "You must not even touch it." Then the serpent follows up with a direct challenge of God. They would surely not die! God, according to the serpent, is threatened. He is afraid that if Adam and Eve eat of the forbidden fruit they will become like God.

Here is the essence of the first temptation. The serpent implied that God had created Adam and Eve naïve, blind, and inferior. They had the potential of becoming like God but God was not going to permit that. On top of this appeal, the fruit was "pleasing to the eye."

The knowledge of "good and evil" that Satan held out to Adam and Eve did not simply refer to an intellectual knowledge of absolute moral values. If it had, it is obvious that God lied, because their eating of the tree did not give them this ability! Instead, the knowledge was an autonomous, experiential knowledge. And tragically enough, experiential knowledge of evil does not make one like God! Von Rad describes this knowledge as follows:

> The Hebrew yd' ("to know") never signifies purely intellectually knowing, but in a much wider sense an "experiencing," a "becoming acquainted with," even an "ability".... For the ancients, the good was not just an idea: the good was what had a good effect; as a result, in this context "good and evil" should be understood more as what is "beneficial" and "salutary" on the one hand and "detrimental," "damaging" on the other. *So the serpent holds out less the prospect of an extension of the capacity for knowledge than the independence that enables a man to decide for himself what will help him or hinder him*[3] (italics mine).

The serpent's appeal, in other words, was that Adam and Eve could be autonomous individuals, free to determine their own fate and decide what was best for them. The appeal was to reject their status as the apex of God's created earthly order and become something they were not designed to be: competitors with God.

[3]G. Von Rad, *Genesis: A Commentary* (Philadelphia: Westminster Press, 1972), p. 89.

DEPENDENCY AND AUTONOMY

Autonomy has different uses in theology and psychology. Psychologists typically use *autonomy* in a positive sense denoting freedom from infantile dependency and the ability to stand on one's own, even in the midst of pressure to do otherwise. Autonomy is thus a sign of emotional maturity and does not necessarily imply the absence of intimate relationships with others. An autonomous person can have intimate *peer* relations without being dependent on others in a parent-child manner.

When theologians use *autonomy* to describe humanity's relationship with God, it has an entirely different meaning. According to Scripture we are created to be dependent *upon God* and we function at our intended best when we acknowledge our real limits as created beings. One of the purposes of the forty years of wandering in the wilderness, for example, was to teach humility and cause the Israelites to recognize their need of God. Moses told the Israelites to

> ... remember all the way which the Lord your God has led you in the wilderness these forty years, *that he might humble you* ... that he might make you understand that man does not live by bread alone but by every word that proceeds out of the mouth of the Lord.[4]

Then he warned them to be careful not to "say in their hearts"

> "*My* power and the strength of *my* hand made me this wealth." But you shall remember the Lord your God, for it is *He* who is giving you power to make wealth, that *He* may confirm *His* covenant which *He* swore to your fathers.[5]

They were to remember the source of their abilities and who it was that delivered them from bondage.

Theologians do not usually use the term *autonomy* in a positive sense. They use it to describe humanity's effort to reject the reality of our created natures and to set ourselves up as our own gods. In the discussion that follows I will be using *autonomy* in this theological sense. In doing this I would like the reader to be

[4]Deut. 8:2, 3.
[5]Deut. 8:17-18.

aware that the opposite of this kind of autonomy is not a helpless, dependent, psychological immaturity, but simply an acknowledgment of our finiteness as created beings, our need of God's redemption and sovereign leading, and a parallel, healthy psychological freedom from childish dependency upon others because we realize we are peers with other created persons.[6] When Adam and Eve ate the forbidden fruit they were not demonstrating a healthy adult independence. They were denying the reality of their created natures and attempting to be something they were not designed to be.[7]

Most secular theorists, of course, reject the possibility that a healthy dependence on God can coexist with psychological independence.[8] Almost by definition they view belief in God as an expression of psychological immaturity and dependency. Since this work is directed largely to Christian readers, I will not here make the effort to fully delineate the distinctions between healthy dependency on God and immature psychological dependency. I would like to suggest, however, that the work of Roland Fleck and that of Allen and Spilka on committed and consensual religion promise to resolve some of the tension between Christian and secular theorists on this point.[9]

THE ORIGIN OF CONSCIENCE

Having completed a brief detour into the meaning of autonomy, we can return to the scriptural narrative of Adam and Eve's sin.

---

[6]Passages like 1 Cor. 12:1-31 describe the absolute necessity of *inter*dependent relationships in the body of Christ. We mature and we minister most effectively when we live and minister collectively.

[7]Jer. 48:7, for example, in condemning the Moabites for their pride, says they "trusted in their own achievements and treasures". Isa. 14:13-15 speaks of the god-like aspirations of the king of Babylon in a passage some believe refers to the fall of Lucifer. And Deut. 8:1-20 indicates that a major purpose of the forty years of wilderness wandering was to teach the Israelites humility, which involved acknowledging their need of God.

[8]See, e.g., Erich Fromm, *You Shall Be As Gods* (New York: Holt, Rinehart, and Winston, 1966).

[9]Roland Fleck, S. Ballard, and J. Reilly, "Development of Religious Concepts and Maturity: A Three-stage Model," *Journal of Psychology and Theology*, Vol. 3, No. 3, 1975, pp. 156-63. R. Allen and B. Spilka, "Committed and Consensual Religion: A Specification of Religion and Prejudice Relationships," *Journal for the Scientific Study of Religion* (1867), 6:191-206.

The moment the fruit was eaten, "the eyes of both of them were opened, and they knew that they were naked; and they sewed fig leaves together and made themselves loin coverings."[10] Adam and Eve's sin immediately placed them in a state or condition of objective guilt. Quite apart from how they now *felt*, they were guilty of sinning against God. Their first emotional reaction to this guilty state was a feeling of guilt (especially shame). Notice that this guilty feeling occurred in the absence of any external punishment or rejection and that it was not the same as fear. Calvin points this out when he writes:

> This opening of the eyes in our first parents to discern their baseness, clearly proves them *to have been condemned by their own judgment.* They are not yet summoned to the tribunal of God; there is none who accuses them; is not then the sense of shame, which rises spontaneously, a sure token of guilt?[11] (italics mine).

Although Adam and Eve were attempting to hide themselves from each other (and later from God), the primary threat was internal. They knew they were not as they should be, so they tried to hide. Here is the first experience of disharmony and disunity in the human personality. Adam and Eve are now inwardly aware of a problem—something gone amiss. They also experience two conflicts growing out of their sinful state. The first is a conflict resulting from the awareness of a gap between what they are as fallen persons and *what they were created by God to be.*[12] The second is a conflict between what they now are as fallen persons and *what they would like to be in their own autonomous existence.* They observe themselves and find themselves lacking. They can neither live as they were created to live by God nor can function harmoniously as the autonomous gods they wish to be in their fallenness.

Alone, in their separation and god-like existence, Adam and Eve have lost their sense of wholeness.[13] Here we also see the

---

[10]Gen. 3:7.

[11]John Calvin, *Commentaries on the Book of Genesis* (Grand Rapids: Baker, 1979), 1:157.

[12]We will see in chapter 11 that the awareness of this gap should result in repentance and godly sorrow.

[13]I refer to their fallen attempts to be god-like in response to Satan's temptation, not the God-given desire to become godly or spiritually mature.

first appearance of what we might consider conscience. In fact, some theologians trace the origins of conscience to the Fall.[14] But whether we trace the origin of conscience to the Fall or simply see this as the first operation of conscience as it now exists, we see both a new process and a new emotion resulting from the Fall. Adam and Eve are now judging themselves and finding that something doesn't measure up. In response to their perceptions of this lack, they experience psychological guilt. *It is important to realize Adam and Eve's psychological guilt is not tied at all to the presence of God or to His divine judgment. It is apparently a natural reaction of fallen man to the awareness of his sinful condition. We should also note that their experience of psychological guilt is in no way portrayed as a positive motivating force. Their guilt feelings did not motivate them to repentance or contrition, and the Bible does not tell us that their feelings came from God. Instead, their guilt feelings motivated them to hide behind some fig leaves!* We will have more to say of this in chapter 10.

ADAM, WHERE ARE YOU?

In Genesis 3, we also see the close connection between the internal experience of guilt feelings and the externally based fear of others. At the same time Adam and Eve felt guilty they also felt a need to hide from each other. Apparently their awareness of their own sinfulness made them vulnerable in each other's presence. Shortly after, they also had their first experience with fear of God:

> And they heard the sound of the Lord God walking in the garden in the cool of the day, and the man and his wife hid themselves from the presence of the Lord God among the trees of the garden. Then the Lord God called to the man, and said to him, "Where are you?" And he said, "I heard the sound of Thee in the garden, and I was afraid because I was naked; so I hid myself."
>
> And He said, "Who told you that you were naked? Have you eaten from the tree of which I commanded you not to eat?" And the man said, "The woman whom Thou gavest to be with

[14]E.g., D. Bonhoeffer, in *Creation and Fall* (New York: Macmillan, 1959).

me, she gave me from the tree, and I ate." And the woman said, "The serpent deceived me; and I ate."[15]

Being afraid of God, Adam and Eve hid among the trees. God was an obvious external source of anxiety. He had promised that the day they ate of the tree they would die, and they were afraid. They knew they were in danger of punishment and punishment creates fear.[16]

Since our current goal is to understand the dynamics of guilt we will not go in depth into either the nature of the fear Adam and Eve experienced or the reality basis for their fear. I would simply like to point out that in response to their sin (and their objective *condition* of guilt), Adam and Eve started experiencing both feelings of anxiety and guilt.[17]

As a result of Adam and Eve's desire for autonomy from God and their fall into sin, their entire identity shifted. Until the Fall they were secure, loved, and confident because they accepted their rightful position in relation to God. They did not have to strive to find or maintain their identity and they didn't have to work to enhance their self-esteem, overcome inferiority, or avoid feelings of guilt. But from the moment of the Fall, they had to be continually *doing* something to mask or cover the gap between who they actually were and who they desired to be or were cre-

[15]Gen. 3:8-13.

[16]1 John 4:18.

[17]I would also like to affirm the historical position of the Church that Adam and Eve were in danger of the wrath of God and that their fear was well founded. See John 3:16; Matt. 3:7; Deut. 32:35; Rom. 2:5; and 1 Thess. 1:10. Since the wrath of God is so often misunderstood and so frequently likened to our own human wrath, it is important to differentiate between the two. G. Berkouwer in *Studies in Dogmatics: Sin* (Grand Rapids: Eerdmans, 1971), p. 359, describes God's wrath as follows: "When we study the biblical witness we soon discover that this wrath of God is not an irrational or an incomprehensible kind. It is not a capricious vehemence which falls upon us and before which we are simply powerless. ... God's anger is the indignation of a God who has 'bent and strung his bow' for the eventuality that man does not repent. ... His wrath is the reaction to apostasy and unchastity and other evils which rightly deserve death (Romans 11:32)." God's wrath, in other words, is a settled opposition of divine holiness to sin and those who fail to repent continue to stand under divine judgment. This real external judgment is the ultimate source of fear while our inner self-judgment is the source of guilt.

ated to be. Adam blamed Eve for his troubles. He said, "*The woman whom Thou gavest to be with me, she gave me from the tree, and I ate.*" And the woman blamed the serpent.[18]

In hiding among the trees and blaming each other, Adam and Eve initiated the process of psychological defense. To try to regain their lost identity on their own, they had to push from awareness the things that did not fit with their autonomous, god-like picture of themselves. They had to deny both their guilt and their finiteness.

At this point the biblical record of the Fall supports a key aspect of the traditional psychodynamic understanding of the nature of neuroses. Specifically, both clinical experience and the Genesis record point to a universal tendency to resort to defenses to ward off guilt that eventually ends up distorting our perception of ourselves and leading to neurosis. This attempt to convince ourselves and others we are not what we really are lies at the core of every neurosis. In some way or another, we all attempt to hide our guilt, to prove that we are acceptable, or as we will see in chapter 10, to pay for our own sins. Although our repressions can include anything, they always include a denial of our finiteness, our dependency, our sinfulness, and at some level, our desire to be like God. All of our defenses are designed to say, "I am O.K." by myself. Like Adam and Eve we want to base our identity on our own performance. We want to be like God.

Sometimes our autonomous attempts to establish our identity involve more than just repressing undesirable features of our life. They also include the development of a lifestyle designed to *earn* an identity through our performance, or at least the holding of ideal expectations in order to merit self-acceptance. For some people this shows up in grandiose or perfectionistic fantasies and striving. We place exhorbitant demands on ourselves and try to live up to our hidden, god-like wishes. Or we blame others for violating our (god-like) rights to *have* what we want, to be where we want *when* we want, or for our failures to achieve up to our expectations. We see this in little things like waiting in line at a checkout stand, being stuck in traffic, or being "bumped" from an airline seat. In each case we believe *we* have a godlike right to be

[18]Gen. 3:12-13.

given the seat, to be in the front of the line, or not to have our progress slowed!

SUMMARY

To pull our above discussion together and apply it to our study of guilt and conscience, let's briefly recap the key insights coming from the biblical record of Adam and Eve's first sin:

1. Adam and Eve were created in a state of harmony with themselves, each other, and God. They knew no guilt (either objectively or subjectively) at this point.

2. The essence of the serpent's temptation was that Adam and Eve might become like God—something they were not designed to be. Specifically, they were tempted to become autonomous, god-like individuals, who could make their own choices.

3. As soon as Adam and Eve sinned, they experienced a split both within their personalities and between themselves and God. This inner division took the form of an awareness of a twofold gap between who they were and who they wanted to be, and between who they were and who they were created to be. The awareness of this gap stirred both feelings of guilt and anxiety.

4. In the biblical record, guilt is not portrayed as a subtype of anxiety. It is seen instead as an inner process of self-accusation set off without external threats in contrast to the objectively based concerns apparent in fear.

5. Adam and Eve's fear (anxiety)[19] was experienced in relation to an external threat (God's wrath), whereas their guilt was experienced primarily in relation to their own self-judgment of being other than what they should or wanted to be.

6. The fact that Adam and Eve had fallen into a state of sin made them objectively guilty before God. This objective condition of guilt, while being related to the psychological ex-

---

[19]For our present purposes I am using *fear* and *anxiety* interchangeably, although we commonly restrict the use of fear to situations with a rather specific object while using anxiety to refer to a more diffuse affective condition with less obvious or concrete referents.

periences of both anxiety and guilt, should not be confused
with these subjective experiences.

7. The origin of Adam and Eve's problems including their use
of defense mechanisms and their experience of anxiety and
guilt originated not in their environment but in their own
sinfulness. The anxiety they experienced had an external
referent (God) but it was based on their own sin.

These facts have important ramifications for our understanding of psychopathology in general and guilt feelings in particular. The experience of guilt is portrayed as at least as important a factor in causing the use of defense mechanisms as anxiety, and both anxiety and guilt are seen as growing out of Adam and Eve's sinfulness. Any view of psychopathology that hopes to be consistent with biblical revelation will have to take these facts into account. From the moment Adam and Eve sinned, each member of the human race has had to struggle with the gap or split between the way they are and the way they were created to be on the one hand, and between the way they are and the way they want to be in their own autonomy on the other. This state is accompanied by anxiety and guilt, which both play important but distinct roles in the development of personality malfunctions.

6

Sin and Psychopathology

In the last two chapters I summarized the traditional dynamic theory of neurosis that sees anxiety as the major cause of maladjustment. I have suggested that the neglect of guilt in that view obscures the moral and spiritual causes of psychopathology and overemphasizes the impact of the environment. In this chapter I want to make a further differentiation between anxiety and guilt and then offer an alternate theory of neurosis that places equal weight on the role of these emotions in personality development.

THE PHENOMENON

A careful analysis of the emotion of guilt supports the proposition that guilt is not simply a subcategory of anxiety but that guilt should be distinguished from anxiety. In addition to a different location of the threat in guilt (internal vs. external), we can observe at least two other differences. *Guilt feelings are always experienced in relationship to some type of inconsistency or duality within oneself.* While anxiety *may* be triggered by this awareness, it need not be. Anxiety can be caused by any kind of external threat apart from the inner sense of inconsistency or failure. If we are about to be run over by a car, we experience anxiety, not guilt. As Oden put it, "guilt is always formally the awareness that what I have done is inconsistent with who I understand myself to be, that my image of myself is challenged by my own behavior."[1]

Guilt can also be differentiated from anxiety by its focus. *Guilt*

[1] T. Oden, *The Structure of Awareness* (Nashville: Abingdon, 1969), p. 50.

always has reference to something past while anxiety has reference to something future. It is impossible to experience guilt over something we have yet to do. We may experience guilt over our *wishes* to do something in the future, but our guilt is over the wishing, now accomplished, and not over the possibility of performing the act. Similarly, we cannot experience anxiety over something past. We may have anxiety regarding the potential consequences of a past act, but the consequences are still future and the anxiety is not over the act itself. Figure 2 summarizes these distinctions.

Figure 2

DIFFERENTIATION OF GUILT FROM ANXIETY

	GUILT	ANXIETY
LOCUS OF THREAT	Internal	External
NATURE OF THREAT	Perceived inconsistency between our goals and our behavior or attitudes.	Any kind of perceived environmental attack.
FOCUS OF THREAT	Past	Future

Oden makes the same point I am attempting to make about the importance of distinguishing between anxiety and guilt.

> Traditional psychoanalysis has tended to view guilt as a subcategory of anxiety.... Even the sharpest critics of the psychoanalytic interpretation of guilt, such as Mowrer, have nevertheless followed Freud in continuing to view guilt as merely a type of anxiety.... Against this whole line of thought espoused by Freud and his critics alike, I argue that guilt is of a fundamentally different genre from anxiety, and in fact, is its precise dialectical opposite analogous in every major aspect. For guilt always refers through memory to something which is already past, just as anxiety always refers oppositely to some possibility

which has not yet occurred. *It is a wholly inadequate observation to see one as absorbed by another or to reduce guilt
merely to a form of anxiety* (italics mine).[2]

A PARALLEL PERSPECTIVE

Based on the biblical and phenomenological considerations we
have discussed above, I would like to suggest that there is a parallel development of guilt and anxiety from infancy on, and that
these experiences play equally important roles in the formation
of the neuroses.

The Role of Anxiety

Because the role of anxiety in psychological maladjustment is well
known I will mention it only briefly here. Careful observers have
long known that all human beings experience anxiety or fear as
a consequence of their interaction with their environment. No
person passes through life—even early life—without encounter-
ing numerous external threats to his or her well-being. Whether
physical or emotional, these threats trigger anxiety that in turn
calls for some form of psychological defense, which, if relied on
excessively, produces neurotic adjustment. These experiences are
inevitable in a fallen world and reflect the effect of others' sins
upon the individual. *Anxiety, in other words, typically arises from
an experience of being sinned against.*

Unfortunately the role guilt plays in the formation of neuroses
has not received careful analysis in the way that anxiety has. As
we have seen, most theorists see guilt as a secondary factor with
a relatively late developmental appearance. I would like to challenge that viewpoint in the following pages.

Guilt in Infancy

Long before infants can either comprehend environmental expectations or internalize parental corrective attitudes, they experience
a rudimentary awareness that things are "right" or "wrong" inside.
Although children cannot conceptualize good and evil in any developed cognitive sense, they do experience a sense of something

[2]Oden, *The Structure of Awareness*, pp. 50-51.

not being quite right when they are irritated, angry, or upset. They also experience a feeling of being "O.K." or "in harmony" when they are calm (but not passive!) and loving. *I suggest that this initial inner psychic awareness of disharmony is a rudimentary form of guilt or at least a forerunner of guilt feelings. These primitive feelings are obviously quite different from those the child will experience after prolonged socialization and maturational processes, but they are their precursors as well as the first expression of what we will later freely call the child's moral awareness and sense of guilt.*

Just as infants experience a primitive form of anxiety when they interact with fallen persons in a fallen world, they also experience a primitive form of guilt when they experience their own fallenness (i.e., rage, demands, etc.). Vitz describes these early experiences:

> I propose that the child is naturally aware of the emotional state of love, normally love for his mother, and for his father. This experience is not primarily an externally manipulated reinforcement. Instead, it is above all an experience involving not only the child's awareness of the mother, but also an awareness of the internal state of cues of love, e.g., feelings of warmth, comfort, trust, happiness. In addition, it seems reasonable to suppose that the child naturally knows that this state is "good." Indeed the previous conditions can be thought of as the domain of experience to which the term "good" first applies in our lives. The second element in the child's experience is of pain, anger, jealousy and occasionally even hate. Again, *there are internal conditions or cues which identify these for the child in ways which I believe are far more important than the externally perceived events that bring them about. These latter experiences serve as the initial basis for the category "bad."* A final element ... is the child's awareness that these two fundamental states conflict, that they are opposites. *Very early, a child understands the desirability of goodness and the disturbing character of badness ... and the basic conflict between them; the two are mutually exclusive, as experiences.*[3]

Although labeling primitive emotions with the term *guilt* and seeing a rudimentary form of conscience operating early in life

---

[3] P. Vitz, "Secular and Christian Moral Education: A Critique and a Proposal," unpublished manuscript.

may initially seem inconsistent with traditional psychological understanding of personality development, I would suggest that it is not. Theorists and researchers in child development have long acknowledged that infants have an undifferentiated psychic experience in the first few months of life. During that period infants have no clear sense of themselves as separate persons. Their perceptions are vague and global and their affective experiences are intense but not yet clearly differentiated.[4]

Based partly on this lack of differentiation, infants do not experience the clear-cut emotions of adults. They experience pleasure and "unpleasure." They experience anger and frustration. And they experience a global emotional response typically labeled anxiety. But the perceptual apparatus necessary to distinguish between oneself and the world, or to perceive the source of one's anxiety or the objects of one's rage, is not yet present. To use psychoanalytic terms, there is as yet no ego or perhaps only a rudimentary ego. Since infants do not yet have a clear picture of themselves as separate persons they also have no developed conscience. Its primitive forerunners are there, but that is all.

This absence of a clear differentiation of the self from others and of a differentiated emotional life has not prevented psychological theorists from discussing the emotions of infants. Theorists from Freud on have attributed to the youngest infant feelings of anxiety, rage, and even depression. We realize that when we speak of the anxiety of infants we are speaking of a very early, diffuse emotional state that only later will take on the more developed quality we experience as adults.[5] Nevertheless we continue to

[4]Spitz, e.g., after carrying out extensive longitudinal studies on the maturation and development of infants using repeated developmental tests, weekly observations, and extensive filming, concludes: "Perception appears to begin as a totality, and various perceptive modalities have to be separated from each other in the course of development" (R. Spitz, *The First Year of Life* [New York: International Universities Press, 1965], p. 56).

[5]Spitz writes "... the 'normal' manifestations of affect in the newborn are not as trifling as we usually like to think of them. We perceive them as minor, because the infant is small and powerless. Therefore, these manifestations are neither as long nor as spectacular as they would be in the adult. We have come to accept that this is the way an infant is, and that this is perfectly 'normal.' True enough. But we should remember all the other implications of this 'normalcy.' We should remember that not only affects are chaotic and undifferentiated in the infant but also 'perception' " (*The First Year of Life*, p. 46).

label a certain constellation of infantile feelings *anxiety. In suggesting that guilt feelings have an early origin parallel to anxiety I am simply looking at guilt the same way we do other infantile emotions like anxiety.*

Students of early mental development like Jacobson and Kernberg have long spoken of "forerunners" or "precursors" of the superego.[6] By these phrases they refer to the fact that the infant's experiences of anger and frustration color both their developing perception of themselves and others,[7] and that these perceptions impact their feelings toward themselves and others.[8]

In recent years other theorists have begun to stress both the presence and importance of primitive feelings of guilt experienced in the first several months of life. Harry Guntrip, for example, writes of guilt arising from the infant's "being destructive to his love-object as a result of the intensity of his greed and hate,"[9] and Winnicott speaks of "fear and guilt stirred by the infant's destructive impulses and fantasies."[10]

These theorists are speaking of a universal experience of inner disharmony arising from within the child rather than the environment and they do not see it as a subtype of anxiety or as internalized fears. Although their formulations differ somewhat, all these theorists see early feelings of guilt growing out of the infant's aggressive and destructive feelings. It is this primitive experience, common to every infant, that is the forerunner of all later feelings of guilt.

SUBSTANCE OR SEMANTICS?

Some of the distinction between guilt and anxiety and their early forerunners may simply be a matter of semantics. The key issue

[6]E. Jacobson, *The Self and the Object World* (New York: International Universities Press, 1964); and O. Kernberg, *Object-relations Theory and Clinical Psychoanalysis* (New York: Jason Arenson, 1976).

[7]Psychoanalysts refer to this as self and object representation.

[8]Later we will look more closely at the connection between primitive guilt feelings and both original sin and objective guilt before God.

[9]Harry Guntrip, *Personality Structure and Human Interaction* (New York: International Universities Press, 1961), p. 372.

[10]D.W. Winnicott, *Through Pediatrics to Psycho-Analysis* (New York: Basic Books, 1975), p. 270.

is certainly not the label we choose to describe a phenomenon but our understanding of that phenomenon. It seems to me, however, that the implications of this viewpoint are by no means insignificant. If we follow the widely held view that guilt develops entirely as a result of a process of socialization and is simply a subcategory of anxiety, we are left with the accompanying assumptions that human nature is intrinsically amoral, that the functioning of conscience is strictly a result of the process of socialization, and that guilt feelings are the consequences of parental and societal influences. Jourard, for example, advocates precisely this view when he writes: "guilt and self-esteem may be regarded as the internalized version of the punishments and rewards which earlier in life were accorded the child by his parents and significant others."[11]

The inescapable conclusion of this viewpoint is that the child suffers guilt because he is a victim of inadequate parenting or improper socialization. This is precisely the view that has led to the tendency to place responsibility for an individual's failures and antisocial acts on everyone and anyone except the individual!

On the other hand, if we posit a basic, though admittedly primitive awareness of "good" and "evil," and an accompanying emotional experience, we can easily work from the accompanying assumptions that man is a moral being, that he has some innate awareness of good and evil that is manifested in increasing measure as developmental processes unfold, and that guilt feelings originate at least in part in the internal psychic world of the child instead of (or in addition to) the environment. To quote Vitz again:

> My thinking here is then opposed to the recent assumption in psychology that the basic concept of morality does not occur in (very young) children and that all that exists is some kind of external "experience" with rewards and punishments. The stage 1 of Kohlberg and Piaget is indistinguishable from models of simple animal learning based on positive and negative reinforcement and implicitly denies that there is anything intrinsically human about a child's moral life.[12]

[11]Jourard, *Personal Adjustment*, p. 250.
[12]Vitz, *Secular and Christian Moral Education*, p. 44.

In giving guilt equal prominence with anxiety I am not suggesting it is more influential. I am simply suggesting that in humanity's fallen state (condition of guilt) we encounter two types of threats and two different affects that can be unpleasant enough to promote psychological maladjustment. One threat is our fallen environment. When an infant's parent is tense, anxious, distant, or angry, the infant senses this and experiences a sense of discomfort that we commonly label *anxiety*. Another way of putting this is when the infant's *needs* for a loving, relaxed, intimate, safe, and caring environment are not met it responds with primitive anxiety.

The other threat is inside the personality. Even though the infant's mother is doing a great job in providing good mothering, the infant may become upset for his or her own internal reasons. The infant may *want* to be fed even though it doesn't *need* to be fed at precisely that moment. When the infant does not receive what it *wants* (as contrasted to what it really *needs*), there is inner discomfort, frustration, and anger, which lead to a primitive forerunner of the emotion we will later label *guilt*. Both anxiety[13] and guilt can thus set in motion the defensive processes that lead to the development of psychological maladjustment.

Figure 3 demonstrates these parallel processes.

Figure 3

PARALLEL ROLES OF ANXIETY AND GUILT
IN THE DEVELOPMENT OF PSYCHOPATHOLOGY

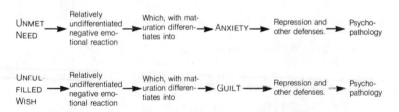

[13]Some of this anxiety may later be converted into guilt through the process of internalization. This is the guilt commonly acknowledged as being a subcategory of anxiety and needs to be differentiated from guilt arising from within the child. The former might be labeled *internalized* guilt and the latter *intrinsic* guilt. The former, internalized guilt, is closer to what Tournier labels *false guilt* and the latter closer to his view of true guilt.

This way of looking at personality places a balanced emphasis on personal and parental responsibility. It also allows us to account for the impact of both personal and societal factors (sin) in the development of psychopathology. Consequently, it has broad ramifications for our understanding of psychopathology, the process of therapy, and our society's struggle to balance personal and societal responsibility in issues like mental illness and criminal insanity. Only a view that sees the developing person as both the *initiator* of destructive patterns and the *recipient* of them can provide this balance. And any view of personality development that has this balance will need to give careful attention to guilt growing out of the person's self-initiated acts as well as fear growing out of conflicted treatment by others.

GUILT, ORIGINAL SIN, AND RESPONSIBILITY

I believe this understanding of the role of guilt in early mental life also sheds light on the nature and extent of humanity's sinfulness. For centuries theologians have debated the concepts of sin and depravity and the presence (or absence) and precise nature of original sin. Without venturing too far into an area where individuals much more deeply trained in theology than myself have failed to reach a consensus, I would like to offer a few observations that may cast a bit of light on this problem.

The first is that to the degree my observations of the emotional lives of infants are accurate, they appear to correspond with the theological concept of original sin. For whatever reasons, every infant, from the earliest days of life, does appear to react with frustration and anger when his or her needs or wishes are not met. Long before infants reach an "age of accountability" in the sense of making conscious moral choices, they have a rudimentary awareness of a sense of right and wrong and experience the forerunners of later guilt emotions in conjunction with their sense of wrong.

In this parallel understanding of anxiety and guilt we also have an insight into the question of responsibility for sin. In the environmental frustration of the infant's God-given *needs* (which leads to anxiety), we see the impact of the sins of others. In the frustration of the infant's *wishes* (which leads to guilt feelings) we see the result of the child's own frustrated desires. This reaction to a frustrated desire for omnipotence could be a forerunner of what we see in later life as pride, selfishness, or god-like aspirations. Infants want to be treated the way they want to be treated, and they become angry if they are not treated that way! This seems to correspond to the desire to be like God.

If sin is present in us before we can make conscious moral choices, responsibility cannot be limited to conscious sins. *We must enlarge our concept of responsibility to refer to the locus or origin of sin as well as our efforts or ability to alter sin.* We obviously cannot say that two- or three-month-old infants are responsible for their sin in the sense that they are mentally able to make a different conscious choice and not sin! We can say, however, that they are responsible in the sense that their desires to have precisely their own wishes met is intrinsic to their nature. To put it another way, the problem is ultimately located in the infant rather than in his or her environment. Even with perfect parenting infants would go through many experiences of frustration, anger, and guilt that lead to psychological maladjustments.

In this sense even the helpless infant is responsible. As we mature we develop increased ability to make conscious choices and our conscious responsibility grows. Neither these latter forms of responsibility, however, nor the responsibilities of parents and others should obscure the earliest, inevitable sin of the person. The failure to attend to this earliest, inevitable sin and guilt leads to superficial solutions to the problem of sin and guilt that are based on confession of "known" sins or on overcoming, avoiding, or atoning for specific, conscious sins through self-effort. A view that takes original sin and guilt seriously demands a more radical act of grace to counteract and help shift our focus from guilt feelings associated with specific sins to the problem intrinsic to our entire nature. It also explains why guilt feelings are so resistant to change. They are part of a pattern intrinsic to our fallen nature. This guilt demands a deeper response than self-inflicted punishment, rejection, and disesteem.

SUMMARY

In this chapter I have suggested an alternative to traditionally held theories of the origin of psychopathology. The view presented here stresses a parallel development of anxiety and guilt that gives them equal prominence in the etiology of psychological maladjustments. I believe this view best fits the biblical record of the Fall of Adam and Eve, phenomenological analyses of anxiety and guilt, the nature of early developmental functioning, the dynamics of psychopathology and the concept of original sin.[14]

Some important therapeutic principles grow out of this understanding of the development of the neuroses. These implications will be explored in future chapters. For the time being I simply want to set before the reader the possibility that much of what we have traditionally considered anxiety may actually be guilt, and that consequently we need to place a much greater emphasis on the role sin and guilt play in personal adjustment than psychologists (even Christian ones) have traditionally done.

[14]There is, of course, a third way of looking at the moral awareness of infants and young children. This is the view that what is unique in the human is the *potential* for developing moral awareness. I suspect that this is the view held by many Christians in the field of psychology. We tend to assume a potential for moral functioning and the development of guilt and then simply layer our traditional understanding of the socialization process on top of this assumption. Since those holding this view tend to accept the traditional view of psychopathology that sees guilt as simply a subtype of anxiety, I have not treated this perspective separately. While this perspective is certainly a viable possibility, it seems to me that the observation of infants, the biblical presentation of man as a moral being, and a phenomenological analysis of anxiety and guilt support a primitive experience of guilt and the centrality of that experience to later, more developed experiences of guilt and to the many psychic maneuvers we use to defend against it.

Perspectives on Guilt and Conscience

Psychologists like Sigmund Freud, Erich Fromm, and Hobart Mowrer have developed theories of personality attempting to explain psychological processes and structures including guilt and conscience. Although these non-Christian theorists have made significant contributions to our understanding of some of the factors involved in guilt, their perspectives are limited by their naturalistic viewpoints. Their rejection of scriptural revelation and the reality of a spiritual realm have left them with a one-sided view of personality. In rejecting the biblical view of human nature, they have distorted or overlooked key ingredients of the dynamics of guilt. Part 2 summarizes the main contributions and limitations of these three non-Christian theorists' views of guilt and conscience.

Freud and the Naturalization of Conscience

The first modern systematic attempt to unfold the psychological dynamics of guilt was made by Sigmund Freud. Born in Moravia of Jewish parents in 1856, Freud was strongly atheistic. In some of his most speculative writings he tried to dispose of the God concept by tracing its origin to early "family conflicts" of primitive human tribes. The idea of God was assumed to be a projection of the feared father that civilization gradually modified to fit a more structured religious system.[1]

Given his negative attitude toward religion, his commitment to psychic determinism, and his penchant for careful psychological analysis, it is only natural that Freud would become the first naturalizer of conscience.[2] That is, Freud was the first well-known psychological theorist to develop an explicit view of conscience as strictly the result of natural events occuring in the early life of the child without any reference to God and man's relation to Him. Although many psychologists today take issue with the specific way Freud formulated his concept of the superego, the vast majority of theorists heartily concur with his belief that the functioning of conscience can be completely explained on naturalistic grounds. Because Freud was the father of most of these later approaches, we will use him as the best representative of the naturalizers of conscience.

---

[1]Freud's views on religion are found chiefly in: "Civilization and Its Discontents," "Moses and Monotheism," "The Future of Illusion," and "Totem and Taboo," *The Standard Edition of the Complete Psychological Works of Sigmund Freud,* J. Strachey, trans. (London: Hogarth, 1961), 21:1-162.

[2]P. Lehmann in *Ethics in a Christian Context* (New York: Harper & Row, 1963) discusses the naturalization of conscience.

THE STRUCTURE OF PERSONALITY

Freud viewed the *superego* as one of the three psychic agencies, or structures (the others being the *ego* and the *id*), containing a group of mental contents and processes. The *id* is the source of all related human drives, impulses, and motivations. The *ego* consists of all the functions having to do with one's relation to the environment and is seen as the more rational part of personality. The *superego* contains all of our moral functions and our ideals and aspirations. Freud viewed man as entirely id at birth, with no reality testing and as yet no hints of conscience. Only gradually do the ego and the superego differentiate out of the amorphous unstructured id. As this happens, they exert increasing control and influence over the person's wishes, desires, and fantasies. According to Freud, when we have an impulse to act (id process), our ego processes come into play. Using our reason and intelligence, we evaluate (ego process) the situation and make a decision on whether or not the id impulse can have its way without doing damage to our person. If an impulse comes, for example, to smash one's head into a concrete wall, our ego processes might perceive the danger and say to the id, "That is not a wise decision." The ego, then, is the rational part of the personality. It includes our perceptions, memory, voluntary motor control, and thinking. It inhibits and restrains the strivings of the id in line with the demands of the world. Freud wrote, "In its relation to the id (the ego) is like a man on horseback who has to hold in check the superior strength of the horse."[3]

According to Freud, the superego (his rough equivalent of conscience) develops out of the ego. It is the center of institutional morality. It scans contemplated and completed actions and doles out varying degrees of self-approval or disapproval, self-love or hate, self-criticism, and self-esteem. The superego includes two sets of processes.[4] The first is known as the *ego ideal*. This is the

[3]S. Freud, *The Ego and the Id* (New York: Norton, 1962), p. 15.

[4]Freud never fully developed and clarified his concept of superego. At some points he distinguished between the ego ideal and the punitive processes. At other times he equated the ego ideal and the superego and at still other points he used the terms conscience and superego interchangeably. For our present purposes we will simply identify the superego as the overall moral system, with the ego ideal and the punitive or self-loving functions as subsystems of the more encompassing superego.

inner mental picture of how we think we ought to be. It develops during childhood out of our needs to grow up and become like respected and powerful adults and out of attempts to avoid punishment by conforming to parental expectations.[5]

The second portion of the superego has no formal name. Its function is to punish when we fall short of our ideals and reward us with love and self-esteem when we fulfill them. Punishment comes in the form of guilt feelings. When we fall short of our ideals, the superego sends out messages like, "You'd better watch out!" "You may be punished!" or "You are bad!" The rewards come through messages like, "That's good!" "You're good!" or "Keep up the good work!" By conjuring up either negative or positive feelings the superego attempts to control the strivings of the id.

ORIGINS OF THE SUPEREGO

So much for the general picture of the conscience or superego. Now we will take a look at how it develops out of the Oedipus complex. Freud utilized the mythical story of Oedipus to describe the struggle he believed all children go through in relating to their parents and in developing their superegos. Oedipus was the son of the king and queen of Thebes who was given to a herdsman at birth because an oracle predicted the infant would murder his father. After being adopted by the King of Corinth, Oedipus grew up and unknowingly murdered his father and married his mother. In this murder of father and love of mother Freud believed he saw a universal human struggle of young males to compete with their fathers. During this period, Freud hypothesized, young boys develop a strong desire to possess their mothers. The boy is thought to want to love his mother (including sexually) and wishes the father were dead so he would have no rival for his mother's love.

At the same time, the boy respects his father's strength and wants to be like him. This gives rise to ambivalent feelings. He both resents and idolizes his father. He wants to be like him, but he also wants to destroy or replace him. His resentment stirs up fear since the boy thinks his father may discern his destructive fantasies and retaliate. One form this fear takes is the fear of castration. What better way could a jealous suitor find to destroy his

[5]See chapter 17 for concepts relating to the ego ideal.

competition! And what greater fear could an aspiring young man have? Because of this great fear the boy renounces and represses his mother love and intensifies his identification with his father. By denying his sexual love toward his mother and becoming like his father he can avoid his father's wrath and the feared castration. In essence, he trades the hope of an immediate love affair with his mother for a future one with someone like her. The way to this goal is to become like father and eventually marry a woman of his own.

Out of this process of desire and fear of punishment, Freud sees the superego developing. The child takes many of his parents' standards as his own because he wants to grow up and be like them. But he also takes in the threats and punishments. If, for example, a boy has strong feelings for his mother his superego immediately sends a warning. This warning is experienced as a vague sense of anxiety (over a prohibited impulse coming to the surface), as a fear of punishment or as a feeling of guilt and self-reproach. The guilt, in other words, functions as a warning or self-punishment. It either prohibits action or (if the action has already taken place), inflicts a self-punishment that beats his father to the draw. Since he has already been punished, he doesn't have to fear further punishment from his father. Freud summarizes his view of the development of the supergo this way:

> For a time these two relationships (mother and father) proceed side by side, until the boy's sexual wishes in regard to his mother become more intense and his father is perceived as an obstacle to them. From this the Oedipus complex originates. His identification with his father then takes on a hostile coloring and changes into a wish to get rid of his father in order to take his place with his mother.[6]

> The broad general outcome of the sexual phase dominated by the Oedipus complex may, therefore, be taken to be the forming of a precipitate in the ego, consisting of these two identifications in some way united to each other. This modification of the ego retains its special position; *it confronts the other contents of the ego as an ego ideal or super-ego* (italics mine).[7]

Although it has many subtle aspects, the classical analytic viewpoint on the development of the superego in the male child can be summarized in the following six-step process.

[6]Freud, *The Ego and the Id*, pp. 21-22.
[7]Ibid., p. 24.

1. The child enters the Oedipal period with his strongest attachment to the mother. This is due to the fact that she has been his primary supplier and his first significant interpersonal relationship.

2. Partly out of his desire to grow up and be like his father, the boy begins to develop a desire to exclusively possess his mother—to be her sole love object.

3. Along with the desire to be the mother's only love comes an increasing resentment of any rivals (especially father) and a desire for their disappearance.

4. The negative feelings toward the boy's father stir up two conflicts. First of all, he fears retaliation (punishment in the form of castration). But since he also loves and admires his father he also fears he will lose his father's love as a result of his possessive and destructive wishes.

5. These twin fears (of punishment and loss of love) in time cause the child to repress his oedipal desires. He (consciously) gives up his desires for his mother and reintensifies his desire to be like his father.

6. In repressing his seductive and destructive oedipal wishes the child changes his actual relations with his parents into identifications. That is, instead of seducing and hating his mother and father respectively (which he fears would bring punishment and abandonment) he becomes like them. He internalizes and adopts their perceived prohibitions and expectations as his own.

The result of this turn of events is the establishment in the child's mind of a set of prohibitions similar to the ones the child experienced in relation to his parents during the oedipal period.[8] Brenner put it this way:

> We see, therefore, that the superego has a particularly intimate relationship to the oedipus complex and that it is formed as a

[8]The girl's situation is a bit more complex according to the traditional psychoanalytic view. She is driven to the father as her predominant love object during the oedipal period because of her disillusionment with her mother when she realizes she has no penis! She is later forced to repress her oedipal wishes, not because of castration anxiety as in the boy, but because of fear of losing her mother's love and because her desires to possess her father must inevitably meet with frustration. She also represses her desires because of the jealousy she harbors toward her father because he possesses a penis (penis envy) and because of her fear of being injured if her sexual wishes toward her father are fulfilled.

consequence of the identifications with the moral and prohibiting aspects of his parents' identifications which arise in the child's mind in the process of the dissolution or passing of the oedipus complex. The superego, we may say, consists originally of the internalized images of the moral aspect of the parents of the phallic or oedipal phase.[9]

This, in brief, is Freud's theory of the development of the superego. Before we go on to other perspectives we will take a look at some of the modifications later psychoanalysts have made on Freud's understanding of the superego and also at some of the major criticisms of the psychoanalytic viewpoint.

FORTY YEARS AFTER FREUD

Much has happened since Freud outlined the major features of his view of the superego. The importance of the first few years of life to later emotional adjustment, the reality of unconscious motivations, and the significance of "slips of the tongue" and dreams are generally accepted. Yet few people today (even psychoanalysts) accept all of Freud's theories, especially his narrow view of the superego. Three major criticisms have been leveled at Freud's view of the superego. Later psychoanalysts have generally incorporated these into a more helpful understanding of the development and functioning of the superego.

Probably the most common criticism of Freud's view of the superego is his emphasis on the centrality of sexual strivings in the formation of the superego. Although practicing therapists consistently find that the intimate relationships of children and parents play a key role in shaping the child's moral thinking, most reject a narrow sexual explanation of this process.

Present-day analysts have also concluded that Freud dated the onset of the superego much later than it actually occurs. They suggest that there are at least forerunners or precursors of the superego present in the first year or two of life. Melanie Klein, for example, traced the origins of the superego to the love-hate polarities of the infant's relations with his mother during the last half

[9]C. Brenner, *An Elementary Textbook of Psychoanalysis*, (New York: Anchor, 1974), p. 113.

of the first year of life.[10] Most analysts now agree that the formation of the superego begins during the first couple of years of life in relation to the infant's interaction with the mother. The dynamics of the oedipal period postulated by Freud are now seen as the later stages of the development of the superego and in some cases, as quite secondary to the intimate relationship of the mother and child.

A third modification of Freud's view of superego development and functioning has to do with his almost exclusive emphasis on the harsh, punitive aspects of the superego. Whether it was due to Freud's own personality or to the fact that most of his theorizing grew out of work with obsessive-compulsive and depressed personalities where the punitive aspects of the superego are prominent, Freud paid very little attention to the loving and affirming functions of the superego. Almost all later psychoanalytic theorists stress the superego's positive function in regulating self-esteem and passing out self-love and self-affirmations.[11]

EVALUATION

It is difficult to give a brief yet adequate critique of psychoanalytic theory as it relates to guilt and conscience. Freud's theories have stirred more antagonism in Christian circles than any single writer's

[10]H. Segal in discussing Klein's view of the genesis of the superego writes: "Melanie Klein saw that what was known of the super-ego in the genital stages was but a last stage of a complex development. . . . In the oral-sadistic phase (1st year of life), the child attacks his mother's breast and incorporates it as both destroyed and destructive—'a bad persecuting internal breast.' This is Melanie Klein's view as the earliest root of the persecuting and sadistic aspect of the super-ego. Parallel with this introjection, in situations of love and gratification the infant introjects an ideal loved breast which becomes the root of the ego-ideal aspect of the super-ego" (*Introduction to the Work of Melanie Klein* [New York: Basic Books, 1973], p. 4).

[11]In an article devoted largely to these aspects of the superego's functioning, R. Schafer writes: "There is a loving and beloved aspect of the superego. It represents the loved and admired oedipal and preoedipal parents who provide love, protection, comfort, and guidance, who embody and transmit certain ideals and moral structures more or less representative of their society, and who, even in their punishing activities, provide needed expressions of parental care, contact, and love" ("The Loving and Beloved Superego in Freud's Structural Theory," *The Psychoanalytic Study of the Child*, 15:1960, pp. 163-88).

with the possible exception of Darwin. And, as with Darwin, people do not tend to be calm and objective in their reactions. They either wholeheartedly endorse or reject the psychoanalytic viewpoint. The rather strong consensus in the evangelical church has been that we should reject it!

There are, however, certain aspects of Freud's clinical observations and theorizing that we must come to grips with. Without accepting his frequently considered dehumanizing view of man, his theorizing about the origin of the belief in God, or his views of the role of sexuality in human adjustment, there are certain aspects of his thinking that have seemed to bear the test of time. If we are to pursue a truly holistic study of psychology and theology, we must move beyond an oppositional stance and attempt to understand these aspects of secular science and theory that can contribute to our fuller understanding of the human personality. In regards to the nature and origins of guilt, it seems to me that psychoanalytic thinking has left us with four basic insights that are essential to any adequate understanding of the topic.

The first and most general of these insights is the fact that feelings of guilt have roots in early childhood. Although it is now obvious to any psychological practitioner that harsh, condemning feelings of guilt have roots in the young child's relationships with his parents, this understanding is relatively new. Prior to the time of Freud there had been no major efforts to unravel the sources of guilt emotions. They were simply assumed to be normal, adult feelings with no significant history. Although some might claim that it was a disservice, Freud once and for all unmasked the early roots of guilt and made it plain that many guilt emotions grow in the context of the child's relationships with his parents in the first few years of life.

A second aspect of Freud's contribution grows out of the first. That is the awareness that the child's feelings of guilt develop at least partially through the taking in (internalizing) of the parents' perceived attitudes and actions. This internalization of the parents' punishing attitudes accounts for the seemingly foreign nature of many of our feelings of guilt. Many clients remark that they wish they could be rid of their self-condemning attitudes. They seem to exist in the brain as intruders, attacking and condemning; they cannot be overcome. One patient said, "I wish I could have brain surgery and just cut out those stupid thoughts!" This feeling comes from the fact that guilt feelings are partly foreign. Many of them are taken in from our parents. For the Christian, this insight has special significance; it means we do not necessarily see the condemning accusations of guilt as coming directly from the Lord. Instead, guilt feelings may originate in the child's relationships with his parents. This forces us to rethink our views about guilt and conviction, and find out what is truly the Holy Spirit, and what is simply the punitive, internalized attitude or action of our parents.

A third contribution that may surprise those who are not rather familiar with Freud's writings has to do with the severity of the superego. Most people believe Freud sees guilt feelings as simply the internalized voice of parental punishments and condemnations. If the parents were harsh, the child developed strong guilt feelings. If the parents were loving, he didn't. The parents, in other words, are responsible for all the problems! This is not the case. In fact, precisely the opposite is true. Based on his understanding of the early mental life of the child and especially the processes of projection (putting out) and introjection (taking in) Freud (and other analysts after him) went to rather great pains to make it clear that the child's condemning self-attitudes are not simply the result of parental mistreatment. They are also strongly influenced by the child's own desires, perceptions, and frustrations.

According to Freud, when the child is in the throes of his Oedipus complex, he fears the same sexed parent's angry punishment and rejection, and takes these perceived threats into his personality as central ingredients of his superego. The attitudes he takes in, however, are not accurate reflections of his parents' attitudes. Instead, they are his parents' attitudes *as he imagines them*. Because the child is highly resentful of the same sexed parent, he tends to perceive the parent as more angry than he or she is in reality. In other words, the child projects, or puts his or her own hostility into the parent, thus distorting the way the parent is viewed. When the child later internalizes the parent's perceived punitive attitudes into his superego, he is taking in the parent's attitudes not as they actually are, but as he has projectively distorted them. He takes them in as angry and punitive as they actually are with his own anger and destructiveness added on top! This is what gives the superego its strong punitive flavor.[12] Alluding to this process, Freud writes:

> If the parents have really ruled with a rod of iron, we can easily understand the child developing a severe superego, but contrary to our expectations, experience shows that the superego may reflect the same relentless harshness even when the upbringing has been gentle and kind, and avoided threats and punishments as far as possible.[13]

This dynamic helps explain why a child with basically well-adjusted parents who do not rely on fear motivation and angry punishment may still develop strong feelings of guilt. If the child does not get what he wants from his parents, he responds with anger. This anger causes the child to distort his understanding of his parent in the direction of an angry and frustrating person. Consequently, when the child takes in his parents' corrective attitudes he is actually reaping the results of his own rage. Children with harsh parents are more prone to developing punitive guilt emotions, but parents can in no way be blamed for all of a child's guilt. Guilt feelings result from the interplay of the child's own feelings of resentment and the actual angry corrections received from parents.[14] Loving and sensitive parents help children modify their propensity to perceive parents in punitive ways and thereby aid children in developing healthier, self-corrective attitudes. Angry and frustrated parents reinforce the child's tendency to perceive parents as punitive and compound the severity of the child's superego.

A fourth significant contribution Freud made to our under-

---

[12]Hanna Segal writes, "The earlier the introjection, the more fantastic are the objects introjected and the more distorted by what has been projected into them." The objects Segal refers to are the images of the parents that the child takes into his own mental picture of himself. To the degree that the child was angry at the parents and consequently distorted his perception of them, his superego will be more severe and harsh than his parents were in reality. Especially with young children these distortions can be extreme (*Introduction to the Work of Melanie Klein*, p. 20).

[13]Freud, *New Introductory Lectures on Psychoanalysis*, J. Strachey, trans. (New York: Norton, 1965), p. 62.

[14]They result, in other words, from the destructive (sinful) wishes of either the parent or the child—and usually both!

standing of guilt is his emphasis on the unconscious nature of much of guilt. Freud was the first psychologist to begin unmasking the hidden sources of guilt and show us that its resolution must be much more than a surface affair. In the compulsive hand-washing of obsessive-compulsive neurotics, Freud saw the results of unconscious guilt that only sensitive poets before him had recognized. In the depressed individual he found guilt over hidden resentments. And in the paranoid he found guilt over long since forgotten wishes that had been projected onto others. Whether or not we agree with all of the content Freud attributes to the unconscious, it is clear that he made a very important contribution in pointing out the presence of influential wishes and feelings operating outside our conscious awareness.[15]

LIMITS OF NATURALISM

In addition to the criticisms secular theorists have made of Freud's views of guilt, the Bible and the observation of individual and social consciences raise other important questions about the adequacy of Freud's concept of the superego. The very naturalistic assumptions that encouraged Freud to search for the developmental factors underlying the formation of conscience and guilt turn out to be a major limitation for his theorizing. Since all secular theorists operate from similar naturalistic assumptions, we will in this section, look at some of the limitations inherent to all naturalistic views although we will be focusing especially on Freud's views.

Freud's (and all other secular theorists) naturalism is hard pressed to account for the fact that people consistently demonstrate moral standards and commitments that are not simply reflections of parental training, societal introjects, or explicable psychological dynamics. The inherent moral nature of humanity as a bearer of the image of God, in other words, is neglected by Freud and other naturalizers of conscience. They simply cannot

[15]This helps us understand why many Christians have difficulty believing they have been forgiven by God after confessing their sins. As long as there are hidden or unconscious sins, guilt continues to rise up and challenge any pronouncement of forgiveness.

satisfactorily account for all of humanity's spiritual ideals and moral commitments on the basis of biological instincts and the socialization process. Cohu put it this way:

> If conscience springs from social utilitarian needs, how does it come about that at every stage of man's history conscience sits in judgment on and breaks the laws of society? If the sense of obligation springs from society itself, why does our sense of duty rise so infinitely above the social standard and refuse to be merged in it? Can a spring rise above its own source? Why does our conscience applaud a Christ who does violence to existing social and religious laws, however time-honored and hallowed their sanctions, and sets them at nought in the interests of society and religion itself? Once more, why does conscience, refusing to be merged in the social consciousness, ever set up for itself an ideal society, a Kingdom of God, a society straining after that justice, truth and love which alone satisfy conscience-needs?[16]

Neglecting this innate source of moral commitment, Freud's naturalistic view of conscience is unable to satisfactorily explain the ultimate source of guilt. Even if Freud's understanding of guilt should prove to be a *necessary* description of the psychological development of guilt, would it be a *sufficient* one? Since we are created by God as moral beings, we have a very important contributor to our ego ideal that is neglected by Freud and that goes beyond that which we gain from the socialization process. Our ideals are not strictly the result of the internalizing of the values of parents and others. They are also significantly impacted by our existence as bearers of the image of God. They contain the law written on the heart.[17]

Similarly, can the internalization of punishments from parents account for all of our guilt feelings? What if we *are* in danger of God's judgment and the fear of parental punishment is merely a reflection of this more basic fear or a parallel expression of it? Or what if our inner self-punishment is an effort to quiet our fears of punishment from God by beating Him to the draw and atoning for our own sins? As Stein put it, "Psychological explanation does

---

[16]J. Cohu, *Vital Problems of Religion* (Edinburgh: T. & T. Clark, 1914), p. 199.
[17]Rom. 2:15

not account for ontological reality, however much it may throw light on it."[18]

This leads to another limitation of nearly all naturalistic views of conscience; they fail to address the problem of objective guilt.[19] In their zeal to root out and resolve unhealthy self-punitiveness, most secular theorists assumed there is no such thing as objective guilt and that guilt feelings are totally unrelated to real sin and guilt.[20] The apostle Paul, for example, did not locate his feelings of guilt in naturalistic environmental factors when he wrote:

> I find then the principle that evil is present in me, the one who wishes to do good. For I joyfully concur with the law of God in the inner man, but I see a different law in the members of my body, waging war against the law of my mind, and making me a prisoner of the law of sin which is in my members. Wretched man that I am! Who will set me free from the body of this death?[21]

And in answer to his rhetorical question Paul wrote:

> Thanks be to God through Jesus Christ our Lord! So then, on the one hand I myself with my mind am serving the law of God, but on the other, with my flesh the law of sin. There is therefore, now no condemnation for those who are in Christ Jesus. For the law of the Spirit of life in Christ Jesus has set you free from the law of sin and of death.[22]

Paul saw both the source of his guilt and the ultimate resolution of his conflicts in his sinfulness and need for the reconciliation to God and to himself that comes through Christ. This does not at all rule out the role of naturalistic insights in the understanding

[18]E. Stein, *Guilt: Theory and Therapy* (Philadelphia: The Westminster Press, 1968), p. 193.

[19]Although some existential theorists and reality therapists speak of objective guilt they generally do not mean by this objective guilt before God, but rather guilt before ourselves and others.

[20]*"The scrupulous, tyrannized superego of the perfectionist is certainly not unrelated to guilt before God. It is an expression of the tension between the way we are and the way we should be, and this tension is at the heart of the religious quest"* (W. Hulme, *The Dynamics of Sanctification* [Minneapolis: Augsburg, 1966], p. 30).

[21]Rom. 7:21-24.

[22]Rom. 7:25-8:2.

and resolution of problems of guilt but it does place them in a radically different perspective and impacts our efforts to resolve them.

The failure of naturalistic theorists to address the issue of objective guilt also means they make some serious errors in their understanding of human nature. Freud, for example, regards man as simply a highly evolved, biologically-driven animal whose problems of adjustment grow out of conflicts between basic biological strivings and the demands of the environment. In contrast, biblical revelation sees the ultimate source of guilt not in an inherent conflict between the individual and his environment but in the rebellion of his inherently moral personality against his own nature and God. This immediately shifts our perception of the nature of all personality conflicts (including guilt) from a biological-environmental struggle to a moral-spiritual one. Knight summarizes the divergence of naturalistic and supernaturalist views of human nature in this way:

> The chief difference between naturalism and supernaturalism as regarding the problem of good and evil seems clear. *The naturalist holds that evil flows from attempts to stifle or violate nature through man's ignorance of nature's laws and his translation of that ignorance into social institutions. ... From the standpoint of the supernaturalist, nature itself is imperfect, and evil is inherent in its constitution.* The creative dialectic then is man's struggle to overcome the imperfections of the City of Man and climb toward the perfections of the City of God (italics mine).[23]

The moral-spiritual perspective does not, of course, rule out either biological or environmental influences. But it does significantly alter our focus. If humanity's problem is strictly one of adaption to the environment, our solutions will focus solely on environmental reconciliations. If it is ultimately one of rebellion against the Creator and the consequent loss of inner wholeness, we will have to grapple with this reality in our therapeutic activities.

Having stressed the limitations of naturalistic psychological

[23]J. Knight, *Conscience and Guilt* (New York: Appleton-Century-Crofts, 1969), p. 76.

views attempting to understand problems of guilt apart from the context of our relationship with God I would also like to point out a problem reflected in the thinking of some Christians. That is the view that since non-Christian therapists do not take the reality of humanity's sinfulness into account that they obviously cannot help *anyone* resolve *any* problems of guilt.[24] Since we are created as social beings we significantly impact the lives of one another. Parents especially, leave lasting impressions on the psychological development of their children. These imprints are passed on in very natural (as opposed to supernatural) ways according to some basic laws. Although alienated from God, non-Christians still possess the God-given ability to comprehend many of these laws and help people grow by understanding how their environment has impacted them.

You need not know, for example, that the entirety of the human race is objectively guilty before God in order to be a caring person and help a depressed person victimized by parental brutality to recognize love and acceptance. You *will* reach a point when it would be helpful to understand the spiritual realities impacting this person's life, but you could help him or her resolve a good deal of neurotic guilt without this knowledge.[25]

A final problem growing out of Freud's naturalistic view of conscience has to do with the lack of an alternative, positive view of motivation. For the Christian, this is a crucial issue. Scripture portrays the highest motivation as a motivation of love growing out of our appreciation of God's love and intervention in our lives. John writes:

[24]This is the stance of theorists such as M. Bobgan and D. Bobgan who posit an inherent conflict between psychology and Scripture (*The Psychological Way/The Spiritual Way* [Minneapolis: Bethany Fellowship, 1979]). For a discussion of the pitfalls of this commonly held perspective the reader is referred to J. Carter and B. Narramore, *The Integration of Psychology and Theology: An Introduction* (Grand Rapids: Zondervan, 1979).

[25]The distinctly spiritual dimension of guilt is more likely to arise with discussion of personal responsibility, the source and nature of values, the basis in reality of one's sense of alienation or separation, a treatment of the gradiose nature of some ideals and the frequently self-atoning nature of many guilt feelings. These are areas where biblical revelation takes us beyond the knowledge secured by naturalistic means.

> Beloved, let us love one another, for love is from God; and every-one who loves is born of God and knows God. The one who does not love does not know God, for God is love. By this the love of God was manifested in us, that God has sent His only begotten Son into the world so that we might live through Him. In this is love, not that we loved God, but that He loved us and sent His Son to be the propitiation for our sins. Beloved, if God so loved us, we also ought to love one another.[26]

John describes love as a response to being loved. He also ties our response of love to Christ's payment for our sins. He suggests, in other words, that our love is a response to what Christ did to free us from guilt! Christ paid the ultimate price to reconcile us to Him and the appreciation of this fact encourages our love for God and others. This view of love elevates the experience of love and the valuing of others far above the biologically based view of Freud that sees all mature forms of love as growing out of sublimations and transformations of basic biological urges.

SUMMARY

In this chapter I have attempted to sketch the fundamentals of the psychoanalytic view of guilt. We have seen that Freud viewed the superego as developing out of the child's desires for posses-sion of the opposite-sex parent and resentment toward the same sexed parent. Later analysts have broadened the psychoanalytic view to make more room for experiences with the mother and for other dynamics than sexual attraction for the opposite sexed parent.

In critiquing the psychoanalytic view of guilt I have suggested that it is possible to reject some very significant aspects of Freud-ian theory (even some of its foundational principles) without throw-ing out all of Freud's insights. Freud's view of guilt is obviously lacking because of its naturalistic assumptions and its failure to see the ultimate source of humanity's guilt as rebellion against God. It seems to me that Freud's biological theory is also entirely inadequate and results in a dehumanizing view of man. In Freud's view man is an instinct ridden animal and his moral views are largely the result of fears of punishment and castration!

[26]1 John 1:7-11.

While I agree that many people are motivated by fears of punishment, and while it may even be the motivation most people are operating under, this view leaves much to be desired. In light of the Christian affirmation that man is a bearer of the image of God and that he is to "walk in love,"[27] an understanding of morality that sees it as simply a result of fears of punishment and rejection is weak indeed!

Another problem with psychoanalytic theory is its emphasis on sex. Although Freud has sometimes been falsely maligned as promoting an irresponsible acting out of sexual urges, it does seem that he has given sexual strivings a much greater role in the formation of personality than the evidence calls for. If we add to these criticisms Freud's attack on organized religion and his views on the development of belief in God, we can see why many Christians have rejected psychoanalytic thinking out of hand. But if we take a more dispassionate look at psychoanalytic theorizing, we can also see some contributions it has made to our understanding of guilt.

Significant insights have helped us understand the role of early parent-child interactions in the development of guilt feelings, the role of identification with parents in the formation of our moral values, the influence of the child's own anger in the development of his feelings of guilt, and the unconscious source of much guilt. We will return to these topics in later chapters when we discuss in detail the psychological development of guilt feelings in the child.

[27]Eph. 5:2.

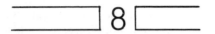

Fromm and the Humanization of Conscience

One of the main alternatives to Freud's psychoanalytic view of guilt is found in the writings of humanistic and existential psychologists such as Carl Rogers,[1] Abraham Maslow,[2] Medard Boss,[3] and Ludwig Binswanger.[4] Although coming from different philosophical roots, humanistic and existential psychologists share some similar views about the nature and functioning of guilt and conscience. They are all dissatisfied with Freud's narrow and pessimistic view of the development and functioning of conscience. They also give man more credit for his ability to consciously select constructive moral standards than Freud, who attributed conscience simply to the interaction of the child's biologically based drives, and the internalizing of parental values and punishments.

Existential and humanistic writers have in general not attempted to develop a careful theoretical understanding of guilt and conscience. Although their writings make frequent reference to the experience of guilt and to man's inner struggles over difficult moral choices, they have resisted the structure of a cohesive theoretical approach to guilt and conscience. One notable exception is Erich Fromm. Consequently we will look at Fromm's writings as a representative of humanistic-existential approaches to

[1]Carl Rogers, *Client Centered Therapy* (Boston: Houghton Mifflin, 1965).

[2]Abraham Maslow, *Toward a Psychology of Being* (Princeton: D. Van Nostrand, 1962).

[3]Medard Boss, *Psychoanalysis and Daseinsanalysis* (New York: Basic Books, 1963).

[4]Ludwig Binswanger, *Being in the World: Selected Papers of Ludwig Binswanger*, J. Needleman, trans. (New York: Harper & Row, 1968).

guilt. Other theorists will be briefly mentioned to elaborate and clarify the major features of humanistic and existential views of conscience.

Born in Frankfurt, in 1900, to a German-Jewish middle-class family, Erich Fromm received early instruction in the Old Testament and Jewish tradition. He received a Ph.D. from the University of Heidelberg and later took psychoanalytic training at the Berlin Psychoanalytic Institute. Coming to the United States in 1933, Fromm taught at the Chicago Psychoanalytic Institute and then began a private practice of psychotherapy in New York City. As an author, Fromm's interests have extended far beyond the areas of psychopathology and psychotherapy to culture, history, philosophy, religion, and sociology. His writings reflect a common thread of emphasis on man's alienation from other men and his frustrated search for freedom from authoritarian controls. Being deeply influenced by the writings of Karl Marx, Fromm edited a book on Socialist Humanism[5] at one point in his career. He was also strongly committed to the philosophical views of the Enlightenment that emphasized the confidence man could have in his own rational processes. This commitment put him at odds with Freud's strong views on man's irrationality and, as we will see, with several aspects of biblical revelation concerning the nature of man.

THE ORIGINS OF CONSCIENCE

Like Freud, Fromm sees the conscience developing mainly during the first few years of life. Unlike Freud, he does not see sexual conflicts as the necessary root of the superego. Fromm sees the origins of conscience in the child's struggle for power against the authority of his parents. Feeling weak and helpless, every child has a life-influencing dilemma. He badly wants the security and protection of his parents and knows the best way to share their power is to be obedient. But he also wants to try out his world and have his own way. If he does, however, he is in danger of displeasing the parents and suffering punishment or rejection.

In much the same way that Freud postulates the resolution

---

[5]Fromm, *Socialist Humanism: An International Symposium* (Garden City, New York: Doubleday, 1965).

of the Oedipus complex and its effects on the formation of the superego, Fromm sees the child identifying with powerful parents in order to avoid their punishment or rejection. The child takes in (internalizes) their values and prohibitions as his own. He also takes in their corrective attitudes. Fromm describes this process as follows:

> The laws and sanctions of external authority become part of oneself, as it were, and instead of feeling responsible to something outside oneself, one feels responsible to something inside, to one's conscience. Conscience is a more effective regulator of conduct than fear of external authorities; for, while one can run away from the latter, one cannot escape from oneself nor, therefore, from the internalized authority which has become part of oneself.[6]

THE AUTHORITARIAN CONSCIENCE

This conformity, based on the fear principle, and the subsequent internalizing of parental expectations, leads to the development of what Fromm calls the "authoritarian conscience." The authoritarian conscience is the conscience of childhood. Its norms are the absolute standards of parents and other authorities and its motivations are fears of punishment and self-rejection. In describing the authoritarian conscience Fromm writes:

> Its strength is rooted in the emotions of fear of, and admiration for, the authority. Good conscience is consciousness of pleasing the (external and internalized) authority; guilty conscience is the consciousness of displeasing it. The good authoritarian conscience produces a feeling of well-being and security, for it implies approval by, and greater closeness to, the authority; the guilty conscience produces fear and insecurity, because acting against the will of the authority implies the danger of being punished and—what is worse—of being deserted by the authority.[7]

Here Fromm is saying the child's conscience is at its best and considered good (by the child) when he is conforming. When he

[6]Fromm, *Man for Himself,* p. 144.
[7]Ibid., p. 141.

rebels (or even considers rebelling!) against the internalized authority whose approval and security he desires, he feels anxious and thinks he has a bad conscience. From this perspective, a good conscience requires the willingness to reject one's independence and acknowledge one's fearful dependency while a bad conscience comes with struggles for individuality and autonomy.

In this sense, Fromm's authoritarian conscience is very similar to Freud's superego. Both are based on the internalization of parental values and on the fear of punishment or rejection by the needed authority. Neither contains maturely selected goals and ideals or healthy attitudes of self-correction. Fromm goes on to say:

> The prime offense in the authoritarian situation is rebellion against the authority's rule. Thus disobedience becomes the "cardinal sin"; obedience, the cardinal virtue.

> Paradoxically, the authoritarian *guilty* conscience is a result of the feelings of strength, independence, productiveness, and pride, while the authoritarian good conscience springs from the feeling of obedience, dependence, powerlessness, and sinfulness.[8]

Needless to say, Fromm is extremely critical of the authoritarian conscience, which, from his perspective, exalts weakness, obedience, and dependency.

THE HUMANISTIC CONSCIENCE

Over against the authoritarian conscience, Fromm places the humanistic conscience. This is the mature conscience, which, according to Fromm, is not based upon the introjection of feared authorities and their values. It is based on one's consciously selected goals and aspirations. Consequently its motivations are different from those of its authoritarian counterpart and its content is likely to be different also. Fromm writes:

> Humanistic conscience is not the internalized voice of an authority whom we are eager to please and afraid of displeasing;

[8]Ibid., p. 148.

it is our own voice, present in every human being and independent of external sanctions and rewards.[9]

For Fromm the humanistic conscience is a reflection of our true selves. He continues:

> (Humanistic conscience) is the reaction of our total personality to its proper functioning or dysfunctioning; not a reaction to the functioning of this or that capacity but to the totality of capacities which constitute our human and our individual existence ... Conscience is thus a re-action of ourselves to ourselves. *It is the voice of our true selves which summons us back to ourselves*, to live productively, to develop fully and harmoniously—that is, to become what we potentially are (italics mine).[10]

Although the humanistic and authoritarian consciences may at times have the same *ethics* (for example, murder is wrong), both the *origins* of the standards and the *motivations* for living up to the standards are different. The person ruled by an authoritarian conscience adopts his standard because authorities taught him, for example, not to murder and because he is afraid of the self-inflicted punishment he would receive for violation. The person with a humanistic conscience arrives at his decision not to murder on the basis of reason and maintains it out of self-interest, which results in a healthy interest in others. As Fromm puts it:

> Humanistic conscience is the expression of man's self-interest and integrity, while authoritarian conscience is concerned with man's obedience, self sacrifice, duty, or his "social adjustment." The goal of humanistic conscience is productiveness, and therefore happiness, since happiness is the necessary concomitant of productive living. To cripple oneself by becoming a tool of others ... is in opposition to the demands of one's conscience.[11]

In stressing the crippling of "oneself by becoming a tool of others," Fromm strikes a chord shared by all humanistic and existential writers—including the century's best-known humanistic

[9]Ibid., p. 148.
[10]Ibid., pp. 158-59.
[11]Ibid., pp. 159-60.

psychologist, Carl Rogers. Although Rogers rarely mentions guilt and conscience in his extensive writings, his theoretical perspectives are consistent with Fromm's stress on the necessity of developing a humanistic rather than an authoritarian conscience. Rogers speaks of the tension created when a person takes in the values of others as if they were based on the person's own "organismic functioning" when in reality they are not. This creates a conflict between the values the individual has arrived at through his own sensory and visceral processes and the introjected values of others. In trying to please the internalized voice of others, the person has to repress or ignore his own true values and reactions and lose touch with important aspects of himself.[12] Rogers's introjected values parallel Fromm's authoritarian conscience while the person's own sensory and visceral reactions (now repressed because of the conflicting introjected values) parallel the roots of Fromm's humanistic conscience. In each case problems arise because of the influence of the environment and the failure to trust the inherently positive directions of the organism.

NORMAL AND NEUROTIC GUILT

Fromm's distinction between the authoritarian and the humanistic conscience leads naturally to a distinction between two forms of guilt common to most humanistic and existential writers.[13] Hammes, for example, distinguishes between normal and neurotic guilt.

> Neurotic guilt is (a) disproportionate to the wrong committed, (b) may induce repression, and (c) is often accompanied by

---

[12]Rogers, *Client Centered Therapy*, 1965, pp. 149-57.

[13]Gordon Allport in *Becoming: Basic Considerations for a Psychology of Personality* (New Haven: Yale University Press, 1960), p. 74, describes the motivation of the "generic conscience," his equivalent to Fromm's humanistic conscience, as follows: "It is the generic self guidance that keeps conscience alive and applicable to new experience. The generic conscience tells us in effect, 'If you do this, it will build your style of being; if that, it will tear down your style of being.' In proportion as the generic conscience becomes the monitor of growth, emphasis shifts from tribalism to individuality, from opportunistic to oriented becoming. Fear becomes ought as appropriate development begins to outweigh opportunistic."

neurotic anxiety. Normal guilt, however, involves full awareness of the moral transgression, the acknowledgement of responsibility and the realization that amends are in order.[14]

Existentialists like Haigh[15] and Boss distinguish between neurotic guilt and existential or true guilt, which "consists in his (humanity's) failing to carry out his mandate to fulfill all his possibilities."[16]

These existentialists, in contrast to most psychoanalytic and humanistic writers, stress objective guilt as well as guilt feelings. In doing so, they come closer to one key ingredient of the biblical point of view of guilt, the reality of objective guilt. Their understanding of objective guilt, however, is rooted in man's alienation from himself rather than his alienation from God. Boss, for example, writes:

> Man is aware of existential guilt when he hears the never-ending call of his conscience. This essential, inevitable being-in-debt is *guilt*, and not merely a subjective *feeling* of guilt.[17]

Boss goes on to say:

> Because of existential being-in-debt (experienced as guilt), even the most skillfully conducted psychoanalysis cannot free man of guilt. Actually, not a single analysand could be found in the whole world who has been transformed into a really guiltless person by psychoanalytic treatment. . . .

> Psychoanalysis, however, can accomplish something else. It can elucidate the past, present, and future of a patient's life to the point where he becomes aware of his existential being-in-debt. This in turn enables him to acknowledge his debt, to say "yes" to it and take it upon himself. He becomes aware of his possibilities for living through listening to the call of his conscience; he can take them over responsibly, stand by himself, and thus make them part of himself.[18]

[14]J. Hammes, *Humanistic Psychology: A Christian Interpretation* (New York: Grune & Stratton, 1971), p. 105.

[15]G. Haigh, "Existential Guilt: Neurotic and Real," *Review of Existential Psychology and Psychiatry* (vol. 1, 1961), pp. 120-30.

[16]Boss, *Psychoanalysis and Daseinsanalysis*, p. 270.

[17]Ibid.

[18]Ibid., pp. 270-71.

Here Boss discusses two fundamental premises of the existential view of guilt: (1) all men are truly guilty, and (2) each individual must take responsibility for his or her guilt and consequently for his or her life. When this true (normal or existential) guilt is fully faced, neurotic guilt disappears because neurotic guilt feelings did not develop from within the person, but were acquired from moralistic parents, educators, and other socializing agents. Once one accepts responsibility for his own guilt, allegiance to this acquired false guilt disappears. Boss and other existentialists see the process of therapy as freeing the person from neurotic, acquired guilt so that he or she can experience true existential guilt.

EVALUATION

Fromm's concept of a humanistic conscience clearly has some advantages over Freud's narrow view of the superego. Although like Freud, Fromm points out the early roots of the punitive superego, he goes beyond this to suggest a viable alternative—the rationally based humanistic conscience. In this way he moves beyond Freud's more "animal" view of man and gives man credit for his ethical choices rather than rooting them solely in the dread of punishment and rejection. In fact, some aspects of Fromm's understanding of morality come close to a biblical perspective. His emphasis on the perils of a morality based upon fear and infantile dependency, for example, certainly has some parallels to the New Testament in Jesus' description of love motivation.[19] So does his call for a morality growing out of concern for oneself and others.[20]

Fromm and other humanistic and existential writers also realize that an immature, conformity based morality actually enables people to avoid taking personal responsibility. In focusing on pleasing parents and others (or their internalized voices) many people avoid facing and making difficult moral choices. When they turn everything into black and white, or into issues of conformity or nonconformity, they do not have to accept the responsibility of struggling in many of the gray areas of life we all encounter. In a

[19]John 14:15-21; 1 John 4:16-21.
[20]1 Cor. 12:1-26; Phil. 2:1-5.

similar way, the existentialist concept of guilt over an unused life also adds a positive side to our understanding of objective guilt. Guilt is not simply doing the wrong. It is also a failure to accept the responsibility to do the right!

The stress that Fromm and other humanistic and existential writers place on listening to our "own inner voice" or "trusting the organism" in order to "become what we potentially are" contains a mixture of truth and error. Since we are created in the image of God, we do have vast untapped ability and potential. And it is true that many Christians have ignored this potential and substituted conformity to outer regulations. This has stifled the Holy Spirit's ability to creatively motivate people to use their God-given gifts and sensitivities and has resulted in a tragic repression of parts of the true self that has caused many to lose touch with their inner resources. But this is only half the story. If human nature were not fallen we could follow Fromm's optimistic exhortations. But because it is, "trusting our inner selves" may lead us to destructive choices as often as it leads us to constructive ones. The Scriptures make it clear that every person has a strong, selfish orientation toward evil (Ps. 53:6; Rom. 3:23). We will have more to say of this later.

Fromm's treatment of dependency and authority is both potentially helpful and misleading. He is certainly correct in pointing out that much of what passes as morality is nothing more than an immature, internalized fear of punishment and rejection. He also rightly sees that religious belief can perpetuate this type of morality. Unfortunately, like Freud before him, Fromm did not see the possibility of the mature, love-based morality espoused in Scripture, which we will discuss in chapter 11. For Fromm, belief in and commitment to a personal God was inevitably motivated by neurotic dependency and fear.

When Fromm attempts to lay the foundation for his humanistic conscience, he runs into several additional problems. The contents of the humanistic conscience, according to Fromm, come solely from man's reason. He rejects any outside authority and substitutes an entirely autonomous morality. He tells us:

> The ideas of the Enlightenment taught man that he could trust his own reason as a guide to establishing valid ethical norms

and that *he could rely on himself, needing neither revelation nor the authority of the church in order to know good and evil.*

Valid ethical norms can be formed by man's reason and by it alone. Man is capable of discerning and making value judgements as valid as all other judgments derived from reason. *The great tradition of humanistic ethical thought has laid the foundation for value systems based on man's autonomy and reason* (italics mine).[21]

While our focus here is more on the structure than the contents of conscience (a task that belongs more properly to the study of ethics) we cannot entirely separate the two. At least three significant difficulties with Fromm's humanistic perspective that impact his view of conscience need to be noted.

To begin with, as we saw in chapters 5-6, it was the desire of man to be ultimately responsible for judging good and evil that set in motion the problems of conscience we have today. Adam and Eve tried to be something they were not designed to be and consequently took upon themselves the impossible burden of establishing their identity on an autonomous basis and trying to effect reconciliation through their own efforts. As a proponent of radical humanism, Fromm is staunchly opposed to any creed or person that in any way suggests placing limits on humanity's autonomy. He writes:

By radical humanism I refer to a global philosophy which emphasizes the oneness of the human race, *the capacity of man to develop his own powers and to arrive at inner harmony* and at the establishment of a peaceful world. *Radical humanism considers the goal of man to be that of complete independence,* and this implies penetrating through fictions and illusions to a full awareness of reality (italics mine).[22]

One of the fictions for Fromm is the belief in a personal, creator God. In *Ye Shall Be As Gods,*[23] he interprets the fall of humanity as a fall upward and sees the first three chapters of Genesis describing a major step forward for mankind. Adam had

[21]Fromm, *Man for Himself,* pp. 5-6.

[22]Fromm, *Psychoanalysis and Religion* (New Haven: Yale University Press, 1956), p. 13.

[23]New York: Holt, Rinehart and Winston, 1966.

the courage to rebel and, "Having been expelled from the Garden of Eden, he begins his independent life; his first act of disobedience is the beginning of human history, because it is the beginning of human freedom."[24] This view of human nature and the Fall, of course, fits nicely with Fromm's view of the necessity of throwing off the authoritarian conscience and making all of one's own decisions.

Tragically Fromm's refusal to face the reality of humanity's sinfulness leads him to confuse slavery with freedom. Instead of seeing that it was Adam's (and our own) choice to reject his position as a created child of God and to attempt to play God that threw the world into chaos and bondage, Fromm steadfastly propounds Adam's fiction—the belief that humanity can live in health and happiness apart from God. And in doing so Fromm cuts us off from the one source that could produce peace and unity—a humble, loving acceptance of the reality that we are created, finite beings made to function in relationship with God.

Fromm's humanistic conscience is actually a call for mankind to follow the path of Adam and Eve. In fact, is there not a very close parallel between Adam and Eve's desire to be like God, knowing good and evil, and Fromm's proclamation that: "There is *no prouder statement* man can make than to say: 'I shall act according to *my* conscience' " (italics mine)?[25]

Both Adam and Fromm propose relying on our own reason and rejecting our finiteness and need of God. As much as we might like to extol the virtue of autonomous man's reason both biblical revelation and centuries of experience tell us there are serious limits to autonomous reason. As a matter of fact, it is paradoxical to try to build a system of ethics or an understanding of humanity's moral nature—both essentially interpersonal endeavors—on a theoretical superstructure that rejects humanity's ultimate dependency! In other words, Adam and Eve's rebellion was essentially an antirelational act. It was a denial of their need to depend upon God. Just like Freud and other naturalizers, Fromm's proposed solution follows the same autonomous path in search of a solution. Man can do it on his own!

[24]Ibid., p. 23.
[25]Fromm, *Man for Himself*, p. 141.

Rather than acknowledging our human limitations and need for dependency—an act that would open us up for both inter- and intrapersonal reconciliation—Fromm posits continued efforts to quiet the painful awareness of our failures by following an autonomous direction. This leaves us in the position of continuing to try to be something we were not created to be—a key source of our inward division and guilt. To put it another way, *since the cleavage giving rise to guilt feelings came about as the result of man's assertion of autonomy from God in the search for moral knowledge, the continued attempt to arrive at this knowledge independently of God can only result in a perpetuation of this cleavage.* No matter what norms are selected (even "correct" ones), the very process of dialogue will maintain the inner sense of division and disunity.

In addition to the problem of autonomy, Fromm's humanistic conscience also leaves us without an explanation for the origin of the sense of obligation, or moral imperative, in the humanistic conscience. If we were not designed to function in a certain way, or if we are not ultimately responsible to a higher being, in other words, why does every human being have some sense of moral obligations or imperative? McKenzie writes:

> Granted that it is a step in advance of Freud's negative conception, we are still left without an explanation of the source of obligation, a sense of ought to which the sense of guilt is psychologically correlated. That, however, is a problem common to all naturalistic ethics. Apart from that, his *summam bonum* is the old theory of self-realization, long ago discarded by ethical philosophers. By self-realization he means the realization of all our potentialities. This is not very helpful. Our potentialities are not all desirable by any means. Are we not potentially evil as well as good?[26]

Fromm offers us neither theological (or philosophical) or psychological answers to this question.[27]

---

[26]J. McKenzie, *Guilt: Its Meaning and Significance* (New York: Abingdon, 1962), pp. 44-45.

[27]A related critique that secular theorists have given concerns Fromm's failure to address specific developmental factors and/or steps in the formation of conscience. He does not really offer us a theory of the development of conscience. Ausubel, for example, writes, "Although a humanistic conscience—in

But the problems with Fromm's humanistic view of conscience do not end with the *process* of searching for valid ethical ideals and the *origin* of humanity's moral conflict and moral imperative. We also cannot expect autonomous man to arrive at the proper *content*. If we take the biblical record of the Fall seriously, we must acknowledge that mankind's ability to reason is seriously impaired as a result of sin.

The effects of the Fall were not limited to some isolated moral sphere. Instead, in trying to play God, Adam and Eve set in motion a cycle of sin that impacts every area of life. Adam's attempt to cover his guilt was a clear case of distorted logic.[28] He blamed God for giving him the woman. And Eve continued the pattern of irrational thinking by blaming the serpent. Knight writes:

> Fromm's major failure has been his neglect or lack of recognition of "the evil" in man, or the dark side of man's life. At this point I am not speaking theologically but psychologically. When man is free, he is free to do evil as well as good. Fromm seems to be telling us repeatedly that man's real freedom depends not upon mastering his own passions and humbling his own pride

which a rational responsibility to abstract principles of justice can supersede uncritical submission to authority—is conceivable in an adult as a final stage of a developmental sequence, it cannot be reasonably expected in a young child, even in a non-authoritarian society, since it is not consonant with known empirical data regarding moral development.

"In ignoring the conditions of moral development, therefore, Fromm dismisses the ontogenesis of ethical behavior, a mistake that is fatal for any psychological theory of ethics. The choice between humanistic or authoritarian ethics insofar as the individual human being is concerned is largely a function of his personal history and developmental capacities; it is not merely the outcome of a struggle between conflicting philosophies or cultural trends as Fromm implies." (Ausubel, *Ego Development and the Personality Disorders* [New York: Grune & Stratton, 1952], p. 396.)

[28] In commenting on the limits of humanity's powers of reason, Carl Henry, in *Christian Personal Ethics* (Grand Rapids: Eerdmans, 1957), p. 154, writes: "The question arises whether this (man's being in the image of God) does not issue in a trust-worthy natural morality—an ethics of natural law. This possibility is ruled out because the image-content is distorted by the sinner in the handling. Whatever propositions from general revelation are a part of the sinner's moral venture—and the combination and recombination of elements of general revelation vary with the preferences of the moral agent—they are always incorporated into a frame of reference forged by one who is in moral revolt."

but upon the reform of society. This surely cannot be the whole truth.[29]

Another limitation of Fromm's concept of humanistic conscience grows out of the problem of autonomous man attempting to establish an ethics of conscience by reason alone. Neither the content nor the development of conscience is strictly an intellectual matter. It involves desires, wishes, feelings, and relationships, since the content of conscience and its affective responses are formed in the soil of intimate personal relationships. Consequently, they do not readily lend themselves to change by purely rational means. Yet this is essentially what Fromm offers. He largely fails to include relational or affective factors in his discussion of the birth of humanity's conscience. And he portrays the shift from authoritarian to humanistic conscience essentially as a philosophical struggle. It is one thing, however, to rationally assert that we will now accept a certain ethic and dispense with all of our childhood fears. It is quite another for these new ethics to be incorporated into the fabric of our personalities and for motives of love to replace those of fear. Only significant, new relationships can help integrate new values at a deep level.[30] Although a broad reading of Fromm's writings shows that he is sensitive to the role

[29]Knight, *Conscience and Guilt*, p. 73; Fromm has attempted to address the issue of the "dark side of man's life" in *Anatomy of Human Destructiveness* (Holt, Rinehart and Winston, 1973). Unfortunately, even there he portrays the evil of humanity as essentially a secondary reaction rather than an intrinsic part of human nature.

[30]Stein writes: "Fromm seems rightly to want to move us from an ethic of fear to an ethic of intelligent self-conscious and loving cooperativeness with some objective value reality in the universe. It is a question whether this can occur by way of shifting the hate-love attitudes toward the self (which flow from the relation to the parental authority) entirely into an unanxious self-love dimension freed to explore some 'inner voice' dispassionately. This appears to be an attempt to shift the feeling aspect of conscience or superego onto a cognitive level, where conscience pain can be avoided by purely rational operations." Stein is here pointing out that true changes of conscience must be rooted in relationships rather than in isolated rational or philosophical activities. We might add that the requirement of another person's involvement in significant changes of conscience is also reflective of an even more encompassing divine relationship in which God lovingly seizes the initiative that can ultimately lead to the most radical resolution of the problems of conscience. (Stein, *Guilt: Theory and Therapy* [Philadelphia: Westminster, 1968], p. 45.)

of relationship and feelings, he does not consider these as important issues to the development of his humanistic conscience.

SUMMARY

Building on the insights of Sigmund Freud, Erich Fromm has suggested that it is possible to throw off the shackles of an immature, punitive, authoritarian conscience and replace this with a loving, rationally based humanistic conscience. While the simultaneous presence of both authoritarian and humanistic aspects of conscience is certainly possible (and indeed the norm), our goal should be in the direction of replacing all ethics arising from outside ourselves with our own rationally selected ethics operating out of self-interest instead of fear.

While Fromm has some valid criticisms of fear-based morality and mindless obedience and while he has made an important contribution in emphasizing the necessity of mature, love-motivated moral choices, his system falls short because of his overly optimistic view of human nature and the naturalistic assumptions that cut him off from an understanding of the ultimate source of guilt. He fails to see that it is man's very effort at autonomous functioning that gives rise to conscience, and that even if an ideal ethical system could be rationally developed, there would be serious barriers to incorporating those values into the personality through reason alone.

Mowrer and the Glorification of Conscience

The last two decades have seen an increasingly negative reaction to the principles of psychoanalysis in many quarters. The length of treatment, the sexual emphasis, and the purported resulting irresponsibility of psychoanalytic psychotherapy have motivated many to look in other directions for an understanding of the human dilemma. Among the most outspoken critics of psychoanalysis in general and its views of guilt in particular are William Glasser and O. H. Mowrer. Mowrer, in his book *The Crisis in Psychiatry and Religion*,[1] was one of the first widely recognized psychologists to entirely reject the viewpoints of psychoanalysis. In criticizing Freud's view that guilt feelings are one potential source of neurosis, Mowrer proposed precisely the opposite. He viewed guilt feelings and the accusations of conscience in a very positive light. Glasser, a California-based psychiatrist, authored the influential *Reality Therapy*, in which he further developed Mowrer's critique of psychoanalysis and offered a clear-cut therapeutic alternative.[2] If Freud can be considered the first systematic *naturalizer* of conscience and Fromm an ardent *humanizer* of conscience, then Mowrer and Glasser, because of their stress on living up to the dictates of conscience, could well be labeled two of the outspoken *glorifiers* of conscience. The two authors that have been most active in bringing the perspectives of Mowrer and Glasser to the attention of the Christian public have been Jay

[1]Hobart Mowrer, *The Crisis in Psychiatry and Religion* (New York: D. Van Nostrand, 1961).

[2]William Glasser, *Reality Therapy* (New York: Harper & Row, 1965).

Adams[3] and John Drakeford.[4] Although these authors (especially Adams) bring many important and distinctively Christian perspectives to their theorizing, their views of psychological maladjustment, guilt, and counseling are sufficiently similar to Mowrer's and Glasser's that we will consider them members of the same school of thought for our present purposes.

MOWRER'S VIEW OF GUILT

The central point of Mowrer's disagreement with Freud's theory of psychopathology centers on the nature of guilt in the neurotic personality. According to Mowrer, psychoanalysis has taught us that the guilt experienced by neurotic individuals is imaginary. In contrast, Mowrer suggests that psychopathology involves real guilt. He writes:

> According to Freud and his followers, the neurotic is in trouble, not because of anything actually wrong which he has done, but merely because of things he would like to do but, quite unrealistically, is afraid to. By contrast, the other view is that in neurosis (and functional psychosis), the individual has committed tangible misdeeds, which have remained unacknowledged and unredeemed and that his anxieties thus have a realistic social basis and justification.[5]

Mowrer uses the diagram on the following page to illustrate his theory of psychopathology. Mowrer suggests that a child is born on the left side (the virtuous side) of the diagram. Not necessarily because he is innately good but because he is loved and respected as he is, the child is considered (and considers himself) virtuous. As the child grows older, parents and others begin to make demands on him. Since their approval must now be earned instead of unconditionally given, the child is gradually socialized. Although he occasionally "sins" he largely respects himself because he has learned how to earn the approval and respect of others. The box at the left end of the solid line rep-

---

[3] Jay Adams, *Competent to Counsel* (Nutley, N.J.: Presbyterian and Reformed, 1970); and *The Christian Counselor's Manual* (Grand Rapids: Baker, 1973).

[4] John Drakeford, *Integrity Therapy* (Nashville: Broadman, 1967).

[5] Mowrer, *The Crisis in Psychology and Religion*, p. 231.

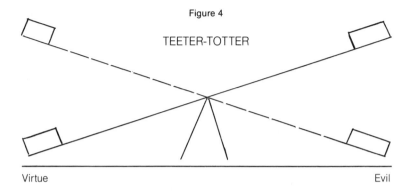

Figure 4

TEETER-TOTTER

Virtue   Evil

resents the credit the child earns. This is experienced as self-respect and a relative lack of guilt.

If, as the child reaches adolescence or young adulthood, he engages in a minimal amount of "sin" (right end of teeter-totter) but then returns to the virtuous end of the teeter-totter, no great harm is done. He may experience a small amount of guilt or apprehension but if he is discrete about it, nothing happens. If he persists in sinful actions, especially if he denies this overtly, credit begins to build up at the right end of the teeter-totter. Finally the teeter-totter tips to the other side (as illustrated by the dotted lines). The result is a "nervous breakdown." The person has lost his emotional balance.

Operating on these assumptions, Mowrer concludes that guilt feelings are constructive ingredients of personality and that therapy should consist of confession of one's "sins" and expiation. As a nontheist, Mowrer's definition of sin deviates significantly from the biblical concept. Sin, for Mowrer, is anything that leads us toward emotional ill health![6]

[6]"Traditionally, sin has been thought of as whatever causes one to go to Hell: and since Hell, as a place of otherworldly retribution and torment, has conveniently dropped out of most religious as well as secular thought, the concept of sin might indeed seem antiquated and absurd. But, as I observed in the Cincinnati paper, Hell is still very much with us in those states of mind and being which we call neurosis and psychosis; and I have come increasingly, at least in my own mind, to identify anything that carries us toward these forms of perdition as sin" (Mowrer, ibid., p. 48).

If we are to overcome the negative effects of "sin" in our lives, Mowrer suggests that we must both confess them and engage in behavioral change and expiation. He says:

> Despite the Biblical exhortation that an honest confession is good for the soul, there is reason to doubt that its benefit is unconditional and necessarily enduring. . . . Voluntary confession of a legal crime may soften the ensuing punishment, but it does not abrogate it. So, may we not assume that confession of an immorality likewise does not end the matter?[7]

Mowrer goes on to contend that society as a whole and Protestantism in particular have been brainwashed by psychoanalysis to remove the need for penalty for misbehaviors. Consequently the neurotic person must search for ways (frequently self-destructive) to work out his or her own atonement. Mowrer sees depression, for example, as one form this self-punishment can take. With this view of guilt, Mowrer sees no need for long-term therapy seeking to untangle the roots of adult maladjustments. Therapy can be of relatively short duration and needs to focus on finding one's misdeeds, gaining a community of people that will support responsible actions, and effecting an appropriate behavioral change. Reparation and confession will result in a greater sense of authenticity and in a lessening of one's guilt.

GLASSER'S REALITY THERAPY

William Glasser's criticisms of psychoanalytic psychotherapy and his basic understanding of the nature and function of guilt are similar to Mowrer's. He presents, however, a much more developed therapeutic picture than Mowrer and in doing so gives us a better insight into the outworkings of this theoretical perspective.

Glasser begins by asking the question, "What is wrong with those who need psychiatric treatment?" He answers by saying the problem maladjusted people face is an inability to fulfill their essential needs. The two most basic of these psychological needs are the need to love and be loved and the need to feel worthwhile. People fail to meet these needs because of irresponsibility, the

[7]Ibid., pp. 97-99.

refusal to face reality and the lack of involvement. In stressing the need for responsibility Glasser places a great emphasis on the morality of behavior. He writes:

> Therefore in order to do therapy successfully, the therapist must acknowledge that standards of behavior exist, standards accepted by both individuals and society as the best means of meeting basic human needs. Patients must be confronted by the disparity between the values they recognize as the acceptable norms and the lives they lead.[8]

Although one would expect Glasser's emphasis on responsibility and reality to lead him to discuss the problem of guilt extensively, his writings are surprisingly sparce in this area. In his discussion of the needs to be loved and to feel worthy, however, he indirectly gives us significant insights into his views of guilt. He writes:

> But, whether we are loved or not, to be worthwhile we must maintain a satisfactory standard of behavior. To do so we must learn to correct ourselves when we do wrong and to credit ourselves when we do right. If we do not evaluate our own behavior, or having evaluated it, we do not act to improve our conduct where it is below our standards, we will not fulfill our need to be worthwhile and we will suffer as acutely as when we fail to love and to be loved.[9]

Assuming that Glasser is here referring to the experience of guilt that undermines our sense of self-worth, he is suggesting that the solution is improved behavior. Guilt functions to show us where we are acting irresponsibly and motivates us to alter our behavior. This is consistent with his view of conscience as described by Mowrer in the foreword to *Reality Therapy.*

> By contrast, the objective of Reality Therapy is to support and strengthen, never to weaken the functioning of conscience; and the method of choice involves honesty, concern, personal authenticity, and confrontation of the kind Mr. Glasser describes.[10]

[8]Glasser, *Reality Therapy*, p. 58.
[9]Ibid., p. 10.
[10]Ibid., p. xxi.

Like Mowrer, Glasser does not see the need to either soften the harsh, punitive attitudes of a condemning conscience or to alter unrealistically high standards. Conscience is viewed as an essentially trustworthy guide and guilt is to be resolved by living up to the conscience's dictates.

CHRISTIAN INTERPRETATIONS OF MOWRER

Perhaps the clearest presentation of the essential features of Mowrer's approach to psychotherapy is contained in John Drakeford's *Integrity Therapy*. After describing his indebtedness to Mowrer, Drakeford summarizes the major postulates of the view of therapy he shares with Mowrer. Those postulates are:

1. Integrity therapy rejects all deterministic theories which make man a victim of heredity, environment, or any other force. Every individual is answerable for himself, and exercises his responsibility in making his personal decisions.

2. Each person has a conscience, or value system, the violation of which gives rise to guilt. This condition is not a sickness but a result of his wrong-doing and irresponsibility.

3. The typical self-defeating reaction to personal wrongdoing is concealment. In this secrecy, guilt throws up symptoms of varying degrees of severity, from vague discomfort to complete immobilization.

4. As secrecy brought on his trouble and separated him from his fellows, so openness with "significant others" is the individual's first step on the road back to normality.

5. The process of socialization involves a group which could be called a microcosm or small world exercising both a corrective and supportive function for the growing individual.

6. Openness by itself is not enough and the individual is under an obligation to undertake some activity of restitution appropriate to his acknowledged failure in life.

7. The only way to continue as a truly authentic person is not only to remain open and make restitution but also to feel a responsibility to carry the message of integrity therapy to other needy people.[11]

[11]Drakeford, *Integrity Therapy*, pp. 4-5.

The key points of interest to our consideration of guilt are 2, 3, 4, and 6. Drakeford suggests that emotional disturbances result from a violation of conscience that produces guilt. Guilt in turn causes symptoms "of varying degrees of severity." The solution to these disturbances is confession and restitution. Conscience in this system is pictured as nearly infallible and guilt as a healthy motivation. Guilt is removed by confession and changed behavior. Drakeford goes on to say that the apparently overguilty person is actually not one who is experiencing too intense a feeling of guilt over misbehavior, but rather one who has other hidden and more serious "crimes." When these deeper misbehaviors are found, confessed, and restitution is made, the seeming oversensitivity to guilt will disappear.

Certainly the most polemic Christian approach to problems of emotional adjustment in recent years has come from Jay Adams. After receiving a doctorate in speech and communication, Adams pastored for a time and then began teaching pastoral theology at Westminster Seminary. In preparing for a course in pastoral counseling he became familiar with Mowrer's work and later spent two months in a training program with Mowrer.

Although Adams is highly critical of Mowrer's atheistic stance and underlying presuppositions, his writings contain striking parallels to Mowrer's. While Adams possesses a different anthropology and ultimately traces all of man's problems to sin, his basic understanding of psychological maladjustments is clearly Mowrerian. He agrees with Mowrer that neurotic individuals are suffering from true guilt rather than imaginary and that the solution to problems lies in confession and altered behavior. Major differences lie in the fact that Adams believes in a personal God and the reality of sin as an offense against God and attempts to bring the resources of Scripture to bear on all problems of adjustment. For Adams, then, confession is not simply confession to another person. Above all it is confession to God. He writes: "The point of the psychosomatic Psalms (5-7, 32, 38), as David clearly indicated, is that God makes us miserable when we hold within the guilt of unforgiven sin."[12]

Adams also rejects Mowrer's emphasis on the role of group

[12]Adams, *Competent to Counsel*, p. 175.

therapy, having come to the conclusion that it is "unscriptural and therefore harmful." He continues to stress a combination of changed behavior and confession, however, as means of altering inner feelings, including those of guilt.

EVALUATION

Evaluating the reality approaches to guilt discussed in this chapter is difficult for two reasons. To begin with, none of the authors discussed here have attempted to outline in any detail their theoretical understanding of guilt and conscience. In taking guilt as a constructive motivation they apparently feel no need to go further and expand on its origins, its exact content and its specific functions in the personality. What they do write in this regard is quite secondary to their major emphases on responsibility, confession, and behavior change. As a Christian, another problem with critiquing these views is that on the surface they seem very consistent with the Scripture's emphasis on sin and personal responsibility. The rallying call of each of these authors is personal responsibility and the overcoming of sinful (or maladaptive) behavior. It is difficult to argue with these ideals!

The main strengths of this point of view are (1) an emphasis on objective guilt (as contrasted to psychoanalytic and many humanistic approaches), (2) a focus on personal responsibility, and (3) a commitment to honesty, integrity, and openness. Each of these authors stands against the prevailing trend of most mental health workers to separate problems of guilt from morality and objective guilt. They also, in contrast to many therapists, stress the primacy of personal responsibility. They see maladjusted individuals more as sinful than sick and more as sinners than sinned against. Given their focus on objective guilt and personal responsibility, they also stress the need for personal honesty and congruence. The goal of therapy is not to overcome the results of overly strict socializing agents but rather to learn to act responsibly. Christian authors like Adams also affirm that feelings of guilt stem from real guilt before God.

On the negative side, all of these theories fail to address the developmental origins of guilt. Although this may be easily corrected, at this point we are left with no suggestion of how the experience of guilt comes into being in the human personality. Is it, perhaps, in the case of Adams and Drakeford, simply the voice of God?[13] Is it, in the case of Mowrer and Glasser, the result of parental and societal conditioning?[14] Or is it a kind of psychological "given" that is inherent in human nature and relatively unaffected by either upbringing or divine conviction? In each case, we are left to wonder. A second weakness of these viewpoints is their failure to discriminate between harsh, punitive, self-condemning attitudes on the one hand and more self-accepting corrections on the other. Although Fromm's humanistic conscience falls short of the biblical view of motivation, it does make a discrimination between the punitive attitudes of the infantile conscience and the more loving and rational self-corrections of the mature conscience. The failure of reality, integrity, and nouthetic theorists to make a distinction of this sort leaves them open to the charge of promoting (or at least not working to lessen) harsh, punitive, and even neurotic attitudes toward self.[15]

To the degree that these authors' use of guilt refers to a love motivated, non-punitive emotional experience (which I will discuss as godly or constructive sorrow in chapter 11) their solutions seem to be largely appropriate. We should respond to our sins and failures with concern and behavior change. It seems, however, that these authors frequently include punitive guilt feelings in

[13]Although Adams indicates conscience "is not a sort of prepackaged box with which each man comes equipped from the creative hand of God," he does not tell us how he views its origin. He also says that because conscience produces "negative emotional warning signals ... the counselor must align himself" with it (Adams, *What About Nouthetic Counseling?* [Grand Rapids: Baker, 1977], p. 77).

[14]Surprisingly, Drakeford seems to take this view when he says a conscience may be defined as "the internalized voice of society" (*Integrity Therapy* [booklet], published by the author, Fort Worth, Tex., p. 3).

[15]While Mowrer fails to make any distinction between healthy and neurotic guilt he does show some awareness of the need for more than simply a superego morality. In commenting on recent developments in ego psychology he states in *The Crisis in Psychiatry and Religion*, p. 34, "Here, instead of stressing superego over severity, we find more reference to the importance of ego adequacy. Here it is not nearly so much a question as it was formerly of how to pare down or reform the conscience; rather the question is, how to get the conscious self-system or ego of the individual to grow and mature so that it is more responsible and more competent to deal with the manifold demands that impinge upon it."

their formulation and that they view these feelings as constructive. Drakeford, for example, says that integrity therapy "rejects all ideas of an over-severe conscience."[16] Commenting on this problem in Mowrer's position Stein says:

> In the effort to emphasize the significance of real guilt as a factor in psychopathology and to redress what he believes is a psychoanalytic bias toward id-release, he gets into a rather uncritical box. It is one that precludes criticism of possible unhealthy superego dynamics or contents and that favors an alliance of the therapist with the patient values, with very little insight into the questions of their genesis or appropriateness.[17]

In Christian circles the failure to differentiate between constructive and destructive responses of conscience is frequently associated with the tendency to equate the voice of conscience with the voice of God. We will see in chapter 10, however, that while the Scripture affirms that the Holy Spirit convicts of sin,[18] it does not equate this conviction with the experience of guilt feelings.

Related to the failure to distinguish between healthy and unhealthy forms of self-correction is the assumption that if maladjusted individuals are indeed guilty (instead of victims) their feelings of guilt are therefore constructive or valid. Although at first glance this conclusion seems logical, it fails to distinguish between man's condition of guilt and the affective experience of it. The assumption that a guilty act or a guilty state should necessarily result in a feeling of guilt in order to motivate us to improved behavior can be seriously questioned from a biblical viewpoint. None of these authors consider the possibility that while people may in fact *be* guilty, their feelings of guilt are not effective means of motivating them to improved behavior.

Perhaps the most serious weakness of reality, integrity, and nouthetic approaches to the handling of guilt lies in their assumption that the resolution of guilt feelings comes through a combination of confession of one's failures or sins and improved behavior. Although this solution sounds biblical at first glance, the

---

[16]Ibid., p. 3.
[17]E. Stein, *Guilt: Theory and Therapy* (Philadelphia: Westminster, 1968), p. 171.
[18]John 16:8.

premise that one must improve his or her behavior to overcome guilt feelings does not appear to be consistent with a scriptural view of motivation. In fact, the issue of motivation cuts to the heart of Christianity and to the essential theological distinction between legalism and grace. As we will see in the next two chapters, the Bible teaches that full freedom from guilt comes solely through the forgiveness afforded us by Christ's atonement.[19] Freedom from guilt is the result of neither improved behavior nor reparation.

In contrast to this, however, glorifiers of conscience suggest that we need to achieve at a certain level in order to be accepted and avoid feelings of guilt or (in the case of Christian glorifiers) that we need to add some works to the forgiveness of Christ. Consider, for example, Glasser's statement about developing a sense of worth: "To be worthwhile we must maintain a satisfactory standard of behavior. To do so we must learn to correct ourselves when we do wrong and to credit ourselves when we do right."[20]

In a similar view Mowrer writes:

> It is surely unrepented and unredeemed actions that destroy our self-respect and moral credit; and *one can hardly escape the conclusion that these cannot be recaptured by any means other than compensating good actions and deeds.*[21]

Few clearer statements that the burden of man's self-acceptance and self-worth lies in his own actions can be found. According to this view, our identity, our worth, our acceptance, and our freedom from guilt come from our own efforts. *If we measure up we can feel accepted and worthwhile. If we do not, we cannot.* The New Testament message suggests this is not true. In Ephesians, for example, Paul spends the first three chapters reciting the blessings God has bestowed upon us. He speaks of our election, our redemption, our acceptance through Christ, our inheritance, and our union with Christ. Only after stressing all of these riches does he begin his challenge, "I therefore, the prisoner of the Lord, beseech you that ye walk worthy of the vocation wherewith ye are called."[22]

[19]See, e.g., Rom. 8:1-4; 1 John 2:2; and Gal. 2:16-18.
[20]Glasser, *Reality Therapy,* p. 10.
[21]Mowrer, *The Crisis in Psychiatry and Religion,* p. 232.
[22]Eph. 4:1 (KJV).

In other words, gratitude over the fact that we are forgiven should result in altered behavior. The essence of Christian motivation is that we are *already* accepted. We are *already* pronounced significant as bearers of the image of God, and our sins are *already* paid for. There is no place for self-expiation or self-atonement. We are to live worthily *because* we have been forgiven and accepted, *not in order to* gain a feeling of worth and acceptance. There *is* discipline or chastisement in the Christian life and there are negative consequences of sinful behavior but this is an entirely different matter from working to avoid guilt and fear. This type of thinking, however, is far from acceptable to Mowrer who tells us:

> Although the Catholic Church has made a mystery and a muddle of many things, in this issue between Paul and James it has been clear-headed and thoroughly Jamesian. It has stressed the importance of good works, with implicit recognition of a "balance sheet" on which our sins and virtues add algebraically. . . .
>
> But the emphasis in the writings of Paul, and in Protestant theology generally, has been on a very different note, namely, that in the Substitutionary Atonement, God wiped the "balance sheet" clean for all time and all men, provided only that they say, "I believe. . . ." In "accepting Christ as our personal redeemer," sin is supposedly banished in our lives and we are, from this point on, "saved." This is what Dietrich Bonhoeffer, in his book *The Cost of Discipleship*, dubs the doctrine of cheap grace, a doctrine which has been a disgrace and a scandal to Christendom. It is a doctrine which holds the deep natural wisdom of the Judeo-Christian ethic in contempt and prevents us from coming to grips effectively with the most profound personal problem of our time, mental illness.[23]

This perspective has very significant therapeutic implications. Stein describes them as follows:

> It is possible for a person to eliminate a guilt feeling by going through an act of restitution—paying a price. A therapist may sit as a judge and encourage such behavior. There is much of this in the approach Mowrer emphasizes. Restitution is not trivial, it is critical. But it leaves the transaction on a payment level unless it is the free loving act of an accepted person . . . .

[23]Mowrer, *The Crisis in Psychiatry and Religion*, p. 189.

> Even in successful cases of reduction of guilt feeling, this may lead to lowered self-esteem, the sense that one's acceptance and hence *worth* lies not in the affirmation of one's being *as he is* but in one's capacity to bribe a favorable response out of another. Love becomes no longer a basic condition of life that is a *gift* but an exaction from life which one extorts.[24]

The distinction Stein suggests basically boils down to the difference between what Pattison has defined as ego and superego morality.[25] We will be discussing this in depth in chapter 18.

One of the main problems in evaluating the contributions of glorifiers of conscience is that so much depends upon the attitude and motivation of the counselor. A sensitive, mature, and gracious therapist may communicate an unconditional acceptance and the fact that the issue in altering one's behavior is an issue of love and congruence, not resolution of punitive guilt feelings. On the other hand, another therapist may imply that behavioral changes should be made *in order to* reduce guilt feelings. Put another way, while these theoretical orientations lend themselves to a superego or legalistic motivation, this problem can be at least in part resolved by sensitive therapists who differentiate between the need for a sense of congruency and a relief from guilt and the means of achieving the two.

In emphasizing that forgiveness and freedom from guilt can never be gained by improved behavior, I do not mean to deny that some inner change of attitude and emotion will not accompany improved behavior. It can and it should. But the inner experience that accompanies altered behavior is a sense of congruence and confidence that comes with knowing we are responding as we should. It is not the resolution of guilt. Coupled with an awareness that our sins are forgiven through Christ, this provides a healthy sense of inner integrity. In fact, the therapeutic perspectives discussed in this chapter can be highly successful in meeting this need for inner integrity. The problem comes when there is a failure to differentiate between self-condemning guilt feelings on the one hand and a love-based motivation on the other.

[24]Stein, *Guilt: Theory and Therapy*, p. 164.

[25]M. Pattison, "Ego Morality: An Emergency Psychotherapeutic Concept," *Psychoanalytic Review*, 55 (2), 1968, pp. 187-222.

Before leaving our discussion of the relation of behavior change to guilt feelings I would like to make one additional observation. *Improved behavior and restitution may (and often does) result in a conscious decrease in feelings of guilt. This decrease, however, is not necessarily a resolution of guilt. It may simply be a repression of guilt that fails to really resolve the problem.* By focusing on desirable behavior and good deeds, we can push the awareness of guilt temporarily from consciousness. In fact, this is precisely the dynamic of legalism. Adherence to rigid standards of behavior and belief help shift the focus from our failures to our successes. Unfortunately the repressed guilt continues to impact our lives in one or more of the disguised expressions discussed in chapter 3.

Christian representatives of integrity and nouthetic counseling, of course, reject Mowrer's attack on the substitutionary atonement. They also believe that we are made acceptable to God entirely by Christ's work on the cross. They sometimes fail, however, to follow through on the logical outcome of our acceptance in Christ. Rather than seeing our self-acceptance coming through the fact that we are image bearers and that we are "in Christ," they either revert to the works mentality propounded by Mowrer, or mix it with an understanding of grace and forgiveness. *If* we are to accept ourselves and feel worthy and free of guilt we must alter our behavior. This seems to be a reversal of the orthodox theological consensus that sees our actions flowing *out of* our acceptance and forgiveness.

This tendency to mix changed behavior and Christ's atoning work is not new in the history of Christianity. It was the problem in the church at Galatia that prompted Paul to ask: "This only would I learn of you. Received ye the Spirit by the works of the law, or by the hearing of faith? Are ye so foolish? Having begun in the Spirit, are ye now made perfect by the flesh?"[26]

The Galatians believed in Christ. They just wanted to add a little something to it! But Paul said, "If righteousness came by the law, then Christ is dead in vain."[27]

[26]Gal. 3:2, 3 (KJV).
[27]Gal. 2:21 (KJV).

Like the Galatians, the evangelical church believes in the efficacy of the Atonement and the doctrine of God's grace. But unfortunately when it comes down to daily motivation we have sometimes reverted to the very works orientation and the fear and guilt motivation that necessitated Paul's rebuke of the Galatian church and the Protestant Reformation. We sometimes live with an intellectual split that allows us to affirm our absolute commitment to God's gracious and unconditional acceptance of the believer on the one hand and to continue motivating the believer to work in order to avoid feelings of guilt and to be acceptable to himself on the other. We will look further at this inconsistency and a possible solution to it in the next two chapters.

A final limitation of glorifiers of conscience is their tendency, in stressing sin and personal responsibility, to minimize the impact of being sinned against by parents and others. In minimizing the importance of the past, advocates of this viewpoint can easily underestimate the impact the sins and failures of others have on our personality development and functioning.

SUMMARY

In this chapter we have surveyed a major alternative to psychoanalytic and humanistic views of guilt. In the writings of Mowrer, Glasser, Adams, and Drakeford we saw an emphasis on the belief that man's emotional maladies stem not from imaginary guilt but from actual guilt. Based on this assumption, we saw a therapeutic strategy that emphasized confession, expiation, and altered behavior as essential ingredients of the therapy of guilt. Because of the emphasis proponents of this view place on living up to the demands of one's conscience and their essential neglect of its fallibility, we have termed this view the glorification of conscience. It tends to exalt the standards of conscience and encourages us to live up to its demands in order to feel worthy, accepted, and free from guilt.

While agreeing with this movement's emphasis on personal responsibility, integrity, confession, and behavior change, I suggested that from a biblical perspective it places the cart before the horse. If confession and change flow out of a love for others and a desire for personal integrity, it is a necessary and vital part of life. If it is done to increase our sense of worth, our freedom from guilt or our self-acceptance, however, it is problematic. To the degree the latter is true, these therapies are inconsistent with the Bible's emphasis on God's grace and unconditional acceptance. Theologically, they reflect a legalistic, works-oriented system of motivation.

Part 3

Christian Motivation or Neurotic Masochism?

Many Christians view guilt feelings as either the voice of God or as a divinely ordained emotion. Yet guilt feelings have often increased personal distress and reinforced neurotic conflicts. These facts have caused many psychotherapists to reject Christianity because they believe its use of guilt encourages repression, rigidity, and a host of other maladjustments. In this section, I explore this conflict and suggest a resolution that grows out of the distinction between our objective condition of guilt before God and the subjective experience of guilt feelings. Then I explore some biblical alternatives to feelings of guilt.

10

Are Guilt Feelings from God?

Against the backdrop of the naturalization, humanization, and glorification of conscience we can begin to set the biblical viewpoint on guilt and conscience.[1] Undoubtedly guilt has been a major means of motivation in the church. Endeavoring to stir people to godly living, church leaders have frequently aroused feelings of disesteem and self-condemnation. This has been especially true of the preaching ministry of the church and of devotional literature where there has often been a major failure to distinguish between objective guilt and guilt feelings and between guilt feelings and constructive sorrow.

Many Christian workers appear to equate guilt feelings with divine conviction. If we can be made to feel sufficiently guilty, or badly enough about ourselves, they reason, the Holy Spirit has done (or is doing) His work.[2] The counseling handbook for a major

[1] I have chosen not to deal with behavioral perspectives on guilt due to space limitations, the tendency for theorists of this persuasion to minimize hypothesized mental structure such as conscience, and the fact that guilt conceptualizations do not tend to play a major role in these perspectives. Although social learning theorists have a distinctive way of conceptualizing guilt feelings, their viewpoint entails many of the same strengths and weaknesses of other naturalistic theories. In stressing the impact of the socialization process on the development of guilt, they minimize or ignore the ultimate nature of sin as an offense against God and the responsibility of the individual in the development of guilt feelings. Those interested in a social learning point of view (which we might label the *socialization* of conscience) are referred to A. Bandura (*Social Learning Theory* [Englewood Cliffs, N.J.: Prentice Hall, 1977]) and A. Bandura and R. Walters (*Social Learning and Personality Development* [New York: Holt, Rinehart and Winston, 1963]).

[2] This particular formulation is especially common in Keswick and Deeper Life Movements.

Christian television ministry tells staff counselors: "Guilt is experienced as God's way of warning us to repent and turn away from sin so He can forgive us, cleanse us and make us entirely guilt free."[3] And spiritual life author Roy Hession writes that Jesus saw us to be ". . . worms having forfeited all rights by our sin, except to deserve hell. And now calls us to take our rightful place as worms for Him and with Him."[4]

The first view equates guilt feelings with the voice of God and the second suggests that Christians are called to be "worms for Jesus!" While there is not a large body of literature espousing such a negative view of personhood, a good bit of pulpit exhortation clearly implies that we should feel guilty for our behavior.

This viewing of psychological guilt and disesteem as a constructive motivation has not been nearly as common in the theological literature of the church. Perhaps because theologians are more oriented to education than to motivation or perhaps because they exercise greater care in treating the data of Scripture, theologians have generally focused on guilt as man's objective condition or state rather than as a subjective psychological experience.

NEUROTIC MASOCHISM?

Confronted with the church's frequent reliance on guilt motivation on the one hand and the causative role of guilt in psychological maladjustment on the other, many psychotherapists have concluded that Christianity helps cause psychological problems. Guilt and fear are seen as tearing at efforts to build self-esteem and as oppressive, inhibiting forms of self-inflicted punishment. In a pamphlet entitled "The Case Against Religion," Albert Ellis gives one of the clearest expressions of this view:

> To the ethical construct of wrongdoing, the traditional religious devotee adds that of sinning—and of humans' deserving to be condemned and punished for their sinning. . . . If it is given a

[3]CBN Spiritual Life Division, *Counseling Handbook for Telephone and Personal Ministry* (Virginia Beach: Christian Broadcasting Network, n.d.), p. 74.

[4]Roy Hession, *The Calvary Road* (Fort Washington: Christian Literature Crusade, 1964), p. 15.

god-given, absolutistic law that you *shall* not, *must* not act wrongly or immorally, you then tend to view yourself as a miserable sinner, a worthless being who deserves to be severely punished (perhaps eternally, in hell) for being wrong or fallible. Religion, by positing absolute, god-given standards of conduct, tends to make you feel self-deprecating and dehumanized when you err; and also encourages you to despise and dehumanize others when they act unethically. Since self-deprecation is the main cause of anxiety, overweening guilt, and depression, and since damning others is probably the chief source of hostility, rage, and violence, religious moralism patently produces or abets enormous amounts of severe emotional disturbance.[5]

And psychiatrist Eli Chesen, in a book entitled *Religion May Be Hazardous to Your Health*, writes:

I would summarize that religion even when loosely practiced by a family, can ... give rise to an inordinate number of double messages to growing children. These messages confuse and frustrate children and often lead to feelings of guilt. This can do nothing less than inhibit, to a varying degree, the normal healthy progress of emotional growth.[6]

I think we can safely say that the views of Ellis and Chesen represent a significant portion of practicing psychotherapists. In fact, they probably also represent the views of some pastors and theologians—especially those of more liberal persuasion! While most therapists are not as outspoken and evangelistic about their views as Ellis, many are convinced that religion is largely a guilt producing phenomenon that contributes to the development of neurotic patterns.

To understand this perspective better, place yourself in the role of a secular psychotherapist. Imagine a number of depressed people coming to you for therapy. All of them are found to be suffering from an acute sense of worthlessness (most neurotics do), failure, and inadequacy. Many of them, it turns out, have some religious background. They either believe in God or at least respect

[5]Albert Ellis, "The Case Against Religion" (New York: Institute for Rational Living, n.d.).

[6]Eli Chesen, *Religion May Be Hazardous to Your Health* (New York: Peter Wyden, 1972), p. 22.

the dictates of their church. Some come from strict religious homes. As these clients pour out feelings of wretchedness, they say things like, "I'm no good"; "I'm worthless"; "I am so sinful." As you attempt to help them build a healthier self-image, they repeatedly tell you how they have fallen short of some unrealistic image others have set for them. They may mention a Bible verse on self-denial or humility or discuss years of experience in a Christian family or church where their feelings of self-worth were undermined by negative religious messages.

After seeing a number of clients like this, you begin to wonder if the church is all it is cracked up to be. Then you pick up a few terms like *total depravity* and *original sin.* By now you are beginning to see a pattern. It seems like religion in general and Christianity in particular tears down self-esteem and reinforces neurotic patterns. The major goal appears to be to make people feel sinful, guilty, and bad so they will repent, conform to the dictates of the church, and accept an other-worldly salvation. You begin to see Christianity as simply a "superego" religion. That is, its primary emphasis appears to be conformity motivated by fears of guilt, punishment, and condemnation. When compared to a humanistic emphasis on self-love and self-acceptance, this form of Christianity seems woefully inadequate. In time, you may even come to see the church (especially the more conservative ones) as mental health's number-one enemy. Ellis, for example, in concluding a lecture on religion, says that it is "... directly opposed to the goals of mental health since it basically consists of masochism, other directedness, intolerance, refusal to accept uncertainty, unscientific thinking, needless inhibition and self abasement."[7]

While Ellis's view is extreme and grossly distorts biblical Christianity it does single out a problem for the Christian pastor, counselor, and theologian. How do we reconcile biblical teachings on sin and guilt with the obvious fact that neurotic problems are reinforced (if not actually caused) by guilt motivation? And how can we lead people to freely acknowledge their sins without getting under a heavy burden of neurotic guilt? Without a successful resolution to these apparent conflicts we are in danger of com-

[7]Albert Ellis, "The Case Against Religion," tape (New York: Institute for Rational Living, n.d.).

municating an oppressive rather than a liberating brand of Christianity and pushing people toward either neurotic conformity or rebellion. Allison echoes this sentiment when he suggests:

> A religion of nagging, of exhorting and rebuking, of law and control, or condemnation and fussing-at is a big part of the picture presented as Christianity, not merely by popular distortions but within the very citadels of scholarly learning.
>
> No wonder Sigmund Freud, Erich Fromm, Herbert Marcuse have opted for a more reasonable and less debilitating set of demands and restrictions! No wonder D. H. Lawrence, Wilhelm Reich, and Norman O. Brown flee from such a soul searching, esteem-diminishing, and guilt producing cold system into the arms of the warm fecundity of nature![8]

Before leaving our discussion of the destructive use of guilt motivation in Christianity I would like to point out that this phenomenon is not at all unique to Christianity. Sit on a bench near a busy section of a shopping mall or department store where parents and young children pass by and you will hear repeated threats and condemnation. Or listen to coaches, parents, and teachers motivating children to higher levels of achievement. You will find that when these leaders reach their level of frustration they too resort to guilt and shame as well as threats of punishment. Guilt motivation is not the unique weapon of the church. It is a common tool of nearly all parents, educators, and leaders regardless of their religious commitment or lack of it! Consequently, as we consider the church's abuse of guilt we need to be careful to realize this problem is not unique to Christianity.

CHRISTIAN MOTIVATION?

Earlier I mentioned the struggle I had as a young therapist relating my understanding of the Christian view of guilt to the problems my clients faced with debilitating guilt emotions. The seeming conflict between my patients' needs for freedom from guilt on the one hand and the churches' emphasis on the importance of guilt as a divine motivator on the other forced me to restudy the biblical

[8]Allison, *Guilt, Anger, and God* (New York: Seabury, 1972), pp. 37-38.

use of guilt and its role in motivation. Before I went far in my study I made a startling (to me) discovery. I found that not once was *guilt* used as an emotion in the entire New Testament! *Guilt* is used in a legal or judicial sense. And it is used to describe our condition as fallen people alienated from God by virtue of our sins. But it is never used in the sense that most of us consider *guilt* today—that inner emotional state of self-condemnation, punishment, and rejection. *The New Testament, in other words, speaks directly of objective guilt but not of subjective guilt.*

The discovery that guilt was strictly a legal term in Scripture led me to other questions. Could it be, I wondered, that the Bible is not suggesting that God motivates us out of feelings of guilt? And if He does not, why is guilt motivation so prevalent in the church? And how does God motivate if He doesn't motivate by guilt? These and other questions ran through my mind. Frankly, I should not have been surprised at all. I had enough theological training that I should have known that *guilt* referred to our condition before God rather than to guilt feelings.[9] But somehow I had not grasped that fact and related it to my understanding of guilt feelings. Later I was to find that the distinction between judicial and psychological guilt was not uncommon in certain religious, psychological, and philosophical writings.[10] At the time, however, it was new to me, and my experience since has shown that it continues to be an unknown, or at least untaught, distinction in many Christian circles.

[9]Charles Hodge, e.g., says that in theological language *guilt* always "means liability or exposure to punishment on account of sin. It is not to be confounded with moral polluting or with mere demerit. It may exist where neither pollution nor personal demerit is to be found. And it may be removed where both remain" (*Commentary on the Epistle to the Romans* [Grand Rapids: Eerdmans, 1950], p. 80).

[10]M. Pattison, "On the Failure to Forgive or to be Forgiven," *American Journal of Psychotherapy,* vol. 19, 1965, p. 106; M. Buber, *The Knowledge of Man* (London: George Allen & Unwin, Ltd., 1965); Tillich, in "Paul Tillich Converses with Psychotherapists," J. Ashbrook, *Journal of Religion and Health,* vol. 11(1), 1972, p. 57., explains, "In German, guilt means 'schuld' and guilt-feelings mean 'schuldgefuhl.' In English, the word 'guilt' is used both for the fact and the feeling. I know from many discussions that this creates a great confusion. Therefore, I always suggest that we consistently use guilt feeling if we want to express the feeling of guilt, and guilt if we speak about somebody who commits a murder and is guilty now. . . ."

Loss of Self-esteem

After gaining this first insight into the biblical use of *guilt*, I decided to look further. Although *guilt* is never used as an emotion in the New Testament, I wondered if I might find its essential ingredients (inner punishment, rejection, and disesteem) endorsed as constructive motivations. But a study of these types of motivation also reveals they are not a part of the scriptural pattern of motivation. Although the Scriptures are at odds with the current humanistic emphasis on self-love on several points,[11] they do make it clear that we have abundant reason for possessing a deep sense of significance, value, and self-esteem. In another place I have discussed seven biblical bases for a positive sense of self-esteem.[12] These include the facts that: (1) We are created in the image of God;[13] (2) we are the apex of God's creative actions;[14] (3) we are given dominion over the earth;[15] (4) we are told that we are made a little lower than the angels and crowned with glory and honor;[16] (5) we were purchased out of sin by Christ's death;[17] (6) we are indwelled by the Holy Spirit;[18] and (7) we have eternity prepared for us.[19] In commenting on the church's failure to teach the importance of a positive sense of self-esteem Frances Schaeffer writes:

> I am convinced that one of the great weaknesses in evangelical preaching in the last few years is that we have lost sight of the biblical fact that man is wonderful. We have seen the unbiblical humanism which surrounds us, and, to resist this in our emphasis on man's lostness, we have tended to reduce man to a zero. Man is indeed lost, but that does not mean he is nothing. We must resist humanism, but to make man a zero is neither the right way nor the best way to resist it. You can emphasize

[11]Secular attempts to root a sense of significance in autonomous man, e.g., fall short of the scriptural view of personhood and lead logically to despair.

[12]Bruce Narramore, *You're Someone Special* (Grand Rapids: Zondervan, 1978). pp. 21-29.

[13]Gen. 1:26, 27, and 1 Cor. 11:7.

[14]Gen. 1 and 2.

[15]Gen. 1:28-30.

[16]Psalm 8:4-6.

[17]1 Peter 1:18, 19.

[18]Eph. 1:13.

[19]John 14:1-3.

that man is totally lost and still have the biblical answer that man is really great.[20]

Self-Condemnation and Punishment

Just as the Scriptures reveal a resource for a positive sense of self-esteem, they also make it clear that fears of punishment and rejection have no place in Christian motivation. There is a place for divine correction (chastisement), remorse, and repentance. But these are distinct from threats of punishment and rejection. Although the Scriptures deal more with the Christian's freedom from *external* punishment (fear of God's wrath), they also suggest that freedom from external fear should be accompanied by a similar *inner* freedom from self-condemnation. Christ's atoning death once and for all paid the penalty for the believers' sins, reconciled mankind to God, removed the danger of divine punishment and rejection, and established the foundation for freedom from self-condemnation. In Romans 5 the apostle Paul writes: "having now been justified by His blood, we shall be saved from the wrath of God through Him."[21] And in chapter 8 he tells us that "there is therefore now no condemnation for those who are in Christ Jesus."[22] Commenting on Romans 8:1, Martin Lloyd-Jones writes: "The Christian is a man who can never *be* condemned. . . . Because this is true of him the Christian should never *feel* condemned."[23] The biblical teaching that the believer has been justified and forgiven, and consequently freed from the fear of external (God's) wrath, should be paralleled by an inner freedom from inner wrath. John tells us:

> We shall know by this that we are of the truth, and shall assure our heart before Him in whatever our heart condemns us; for God is greater than our heart and knows all things.[24]

[20]Frances Shaeffer, *Death in the City* (Downers Grove: Inter-Varsity, 1969), pp. 80-81.

[21]Rom. 5:8-11.

[22]Rom. 8:1.

[23]Martin Lloyd-Jones, *Romans: The Law: Its Functions and Limits* (Grand Rapids: Zondervan, 1974), p. 271.

[24]1 John 3:19-20.

While believers may be condemned by their hearts, we can assure our hearts by recognizing that God who has forgiven our sins is greater than our hearts. Quite clearly, Scriptures do not suggest we should see self-punishment and condemnation as God-given. In fact, we are told that the process of self-condemnation is contrary to divine design. The believer is totally free from divine punishment and this should lead to inner freedom from self-inflicted wrath.

Although the believer's sins have been completely paid for and we are in no danger of punishment, the Scriptures do teach a fatherly chastening or correction. But this is entirely different from punishment or rejection. Punishment has as its purpose divine justice while discipline's motive is correction and improvement of behavior. Punishment focuses on past misdeeds while discipline or fatherly chastisement focuses on future correct deeds. And punishment is done in anger whereas discipline is done in love. Strong, for example, says: "Punishment is essentially different from chastisement. The latter proceeds from love. . . . Punishment proceeds not from love but from justice."[25]

Unfortunately many Christians are as confused about the role of fear in their lives as they are of guilt. Although we do not have time to develop the biblical use of fear I would like to remind the reader that God never motivates His children through threats of punishment, rejection, or dreadful feelings of fear. John tells us

> By this, love is perfected with us, that we may have confidence in the day of judgment; because as He is, so also are we in this world. There is no fear in love, but perfect love casts out fear, because fear involves punishment, and the one who fears is not perfected in love.[26]

A great deal of neurotic anxiety and suffering has come from the failure to distinguish between biblical passages directed to believers and nonbelievers and between fear as an awesome respect for a holy God and fear as a dreadful anxiety. W. L. Walker summarizes this distinction when he writes:

[25]A. Strong, *Systematic Theology* (Old Tappan: Fleming H. Revell, 1907), p. 653.
[26]1 John 4:17-18.

> In the New Testament dread, or fear of God in the lower sense, is removed; He is revealed as the loving and forgiving Father, who gives to men the spirit of sonship (Romans 8:15; 2 Timothy 1:7; 1 John 4:18); we are invited even to come "with boldness unto the throne of grace. . . ." but there remains a filial fear and sense of awe and of the greatness of the issues involved (Romans 11:20; Ephesians 5:2; 1 Timothy 5:20; Hebrews 4:1); all other fears should be dismissed.[27]

Self-rejection

Perhaps the most difficult aspect of the biblical answer to guilt feelings for many to experience is freedom from fears of rejection or alienation. There is a tendency to feel that we must *do* something to be acceptable both to God and to ourselves. Even though we intellectually know we are acceptable to God through Christ, we easily lapse into a pattern that says we must do something to maintain our acceptance. Once again, a biblical basis for this fear is lacking. Scripture indicates we gain acceptance by God on one basis alone—the righteousness of Christ. Paul writes: "Not having mine own righteousness, which is of the law, but that which is through the faith of Christ, the righteousness which is of God by faith."[28]

In another place, Paul says,

> Being justified freely by his grace through the redemption that is in Christ Jesus. Whom God hath set forth to be a propitiation through faith in his blood, to declare his righteousness for the remission of sins that are past, through the forbearance of God.[29]

According to these passages God not only forgives sinners but also imputes to us all of the righteousness of Christ. From the moment of salvation the Christian is once and for all acceptable to God. While our sins may necessitate fatherly correction—even painful correction—we are never for a moment rejected by God or put in a state of psychological isolation or alienation. Lloyd-Jones states: "Condemnation and separation are an utter impos-

---

[27]W. L. Walker, "Fear" in *The International Standard Bible Encyclopedia*, James Orr, ed. (Grand Rapids: Eerdmans, 1956), 2:1102.

[28]Phil. 3:9 (KJV).

[29]Rom. 3:24-25 (KJV).

sibility for the Christian."[30] In fact, Paul's reference to those who "delight in self abasement"[31] and the fact that the believer is unconditionally loved by God seem to clearly rule out self-hatred or rejection as godly motivations. *Not only do we never find exhortations to psychological guilt in the New Testament; we also do not find exhortations to experience any of its constituent ingredients.* Far from portraying guilt feelings as a God-given stimulus to spiritual growth, the Bible teaches that guilt feelings should have absolutely no place in the Christian life. Christ's death once and for all provided the foundation for freedom from both external threats and from the condemnations of a guilty conscience. In fact, we are told that Satan (not the Holy Spirit) is the "accuser of the brethren."[32] Christians should respond to their sins with deep repentance, but guilt feelings in the Christian life should never be seen as the Holy Spirit's tool. They are actually the result of a reversal to life under law.

RESULTS OF GUILT MOTIVATION

As part of humanity's autonomous attempt to solve the problem of being less than we should be, guilt feelings always have some negative results. In fact there are only four basic alternative responses to guilt feelings.

The first response is to give in to the accusations of a guilty conscience and suffer the resulting self-punishment and loss of self-esteem. This was the way of Judas, who went out and hanged himself. The second response is to attempt to hide, rationalize, or in some other way repress both our guilt feelings and our actual guilt. That was the way of Adam who hid among the trees of the garden. Even though his guilt feelings attested to an awareness that something was wrong he continued hiding to try to silence his conscience.

A third common reaction to guilt feelings is rebellion. Like many children who rebel against punitive parents, adults can rebel against their punitive consciences. Our attempts to pay for

[30]Lloyd-Jones, *Romans*, p. 272.
[31]Col. 2:18.
[32]Rev. 12:10.

our own sins set a vicious cycle in motion. We sin, we punish ourselves just as our parents did, and then we sin more in response to our self-payments just as we rebelled (or wanted to) against our parents when they punished us. Sometimes this rebellion is active and overt as it is in young adults who in reaction to the guilt learned from parents, throw off their values and adopt an alternative lifestyle. More frequently rebellion takes a passive form in which the guilt-laden person loses his or her motivation for Christian service, gives up trying for fear of further failure, or simply goes through the motions of religious ritual. This is similar to the situation of an adolescent who resigns himself to living with pressuring parents and goes through the motions of external conformity without any real interest or commitment.

The final possible response to guilt feelings is to confess and alter one's behavior. Although this initially sounds like a positive resolution, it also leaves much to be desired. Since the goal of changed behavior is to reduce guilt feelings, the motive underlying confession is selfish and the "solution" is self-effort. The goal is to rid ourselves of guilty feelings by our own actions, not to become holy as a result of true repentance. This solution also perpetuates a view of God as a coercive parent who relies on fear and guilt to push us into conformity rather than relying on a gracious God who lovingly but firmly seeks our welfare. Although this type of confession can result in a great deal of outwardly Christian actions and even successful Christian service, individuals operating on this emotional motivation typically suffer some of the pressures and symptoms of hidden guilt discussed in chapter 3. Not only are guilt feelings never encouraged in the Bible, they are actually an impediment to a life of faith.[33]

GUILT FEELINGS AS SELF-ATONEMENT

If we pause to analyze the hidden dynamics of guilt we come to another surprising conclusion. Not only is the feeling of guilt not a God-given form of motivation; it is actually a form of omnipotent self-atonement. In experiencing psychological guilt we are in effect saying, "Christ's death and God's forgiveness are not sufficient to

[33]Gal. 3:1-5, 26.

take care of my sins. *I* will pay for them by inflicting some inner psychic pain upon myself." In the non-Christian this form of self-punishment is understandable. Standing outside the circle of God's forgiveness the natural man is compelled to satisfy the demands of conscience through acts of self-propitiation. In refusing to accept the substitutionary atonement, he is forced to find within himself some way of quieting the qualms of conscience. For some, alcohol provides this temporary relief. For others, success, achievement, security, or humanitarian efforts do the same. But underneath every relatively successful effort to silence one's conscience and say that one is acceptable or okay, lies the hidden expectation of deserved punishment. Tournier reminds us to:

> Think of the innumerable multitudes of Hindus who plunge into the waters of the Ganges to be washed from their guilt. ... Think of all the penitents and pilgrims of all religions who impose upon themselves sacrifices. ... In a more secular sphere, less aware of its religious significance, think of all the privations and all the acts of charity which so many people impose upon themselves, in order to be pardoned for the more or less unfair privileges they enjoy. ... The dreadful agony of this inexhaustible guilt ... is a kind of expiatory sacrifice which they are rendering.[34]

In the Christian we have a potentially very different matter. Standing inside the circle of God's grace we have no need to pay for our sins. Christ has already paid and we are freed from the need for self-expiation. To punish ourselves further is tantamount to a denial of the efficacy of the Atonement.

The attempt to atone for one's sins through self-punishment is actually a form of self-effort common to all non-Christian religions. In an admittedly pious appearing manner, we are saying, "I will be as God. Not only will I know good and evil, I will also take it upon myself to make regular payments to settle the debt I owe."

SUMMARY

In answer to the question, Are guilt feelings a form of Christian motivation or are they a neurotic masochism? we must say that

---

[34]Tournier, *Guilt and Grace* (New York: Harper & Row, 1962), p. 175.

guilt feelings are definitely not a Christian motivation. They are a form of masochism. But even beyond this they are a form of self-worship and omnipotence. Guilt feelings show us something is wrong within our personalities and in that sense we can learn from them. But they can never motivate us to genuine repentance. As with Adam and Eve, guilt feelings motivate us to hide or offer our own self-punishments or solutions in the place of God's forgiveness. They are an attempt to place the responsibility for reconciliation squarely upon our own autonomous shoulders and are consequently a denial of our dependency on God.

When viewed in this light, we can see another reason it is insufficient to view the guilt-laden person as simply a victim of parental mistreatment and societal conditioning. While these factors are important, we also need to look beyond them to the deep religious instinct of self-worship and the desire to assume the role of deity lying within every personality. To understand the dynamics of guilt, we must see that far from being God's means of motivation, guilt feelings actually flow from the very essence of our sinful desires for autonomy and control of our lives. In chapter 11 we will look at the biblical alternative to these self-atoning feelings of guilt.

An Alternative to Guilt

Our survey of the New Testament use of guilt leads to an important distinction between different types of guilt. The emotion of guilt we have been discussing so far is best labeled *psychological guilt* or *guilt feelings.*

GUILT FEELINGS

Psychological guilt is the inner subjective experience of condemnation. Comprised of self-inflicted mental punishment, rejection and disesteem, psychological guilt is neither portrayed in Scripture as a positive motivation nor attributed to divine conviction. Even when guilt feelings motivate altered behavior, they tend to cause repression, depression, rebellion, or other personality dysfunctions. In this way guilt feelings function like the law. They can promote guilt-based conformity or drive us to despair but they have no power of positive motivation! Guilt feelings affect us the same way they did Adam and Eve. Their guilt showed them something was wrong but it did absolutely nothing to motivate them to repent. It only caused them to hide.

OBJECTIVE GUILT

In contrast to guilt feelings is the objective condition of guilt. Whether *civil* guilt due to the violation of a human law or guilt before God, this objective guilt is entirely different from guilt feelings. It is an objective state or condition rather than a subjective experience. We *are* legally guilty when we are pronounced guilty by a court of law, whether or not we *feel* guilty. History is replete with cases of violent criminal deeds over which the criminal apparently had no *feeling* of guilt. Similarly, Scripture makes it clear that all persons *are* guilty before God whether or not they *feel* guilty or have a conscious awareness of their guilt. We have rebelled against His authority, violated His divine law and been judged guilty. Like civil guilt, guilt before God is an objective state or condition. While it may be accompanied by guilt feelings (or fear, or a variety of other emotions for that matter), it is not a feeling. It is a condition, or state, of being. Brown, for example, writes that "... guilt is a legal and judicial term which implies criminal responsibility in the eyes of a court of law, whether that court is human or divine."[1]

SIN AND GUILT

Since all guilt feelings grow out of humanity's fallen condition, it is impossible to comprehend the nature of guilt apart from the doctrine of sin. It is sin that both places us in a condition of guilt and causes guilt feelings.

At the foundation of all sin is our rejection of and rebellion against the Holy God who brought us into existence,[2] who prepared a world for us to inhabit,[3] who lovingly created helpmates for us,[4] who upholds the entire world by His power,[5] who has made provision for all of our needs,[6] and who loves us so infinitely that He was willing to die for us.[7] In creating us in His own image, God wonderfully made us[8] to function harmoniously, happily, and holily. All we had to do was respond to His gracious love in the way we were created to function—as His appointed rulers of the planet earth. But we refused and attempted to exalt ourselves to

---

[1]C. Brown, "Guilt," *The New International Dictionary of New Testament Theology* (Grand Rapids: Zondervan, 1976), 2:137.

[2]Gen. 1:26-27.
[3]Gen. 1:28-31.
[4]Gen. 2:18-20.
[5]Heb. 1:3.
[6]Phil. 4:19.
[7]John 3:16-17.
[8]Ps. 139:14.

the level of God Himself. In doing so we violated our relationship with Him, with our own created natures, and with others.

It was the decision to violate our natures as they were created and attempt to be something we were not designed to be that led to all later offenses and to problems of guilt. This attempt impacted the entirety of our personality because sin is not simply an offense against God. It is a pattern of personality functioning that goes against our very natures.[9] In trying to be something we were not created to be, we create a division within our own personality that stirs up fear and guilt and constant efforts to close the gap between who we are and who we want or ought to be. Our sinful attempts to be like God are like those of a bear who decides she wants to be a ballerina. The bear is beautiful in her own right and as long as she is living as she was created to live she gets along well. If our hypothetical bear had the mental processes to aspire to be a ballerina, however, think of the inner struggle she would have. She would continually be striving yet always doomed to fail! When she failed she would either experience fear or guilt for not living up to her expectations!

Seen in this light sin is not a passive experience that has happened upon the human race. It is an active, ongoing problem deep within the life of every person that continually gives rise to feelings of guilt. If we were not separated from God by trying to run our own lives in god-like fashion, we would neither be setting our own unrealistic (god-like) standards nor attempting to atone for our own sins through self-inflicted psychic pain.

This understanding of sin being ultimately rooted in an interpersonal offense against God that is accompanied by an offense against ourselves as we were created to be is the link that ties objective and subjective guilt together. It is because we are trying to function in ways contradictory to our created natures that we are guilty before God. It is this same desire that creates the inner

[9]L. Berkhof writes, "This change in the actual condition of man also reflected itself in his consciousness. This was, first of all, a consciousness of pollution, revealing itself in the sense of shame, and in the efforts of our first parents to cover their nakedness. And in the second place there was a consciousness of guilt which found expression in an accusing conscience and in the fear of God which it inspired" (L. Berkhof, *Systematic Theology* [Grand Rapids: Eerdmans, 1964], p. 226).

tension and disunity we experience as guilt feelings. Knowing we aren't what we ought or desire to be, we punish ourselves in a vain attempt to solve our self-created problems. The internalized voice of parents and other authorities adds to our basic unrest about ourselves. But if there were no fundamental disunity in the personality, these environmental inputs would not cause so many problems. Environmental judgments take root in the soil of our awareness that we are not all that we ought to be.

CONSTRUCTIVE SORROW

In stark contrast to the punitive, atoning nature of psychological guilt is a positive corrective attitude the apostle Paul calls godly sorrow. Paul writes of this experience in 2 Corinthians 7:9-11 where he reminds the Corinthians that there is a difference between a worldly sorrow (which leads to death) and a godly sorrow (that leads to righteousness). Constructive or godly sorrow is a love motivated emotion that is the biblical alternative to psychological guilt. Whereas psychological guilt is essentially a self-punitive process designed to atone for one's sins, constructive sorrow is a love-motivated desire to change rooted in concern for the offended person and one's relationship to God.

Peter's reaction after he realized he had denied Christ three times is a good biblical illustration of constructive sorrow. "He went out and wept bitterly."[10] Peter apparently felt deep remorse and contrition but we have no evidence he engaged in a process of self-debasement and condemnation. He knew he had not lived up to his confident promise, "Even if I must die with you, I will not deny you."[11] He knew he had been disloyal to Christ and placed concern for his own safety above his love for Christ. But his godly sorrow did not bind him into a defeatest pattern of depression and self-hatred.[12] Rather than going out and hanging himself like Judas,[13] Peter used his failure to promote his maturity. He allowed the experience of failure to deepen his love and

[10]Matt. 26:75.
[11]Matt. 26:35.
[12]2 Cor. 7:9-10.
[13]Matt. 27:1-5.

commitment so that he would go on to become one of the boldest of the apostles.

I prefer the term *constructive,* or *godly, sorrow* to terms like *true guilt,*[14] *intrinsic guilt,*[15] or *existential guilt,*[16] because this experience is based on precisely the opposite dynamics of psychological guilt and because there is such a universal tendency to confuse the two. Other labels that appropriately describe what I am calling constructive or godly sorrow are remorse and contrition. Pattison contrasts some of the fundamental distinctions between psychological guilt and constructive sorrow under the topic of remorse when he writes: "Remorse is the motivating spur to reconstitutive action rather than the occasion for self flagellation."[17]

And Maslow, in discussing his concept of intrinsic guilt, sheds further light on the healthy nature of constructive sorrow when he writes that it is ". . . the consequence of betrayal of one's own inner nature of self, a turning off the path of self-actualization, and is essentially qualified self-disapproval."[18] Although Maslow's concept of intrinsic guilt as a betrayal of one's inner nature (a concept common to existential theorists) is not fully consistent with Scripture it does bring two key concepts into focus. To begin with, it sees this reaction as justified self-disapproval. It is not self-contempt or condemnation but a regret based on a true evaluation of one's self. Maslow's second contribution is his focus on intrinsic guilt as a result of the betrayal of one's inner nature. Given a biblical understanding of our inner nature I would suggest a major modification of Maslow's definition to read "a betrayal of one's inner nature *as God created it."* In other words, since the Fall we can try to actualize either our basic God-given patterns or our own sinful dispositions. Maslow gives no room for the latter.

The differentiation I am attempting to make, of course, is not an entirely new one. Existential and other theorists have stressed the necessity of distinguishing between experiences variously labeled, *pathological guilt* and *normal guilt; true guilt* and *false*

[14]P. Tournier, *Guilt and Grace* (New York: Harper & Row, 1962).

[15]A. Maslow, *Toward a Psychology of Being* (Princeton: D. Van Nostrand, 1962).

[16]J. Knight, *Conscience and Guilt* (New York: Appleton-Century-Crofts, 1969).

[17]Pattison, "On the Failure to Forgive or to Be Forgiven," *American Journal of Psychotherapy,* vol. 19, 1965, pp. 100-15.

[18]Maslow, *Toward a Psychology of Being,* p. 182.

guilt;[19] neurotic guilt and existential guilt.[20] Yet while each of these theorists have made some helpful distinctions, I find each of them lacking in some degree. Tournier, for example, concludes that the essential difference between true and false guilt is the source of the guilt. He writes: " 'False guilt' is that which comes as a result of the judgments and suggestions of men. 'True guilt' is that which results from divine judgment."[21]

Although this distinction is of some help it fails to account for the fact that people may respond to the judgments of God with either godly sorrow or self-punitive reactions. This is precisely the point Paul had to clarify with the church at Corinth. The problem was not the source of the judgment but the nature of the emotional response to the judgment.

Whereas Tournier sees the essential distinction between true and false guilt lying in their different sources, others see the distinction lying in the type of standard violated. If the emotion grows out of the violation of a God-given or realistic standard (such as stealing or murder), the guilt emotion is considered normal. If it grows out of an unrealistic standard or expectation (like swimming on Sunday or attending a "G" rated movie) the feeling is considered false or neurotic guilt. This view has limitations similar to Tournier's since it ignores important differences between the affective experiences of guilt feelings and constructive sorrow and the thought processes underlying them. Neither one of these views distinguishes between the punitive nature of guilt feelings and the love orientation of constructive sorrow.

Other authors differentiate between positive and negative guilt on the basis of the severity of the emotion. Deep feelings of self-condemnation are seen by authors such as Jourard[22] to reflect neurotic guilt, whereas guilt experienced in lesser degrees is considered normal.

It is my opinion that existential theorists have in some ways come closest to the differentiating factors between constructive and destructive responses to the awareness of our objective guilt.

[19]Tournier, Guilt and Grace.

[20]M. Boss, Psychoanalysis and Daseinsanalysis (New York: Basic Books, 1963).

[21]Tournier, Guilt and Grace, p. 67.

[22]Jourard, Personal Adjustment (New York: Macmillan, 1963).

Although they generally do not relate experiences of guilt to a divine-human encounter or to humanity's sinful condition, they do carefully distinguish between neurotic guilt, which is seen as originating from the outside (judgments of others), and existential guilt, which is an awareness of one's inevitable condition of being in debt. The focus of existential guilt is not on self-punishment, but the reality of our frail condition. In a general way this approaches the biblical concept of constructive sorrow. The failure of most existentialists to relate this existential guilt to our alienated relationship with God and the tendency to find the solutions to it in the courage to stand and face one's choices responsibly by oneself, however, are seriously divergent from the biblical view of both objective guilt and constructive sorrow.

GUILT FEELINGS AND CONSTRUCTIVE SORROW

Our discussion of the differences between godly sorrow and psychological guilt are not merely theoretical. As long as guilt is seen as a form of punishment or disesteem we are prone to confess our sins, not as a part of a process of deep inner repentance and remorse, but more to remove the fear of punishment or self-inflicted condemnation. This is why many Christians go through repeated cycles of sin, guilt feelings, confession, temporary relief, and more sin. The confession was not accompanied by true repentance or remorse. It was designed to give them a bit of inner peace until they sinned again—a rather selfish motivation!

This process has become almost institutionalized in some churches. For some Protestants, 1 John 1:9 has come to be used as a kind of psychological spot remover for emotional guilt. Any time we feel guilty we confess our sins and receive assurance that we are forgiven. But we fail to change because we didn't experience constructive sorrow. We just confess, as one patient put it, to "get God off my back." Catholics can abuse the confessional the same way. McNulty and Wakin write:

> Catholics have gradually sensed that they were making the same kinds of Confession that they had made at the age of eight or nine. ... What was happening was the use of a sacrament to absolve superego guilt. Individuals were going to

Confession so that religious authority (personified by a priest) would not punish them by withholding approval and acceptance. With Confession, they felt they were winning back approval.[23]

Paradoxically, it is often those who focus most on their sins and feelings of guilt and confession that fail to grapple with the depths of their sinfulness. The focus on specific *sins* (plural) masks the deeper problem of *sin* (singular) as a very basic alienation of affection from God and a self-centered direction to one's life. Once we truly see the depths of our sinfulness we are not so naïve as to believe that we can keep a clean slate with God by periodically asking forgivness of all "known" (or even unknown for that matter!) sins. We realize instead that Jesus has once and for all paid the penalty for our sins and that the agony of that payment calls us to face directly the fact that our entire nature tends to be at enmity with God and that we need a continual awareness of Christ's presence in our lives. This goes much deeper than confession to remove guilt feelings. It is a true repentance involving godly sorrow and a significant change of mind.

It is this experience of constructive sorrow that is the primary biblical alternative to psychological guilt. In fact, one of the main goals of therapy is to help people replace feelings of guilt with a God-given, love-based motivation of constructive sorrow. Since guilt feelings and godly sorrow are based on opposing personality processes, it is difficult to experience them simultaneously. Consequently guilt feelings stand in the way of true repentance. Guilt feelings are punitive. Constructive sorrow is loving. In psychological guilt *we* take the initiative to atone and punish ourselves. In constructive sorrow we respond because *God* has taken the initiative. In psychological guilt we change because *we* don't like to feel badly (guilty). In constructive sorrow we change because we have a concern for God or others. Because we see that God has taken the initiative by providing acceptance and forgiveness, we are free to respond in love and deep appreciation! The table in figure 5 summarizes these distinctions.

[23]F. McNulty and E. Wakin, *Should You Ever Feel Guilty?* (New York: Paulist Press, 1978), p. 59.

Figure 5

COMPARISON OF PSYCHOLOGICAL GUILT AND
CONSTRUCTIVE SORROW

	PSYCHOLOGICAL GUILT	CONSTRUCTIVE SORROW
PERSON IN PRIMARY FOCUS	Self	Both the offended party and oneself (the violated relationship).
ATTITUDES OR ACTIONS IN PRIMARY FOCUS	Past misdeeds	Damage done to others or future correct deeds and attitudes.
MOTIVATION FOR CHANGE (IF ANY)	To avoid feeling bad (guilt feelings).	To help others, to promote our growth, or to do God's will (love).
ATTITUDE TOWARD GOD	Autonomy (I will pay).	Constructive dependence.
ATTITUDE TOWARD ONESELF	Anger and frustration.	Love and respect combined with deep concern or contrition.
RESULT	a) External change (for improper motivation). b) Stagnation due to paralyzing effect of guilt. c) Further rebellion.	Repentance and change based on an attitude of love and respect.

THE HOLY SPIRIT AND CONVICTION

Many Christians are confused about the role of the Holy Spirit in conviction. They equate divine conviction with feelings of psychological guilt. Scripturally, however, conviction[24] simply means to expose, to reprove, or to bring to awareness. To equate psychological guilt (or constructive sorrow for that matter) with conviction is to confuse the two. Conviction means to bring to light or reveal. We can respond to conviction with anger, guilt feelings, constructive sorrow, or a variety of other feelings but these feelings are not a *part* of conviction. They are our *responses* to the Holy Spirit's conviction and should not be confused with it.

The role of the Holy Spirit in the entire process of moral functioning is both a central one and a difficult one to comprehend. It is easier to delineate what the Holy Spirit does not do (e.g., implant guilt feelings) and what He is not (the voice of conscience) than to define precisely his function in our moral functioning. In Jesus' discussion of the coming of the Holy Spirit with His disciples, however, we gain some insight into the role and ministry of the Holy Spirit:

> But I tell you the truth, it is to your advantage that I go away; for if I do not go away, the Helper shall not come to you; but if I go, I will send Him to you. And He, when He comes, will convict the world concerning sin, and righteousness, and judgment; concerning sin, because they do not believe in Me; and concerning righteousness, because I go to the Father, and you no longer behold Me; and concerning judgment, because the ruler of this world has been judged. I have many more things to say to you, but you cannot bear them now. But when He, the Spirit of truth, comes, He will guide you into all the truth; for He will not speak on His own initiative, but whatever He hears, He will speak; and he will disclose to you what is to come. He shall glorify Me; for He shall take of Mine, and shall disclose it to you. All things that the Father has are Mine; therefore I said, that He takes of Mine, and will disclose it to you.[25]

It is interesting to note that the Holy Spirit's convicting activity is here related not to the believer, but to the world—to those who do not believe in Him. Rather than relating the convicting function

---

[24]*The International Standard Bible Encyclopedia*, e.g., suggests, "The basic meaning of *elencho* is 'show' or 'demonstrate'; the further legal sense 'prove guilt' is evident from the context" (G. Bromiley, *The International Standard Bible Encyclopedia* [Grand Rapids: Eerdmans, 1978], p. 770).

[25]John 16:7-17.

to the work of the Holy Spirit in the lives of Christians, Christ relates it to the Spirit's work in arousing an awareness of sin and the demands of righteousness and judgment in the unbeliever's life. Then Christ goes on to describe the Holy Spirit as the Spirit of truth and tells the disciples the Holy Spirit will guide them into all truth. Above all else, the Holy Spirit is the Spirit of truth. In this role, He especially communicates truth that glorifies Christ (v. 14) and alters our lives.

When Paul challenges us to walk in the Spirit so that we will not carry out the desire of the flesh (Gal. 5:16) it is in the context of Christ's atoning death that frees us from slavery to the law. In Galatians 5:1, for example, he writes, "It was for freedom that Christ set us free; therefore keep standing firm and do not be subject again to a yoke of slavery." Then he follows this in verses 16-18 by saying:

> But I say, walk by the Spirit, and you will not carry out the desire of the flesh. For the flesh sets its desire against the Spirit, and the Spirit against the flesh; for these are in opposition to one another, so that you may not do the things that you please.

The Spirit motivates us to holiness by reminding us of our position in Christ and of our freedom from the law and its accompanying condemnation. We find precisely the same relation between the work of Christ, the work of the Holy Spirit, and our holiness in Romans 8, "The Spirit Himself bears witness with our spirit that we are children of God."[26]

> And in the same way the Spirit also helps our weakness; for we do not know how to pray as we should, but the Spirit Himself intercedes for us with groanings too deep for words; and He who searches the hearts knows what the mind of the Spirit is, because He intercedes for the saints according to the will of God.[27]

Combining these passages, we see three aspects of the ministry of the Holy Spirit. First, He convinces us of truth, both about ourselves and Christ. In doing so He glorifies Christ, especially in relation to His holiness and gracious atoning work. Second, He

[26]Rom. 8:16.
[27]Rom. 8:26, 27.

bears witness to the believer's position as children and heirs of God and on that basis motivates us to holy living. Finally, He comes to our side in our weaknesses and comforts and encourages and intercedes for us.

Without going into other aspects of the Holy Spirit's ministry (such as His work in conversion and in illuminating the Word of God), we can say that in relation to conviction of sin and motivation to holiness He does everything Christ did during His earthly ministry. He makes our sins known to us and witnesses to the fact that Christ has paid for them. He comforts and encourages us in our weaknesses and He lovingly motivates us to respond in love to God's limitless love and grace.

RESPONSIBILITY AND GODLY SORROW

Some Christians fear that the distinction between guilt and godly sorrow minimizes the severity of sin or does not take sin seriously. They assume the alternative to self-belittling and condemning guilt feelings is a laissez faire mental assent to our sinfulness that leads to license. This concern is not a new one. Anticipating the charge that liberty growing out of Christ's atonement and our freedom from the law equals license Paul wrote, "What shall we say then? Are we to continue in sin that grace might increase? May it never be."[28]

While there is a danger of disfiguring liberty into license, the concept of a godly or constructive sorrow is the very antidote to that. *Constructive sorrow is not an absence of emotion or a laissez faire attitude toward our sin. It is a different emotion. It is a deep feeling of concern over one's attitudes and actions arising from true repentance based on seeing ourselves in the light of God's holiness and Christ's redemptive work.*

Frankly, I suspect that some who are most afraid of what Christians will do if they aren't motivated by guilt have not truly experienced godly sorrow in their own lives. Some Christians are so habituated to a cycle of guilt that they can't emotionally conceive of a nonpunitive alternative. They may even feel insecure without it! As a counselee put it, "If I don't feel guilty then who is

[28]Rom. 6:1, 2.

going to punish me so I can feel better about myself?" In reality, people like this have become so oriented to external conformity growing out of fear and guilt motivation they have lost touch with the inner feelings of caring and gratitude that could lead them to a loving morality free of the pressures of guilt and condemnation. Underneath their guilt-based conformity they would actually like to rebel. They fear that the elimination of guilt feelings will result in the license to act on the sinful desire they have covered up with conformity. Their need for self-imposed guilt to motivate conformity belies their hidden rebellious wishes. Martin Luther saw this when he wrote:

> For even though you keep the law outwardly, with works, from fear of punishment or love of reward, nevertheless you do all this without willingness and pleasure and without love for the law, but rather with unwillingness, under compulsion; and you would rather do otherwise, if the law were not there! The conclusion is that at the bottom of your heart you hate the law.[29]

Psychological guilt is based on fear, self-punishment, and comparison with others. Constructive sorrow is a deep feeling, but it is oriented to changed attitudes and actions rather than removal of guilt feelings. Constructive sorrow also allows a much deeper feeling of concern for the person we have offended than psychological guilt, which is more concerned with our own feelings of failure. Edward Stein put it this way:

> What genuine guilt (what I am calling godly sorrow) cares about is that a personal relationship has been broken, love has been wronged. The sadness that ensues is normal and natural, as when a friend has gone or been injured. What neurotic guilt cares about is that the self may be punished or love must be recovered. It is narcissistic and concerned about the punishment more than reconciliation with the other.[30]

Unfortunately it is not always easy to move from guilt feelings to constructive sorrow. Many of us have a tendency to cling to

---

[29]Martin Luther, *Commentary on Romans*, T. Mueller, trans. (Grand Rapids: Kregel, 1976), p. xiv.

[30]Edward Stein, *Guilt: Theory and Therapy* (Philadelphia: Westminster, 1968), p. 166.

guilt feelings. Even though they are painful—sometimes even to the point of suicidal depression—they do provide a sense of security. Without them we feel much like a young adult who leaves a home where parents have enforced conformity through fear, punishment, and pressure. Suddenly there is opportunity to try new things and to make one's own choices—even wrong or sinful ones. The freedom is appealing yet frightening. In some ways this person wants to go on and become a responsible, choosing adult. But the fear of his own wishes may drive him back to the safety of external controls. Some are actually willing to trade the anxiety they experience over responsibility associated with freedom for the security they have in bondage! Consequently they either seek out authoritarian people to rule their lives or rigidly control themselves through guilt. In fact this is precisely the problem faced by the Galatian Christians and all who give in to religious legalism. Their security is self-effort and self-atonement.

Moving from the security of psychological guilt to the uncharted waters of godly sorrow is a bit like flying from one trapeze to another. For one terrifying moment we must give up our grasp on the only thing supporting us if we are to move on to something new. But no matter how frightening it is to let go, we cannot know the freedom of a loving morality unless we let go of the old. As one client put it, "Without guilt, what would I do! I would feel completely at sea!" Yet no matter how new or frightening, it is only at this point that we can begin to switch our motivation from the selfish goal of security through conformity and atonement through self-punishment to a truly Christian motive.

Godly sorrow is not content with atoning for our own failures or appeasing ourselves or others through conformity. Godly sorrow wants to be different from the depths of our being. It involves real repentance and a deep change of heart. As one client put it, "When I experience godly sorrow I feel uncomfortable. I can't just become obsessed with my failure. I feel a tremendous responsibility to *do* something." This young man's urgency to "do something" reflects the power of godly sorrow to motivate us to responsible action. When we see the depths of our sin and the extent of God's grace, we are impelled to live rightly from gratitude. This is so radically different from the self-atoning nature of psychological guilt that the latter can only be seen as a cheap substitute.

THE SENSE OF GUILT

Before leaving our discussion we need to mention one other type of guilt. This is what we might call a "sense of guilt." A sense of guilt is simply the awareness of having sinned or fallen short. It is the stage between our condition of guilt and our emotional response of either psychological guilt or constructive sorrow. It is the perception or awareness of our objective guilt. Without it we would be unaware of our failures. A sense of guilt is not necessarily a strong emotional reaction, but an awareness of our guilt. It can lead to either deep feelings of repentance or to hiding and self-atonement.

Figure 6 demonstrates the relationship between objective guilt, a sense of guilt, guilt feelings, and constructive sorrow. It also shows how an awareness of our sinful condition can lead either to genuine, life enhancing repentance or to debilitating guilt emotions.

The process starts with our sin, which places us in an objective condition of guilt. The next step in the process is either to acknowledge our objective guilt or to deny it. The lower half of the figure represents the processes that follow when guilt is denied or repressed; the top portion represents what happens when we acknowledge our guilt. If we deny awareness to our objective guilt, we either harbor unconscious guilt feelings or experience conscious guilt feelings over false issues. In the latter case our guilt feelings are first repressed and then displaced from their original source to some "safer" attitude or action.

The top portion of Figure 6 demonstrates the directions acknowledged objective guilt can take. If we face our sin and objective guilt, we can either respond with conscious self-punitive guilt feelings or with godly sorrow. If we experience guilt feelings we are led to legalistic conformity, rebellion, depression, or other symptoms. If we experience godly sorrow we are led to true repentance and inner harmony.

This diagram also illustrates the two main choice points or key steps where intervention can occur in the guilt process. The

Figure 6

GUILT AND GODLY SORROW

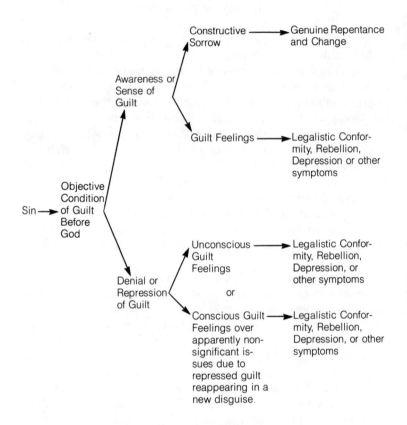

first is at the choice between awareness and denial and the second is between guilt feelings and constructive sorrow. Although one's immediate ability to make alternative choices at these points may be impaired by parentally or societally induced repression or guilt feelings it is at these points that effective intervention must be made to resolve guilt feelings.

Figure 6 illustrates the development of guilt feelings growing out of objective guilt before God. Since guilt feelings may also grow out of perceived guilt in relationship to one's parents, we need to modify Figure 6 in order to represent the course of guilt feelings growing out of the sins of others and the parent-child relationship. We can do that by substituting for steps one and two (sin and objective condition of guilt before God) the failure to live as parents or others expect us to live and the resulting condition of being guilty in their eyes. Figure 7 demonstrates how the failure to live up to societal standards and the fact that one is peceived as objectively guilty by other significant persons set in motion essentially the same process as does objective guilt before God.

Figure 7

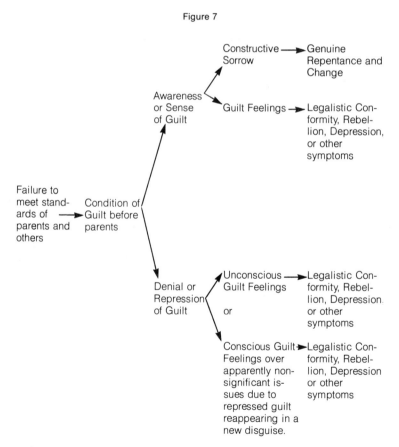

Although most of the process is the same in figures 6 and 7, it is important to realize that the failure to meet either God's standard or the standards of others can set the cycle of guilt in motion. Most psychologists ignore the possibility of guilt before God while many Christians assume all guilt is set in motion by personal sin rather than by the sin of others. A grasp of both of these processes is essential to a proper understanding of guilt feelings.

SUMMARY

I believe the failure to consistently and clearly distinguish between objective guilt, an awareness of objective guilt, guilt feelings, and constructive sorrow has been one of the greatest failings of the Christian church. Confusion on this point has often caused the church to compound rather than relieve destructive guilt emotions. The sad fact is that a very large number of Christians, when they hear the goals and ideals of Scripture expounded, assume that they should undergo a period of psychological suffering (guilt) until their behavior is brought into conformity. And many others, while not living under long periods of guilt-induced suffering, experience either repeated short bouts with it or develop a personality style (see chapters 3-5) that wards off a conscious awareness of their guilt feelings.

Not until parishioners, pastors, patients, and psychotherapists become aware of the difference between our condition of guilt before God, psychological guilt, and constructive sorrow, will we begin experiencing the release from guilt that is made possible through the grace of God. Guilt feelings essentially reflect a failure in our ability to love and be loved. When we truly see how we are loved by God, we are free to give up our omnipotent self-atoning processes and live life out of a motivation of love and constructive sorrow.

Morality or Moralism?

Since the time of Freud, therapists have tended to associate morality in general and Christianity in particular with punitive feelings of psychological guilt. Failing to differentiate between guilt feelings and constructive sorrow, many psychotherapists have a strong anti-Christian bias. They have also attempted to exclude consideration of moral issues from the psychotherapy process. They have, in other words, equated morality with moralism.

SUPEREGO MORALITY

According to Freud, the superego is the seat of the moral prohibitions internalized from parents and significant others. As the seat of parental and institutional morality the superego develops largely as a result of internalizing our parents' values and prohibitions and their threats of punishment. Consequently, adult morality for Freud is essentially a continuation of childhood prohibitions (modified somewhat by maturity and healthy sublimations) now carried out by our superego instead of our parents.

The values of the superego are largely extrinsic since they are taken in from authority figures without any great amount of personal choice on the part of the growing child. Similarly, the motivation for living up to one's internalized superego (ego ideal) standards is the internalized fear of punishment, rejection, or self-condemnation. As the child first learns to conform in order to avoid the parents' punishment, he or she now behaves morally in order to avoid self-inflicted mental suffering. Fenichel, for example, tells us:

The superego is the heir of the parents not only as a source of threats and punishments but also as a source of protection and as a provider of reassuring love. Being on good or bad terms with one's superego becomes as important as being on good terms with one's parents previously was.[1]

Another characteristic of Freud's superego is its unconscious nature. Having their origins in early life, the exact nature of our prohibitions and punishments is obscured by years of repression and/or habit. Consequently the standards of the superego tend to be arbitrary. Similarly, since the superego's stress is on conformity to please an internalized authority figure, it also allows little room for personal grappling with moral choices and tends to make everything black or white.[2]

Unfortunately Freud's view of the superego focuses almost entirely on the punitive dynamics leading to moral conformity. Perhaps because he worked largely with disturbed individuals suffering excessive guilt feelings or perhaps because of his commitment to a highly individualistic (autonomous) morality, Freud failed to develop a positive view of morality. Even in his discussions on the necessity of values and morals for the survival of culture he failed to develop a positive understanding of the unifying, integrative potential of morality. As Pattison put it:

When Freud wrote specifically on morality it was usually in regard to the psychopathologies of the superego. In *Future of an Illusion, Civilization and Its Discontents* and *Moses and Monotheism*, Freud identifies morality with institutionalized religion; and both were ultimately related to superego development consequent to the resolutions of the Oedipal conflict. Thus religion and its moral imperatives were an oppressive force that served to constrict man's freedom and foster illusionary denials of his basic nature and function.[3]

[1]O. Fenichel, *The Psychoanalytic Theory of Neurosis* (New York: Norton, 1945), pp. 105-6.

[2]The superego morality is essentially the same as Fromm's *authoritarian conscience*.

[3]Pattison, "Ego Morality: An Emerging Psychotherapeutic Concept," *Psychoanalytic Review*, vol. 55(2), 1968, pp. 187-222.

With Freud's conception of the origin and nature of morality we can see why many psychoanalytically-oriented psychotherapists have viewed morality as negative and inhibiting and have been highly critical of religious belief. Superego morality *is* oppressive. And it *can* lead to neuroses. But this type of morality is more *moralism* than *morality*. It is the perpetuation of a childish form of compliance motivated by fears of punishment and rejection with little thought given to real moral issues. Unfortunately, this truncated view of morality is the only one that many psychotherapists have encountered or considered. Hoffman, for example, concludes that for both Freud and Rogers "morality is unavoidably moralistic."[4]

> The conscience for Freud ... became both prohibitive and threatening. Though conceptualized in less dramatic language, morality as described by Rogers operates in an equally moralistic fashion. His scrupulous rejection of any "judgmental frame of mind" and his description of introjected values as "conditions of worth" clearly rest upon such an assumption.[5]

EGO MORALITY

In recent years a number of theorists have begun to see an alternative to Freud's moralistic superego morality. Mansell Pattison, for example, introduced the term "ego morality" in a paper titled "Ego Morality: An Emerging Psychotherapeutic Concept."[6] In contrast to the rigid, punitive-based morality of the superego, Pattison posits an ego morality built more on consciously chosen adult moral values than Freud's superego morality. Pattison suggests morality includes the rational, perceptual processes of the ego in addition to the early parental introjects. While acknowledging the powerful nature of the early internalization of parental values and punishments, this view allows much more room for later, more mature moral choices.

Whereas superego morality is initially extrinsic, ego morality

---

[4]J. Hoffman, *Ethical Confrontation in Counseling* (Chicago: University of Chicago Press, 1979), p. 55.

[5]Ibid.

[6]Pattison, "Ego Morality: An Emerging Psychotherapeutic Concept."

is more intrinsic. Ego morality involves choosing to do the right because we want to be helpful or respond lovingly rather than simply to avoid self-punishment and condemnation. This morality contains more consciously chosen values than the unconscious ones of the superego. And the goal of ego morality is not blind conformity but rather the desire to function optimally for the welfare of oneself and others. Ego morality flows out of the total life experience of the individual and is built on the assumption that the infant comes to this world as more than simply a bundle of reflexes and id impulses that will become socialized through the internalization of parental prohibitions and punishments.[7]

Psychologists utilizing Freud's structural view of the personality (id, ego, and superego) are increasingly realizing that a healthily functioning ego is the key to moral behavior. The superego may yield forced conformity but it does not produce healthy inner motivations. And the pressures of the superego often cause depression or lead to passive or overt rebellion. In their place ego functions such as the ability to delay immediate gratification for a long-term gain, the ability to perceive the consequences of one's acts, the ability to control impulses, and the ability to focus one's attentions on a single task are seen as the essential prerequisites for mature morality.

The increasing awareness of psychoanalytically-oriented therapists to the possibility of a healthy, nonpunitive morality parallels Fromm's suggestion of a humanistic conscience. Although the developmental and dynamic formulations differ, they converge at the point of suggesting a positive form of morality based more upon a consideration of one's own and others' needs. From differing theoretical perspectives then, most naturalizers and humanizers of conscience now posit the need for a morality that is more than simply the internalization of parental punishments and values. The foundations of this morality are generally seen as including the child's own innate moral nature, the possibility of truly love-motivated moral choices and the impact of later relational experiences and conscious moral choices.

[7]E. Jacobson, e.g., speaks of "the more and more individualized conscious value concepts and ideals which are built up during and after adolescence under the growing influence of the autonomous ego" (E. Jacobson, *The Self and the Object World* [New York: International Universities Press, 1964], p. 187).

The table in Figure 8 contrasts the essential differences between the punitive morality of the superego and an ego-based morality.

Figure 8

SUPEREGO AND EGO MORALITY

	SUPEREGO MORALITY	EGO MORALITY
Origins of Standards	Extrinsic: Parents and others	Intrinsic: Perceived welfare of self and others
Purpose of Moral Behavior	Avoid internalized punishment, rejection, and disesteem	Welfare of self and others
Awareness of Origin and Nature of One's Morality	Largely unconscious with many conscious rationalizations	Largely conscious with early unconscious roots
Nature of Morality	Focus on conformity, details, absolutes, and law keeping	Focus on welfare of others and the effects of one's behavior
Onset of "Adult" Values	Childhood	The entire developmental span
Attitude to Those with Differing Views	Fear, anger, or condemnation	Sensitivity and at least some understanding of the other's logic even when differences are strong

IDENTITY-BASED MORALITY

The mature ego-based morality now being espoused by a number of psychotherapists is a major advance over Freud's superego morality. It fails, however, to present a full picture of constructive motivation because it neglects biblical data. Fromm and Rogers, for example, posit a highly autonomous view of morality due to their overly optimistic view of human nature. In doing so, they fail to address the need for moral direction that surpasses our own wisdom and takes into consideration our sinful propensities. And although ego psychologists have described many of the functions, dynamics, and developmental factors in morality, they have provided neither a satisfactory *context* in which to set these factors nor an ultimate *motivation* for being moral.

In ignoring the fact that we are created in the image of God, they have failed to address the ultimate origin of humanity's moral nature.[8] And in ignoring the fact that we were created for intimate fellowship with God, they have defined morality as an issue between one or more individuals instead of being most fundamentally an issue between God and man. When David confessed, "Against thee, thee only, have I sinned," he acknowledged the deep truth that all sin is ultimately an offense against God.[9] Morality for the ego psychologist is simply based upon social necessity and the normal developmental unfoldings of personality. It is a matter of pragmatism, not sin and holiness.

My colleague at Rosemead, Dr. John Carter, has suggested a model of counseling built upon a scriptural understanding of morality that goes beyond these emerging ego psychology views of morality. In describing what he labels an *identity based morality*, Carter emphasizes the fact that problems of psychopathology are ultimately problems of morality. Much as I have outlined the development of psychopathology in chapters 4, 5, and 6, he sees sin (both the individual's and the individual's socializing agents') as the ultimate cause of all nonorganically based maladjustment. Specifically, it is our tendency to try to be what we were not created to be that sets in motion the fear and guilt that motivate excessive reliance on defense mechanisms and cause the various psychopathologies. The essence of our moral failure, in other words, is our desire to become what *we* want to be rather than what *God* created us to be. Put another way, it is a conflict between

[8]Gen. 1:26-27.
[9]Ps. 51:4.

actualizing the image of God or actualizing our sinful, autonomous desires and directions.

Carter then draws upon the biblical concepts of flesh and spirit to demonstrate how we attempt to resolve this basic moral flaw. He suggests that scripturally the flesh represents all our efforts to direct our lives apart from God.[10] The flesh, in other words, is our god-like, omnipotent, and autonomous tendency. This basic sin principle expresses itself in two very different ways—either in impulsive acting out or in legalistic conformity. In Romans 6:12 (NASB), Paul emphasizes the impulsive, bodily expression of our sinful, autonomous functioning: "Do not let sin reign in your mortal body that you should obey its lusts, and do not go on presenting the members of your body to sin as instruments of unrighteousness." In contrast, in Colossians 2:20-23, Paul discusses a legalistic expression of our sinful autonomous functioning when he asks:

> Why do you submit yourself to decrees such as, "Do not handle, do not taste, do not touch" (which all refer to things destined to perish with the using)—in accordance with the commandments and teachings of men. These are matters which have, to be sure, the appearance of wisdom in self made religion and self abasement and severe treament of the body, but are of no value against fleshly indulgence.[11]

Here we have a legalistic, performance-based style of morality that, at first glance, appears to be the precise opposite of an impulsive, lustful style of morality. When viewed from another perspective, however, these two orientations can be seen to have a great deal in common. They are actually alternative ways of expressing the same fleshly (sin) principle. Carter illustrates this twofold nature of the flesh and these usually hidden similarities in Figure 9.

---

[10]Carter, "Toward a Biblical Model of Counseling," *Journal of Psychology and Theology*, vol. 8(1), 1980, pp. 45-52. This description of Carter's view of identity based morality goes beyond his published works and includes our personal conversations on this topic.

[11]Paul further describes this conflict in Gal. 5:16-18, "But I say, walk by the Spirit, and you will not carry out the desire of the flesh. For the flesh sets its desire against the Spirit, and the Spirit against the flesh; for these are in opposition to one another, so that you may not do the things that you please. But if you are led by the Spirit, you are not under the Law."

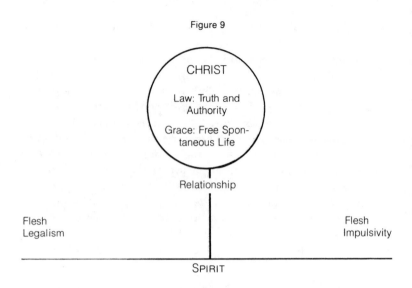

Figure 9

The horizontal base line represents the flesh or sin principle of autonomous, god-like functioning. On the impulsive side, our god playing takes the obvious form of denying God's claims on life, choosing our own values and acting as we wish. On the other end of the continuum, the expression of the flesh is initially not so obvious. The god playing on this end is not necessarily in selecting unscriptural goals or in an uncontrolled, impulsive lifestyle. It is found instead in the belief that we can do something to merit God's favor, or to add to Christ's atoning work by maintaining certain standards of performance. It is also reflected in the self-atoning nature of the guilt feelings that we experience for failing to live up to our expectations. Individuals can live out their fleshly sin principle either through fulfilling the lusts of their flesh or through their own works.

Both expressions of the flesh manifest a basic misunderstanding of both authority and redemption. The impulsive style of fleshly living says, "*I* am the authority; *I* will choose my own values—*I* need no salvation." The legalistic (Pharisaical) expression of the flesh says, "*I* am the authority regarding criteria of spirituality; *I* will define it as conformity to certain standards." Then the fleshly legalist says, "*I* will be my own savior (or at least my own sanctifier) by living up to my own criteria of spirituality."

The impulsive expression of the fleshly principle might be called an *id morality* (where impulses are unrestrained); the legalistic view could be called a *superego morality* (where acceptance and forgiveness are worked for). The common factor to these perspectives is their rejection of the Spirit. The Spirit dimension in Christ incorporates both law (as the law of God, not as punitiveness or legalism) and grace (not license or permissiveness). It is based not on works but on a response to the gift of God. By focusing on the fact that Christ embodies both grace and truth, we can see that fleshly legalism and fleshly impulsivity are distortions of one or the other of these attributes. Legalism, in focusing on conformity, is actually a perverted substitute for truth, while impulsiveness is a distortion of grace.

Carter then points out that the context for Paul's discussion of the flesh and spirit in Romans 6 and Colossians 2 is the believer's identity in Christ. We have been given a condemnation-free position in Christ (Rom. 8:1), we have an identity with Christ (Rom. 6:4-11), and we are in the process of having the image of God renewed in us (Eph. 4:24; Col. 3:10). Paul reminds us, for example, that we "have been buried with Him through baptism,"[12] "become united with Him,"[13] "have received Christ Jesus as the Lord,"[14] and have been made "alive together with Him."[15]

It is only *after* these reminders of our position and identity in Christ that we are challenged to behave morally. While we are not to live under the sway of sinful lusts, our motivation for this is not to avoid condemnation—an equally fleshly desire. Our motivation is to live consistently with our position. Carter puts it this way:

> Identity is always a product of a relationship, i.e., there is no identity without relationship. Hence, the biblical morality is a being-congruent morality rather than an achievement-perfor-

[12]Rom. 6:4; Col. 2:12.
[13]Rom. 6:5.
[14]Rom. 2:6.
[15]Col. 2:13.

mance morality because the believer is commanded to act congruently with his positional and personal identity with Christ instead of performing in order to obtain an identity.[16]

This identity-based morality is another way of looking at Paul's concept of a clear conscience, which we will consider in chapter 16. This view compliments both the biblical concept of godly sorrow and Pattison's concept of ego morality. In each instance morality is viewed as a function of the total personality operating out of motives of love for the welfare of all concerned. This type of morality is in no way inhibitory, repressive, or neurotic, and it does not bind or enslave. It sets us free to become what we were created to be.

Although my purpose in this volume is not to write a psychology and theology of ethics, I would suggest that a basic understanding of these fundamental ingredients of biblical morality is essential for all counselors and pastors. If we are not sensitive to the differences between punitive moralism and positive morality it will be difficult to lead others beyond the repressive restraints of fleshly legalism to a healthy, productive moral existence. It will also be difficult to lead the impulsive, acting-out person to an awareness of the need for redemption and responsibility.

SUMMARY

In this chapter I have suggested that many non-Christian (and perhaps even some Christian) counselors have avoided moral issues for fear of reinforcing punitive, immature, and constricting superego processes. By distinguishing between morality and moralism, we remove the grounds of this fear and free ourselves (and our counselees) to positively address these vital issues. A biblical understanding of the Christian's identity provides a growth-enhancing way of looking at constructive motivation.

Although we do not have the space to develop all of the ingredients of a positive biblical morality, it seems to me that this must include a clear understanding of the following: our identity in relationship to God (both as created and redeemed children),

---

[16]Carter, "Toward a Biblical Model of Counseling," p. 49.

our human potential for both good and evil, the limits of human reason, the necessity of biblical revelation, the forgiveness of sins, and the impact of both the Spirit of God and fellow Christians in a convicting and encouraging role. When these elements are present, we have the potential for a positive morality that is attractive because it means functioning as we were created to function out of love, rather than functioning out of fear or guilt as an external source says we ought to live.

Part 4

Christ and Conscience

Just as Christians have tended to see guilt feelings as coming from God, they have also viewed conscience as God-given. Part 4 suggests that some of its functions are actually the result of the fall of Adam. As such, they are a part of humanity's efforts to run our lives apart from God. Reliance on these functions of conscience perpetuates both personal maladjustment and our sinful condition. The solution to this problem is a new understanding of our relationship with our conscience based upon the reconciling work of Christ.

13

Conscience and the Fall

Since conscience is generally viewed as the source of guilt and moral judgment, I followed up my study of guilt and godly sorrow with a biblical study of conscience. Considering the widespread usage of the term, I was surprised to find that there are few thorough theological studies of conscience. Perhaps this paucity of studies is explained by the fact that the term *conscience* (*syneidēsis*) appears only thirty-one times in the New Testament, or perhaps it is because we assume *conscience* is so universally understood it needs little definition or clarification. After all, if we were to take a survey of almost any group of people in order to learn the meaning of *conscience*, we would probably receive rather consistent definitions. "Conscience," they would say, "is that inner faculty or process that judges right and wrong, that makes us aware of our moral failures, and inflicts psychic pain or penalty when we fall short of our moral standards." And if the survey group were composed of Christians, the individuals might add a statement to the effect that conscience is the voice of God or that conscience was implanted in man by God to lead us to desirable behavior. In the most widely quoted theological work on conscience, Pierce gives us almost this same definition when he calls conscience

> the internal counterpart and complement of the wrath. It is the painful consciousness that a man has of his own sins, past or, if present, begun in the past. It is of God in that it is the reaction of man's nature, as created, and so delimited, by God, against moral transgressions of its bounds.[1]

[1]C. Pierce, *Conscience in the New Testament* (London: SCM Press, 1955), p. 111.

Unfortunately, when I studied the scriptural use of *conscience*, I found no such easy definition. Biblical writers evidenced little concern for either theological systematization or psychological clarification in their use of the term and theologians differ greatly in their understanding of conscience.[2] As Barabas put it, "Nowhere in the New Testament is there a clearly defined doctrine of conscience, or even a description of it."[3]

Many authors agree that *conscience* involves a process of knowledge, but beyond this there is great division of opinion. Theologians have argued over the *origins* of *syneidēsis* (Stoic or Hellenistic), over its *focus* (past, present, or future), over whether it evaluates only one's own actions (rather than others'), and over the relationship of its biblical and extrabiblical usage. Concerning Paul's meaning for *syneidēsis*, for example, Osborne writes, "I find no justification for the view of certain scholars that the word and concept sustained at his hands an enrichment and development of meaning."[4] Yet Maurer claims:

> ... one may say that Paul takes *suneidesis* with a comprehensive breadth and variety not found in any of his predecessors.... Paul raises the whole problem of act, being, and knowledge in anthropology—a step of momentous significance for centuries which followed.[5]

The inability of theologians to agree on some fundamental questions makes me reticent to tackle this issue. Since it is crucial to our understanding of the operation of guilt, however, I will attempt to outline a biblically consistent understanding of the topic in this and the next four chapters. We will begin with a brief discussion of the use of *conscience* in the Old Testament. Then I will offer an initial definition followed by a discussion of the concept as a mental faculty and a look at the origins of the term. In chapters 14 and 15, we will examine the biblical understanding

---

[2]Similarly, analyses of the use of *syneidēsis* in secular Greek and the relationship of this usage to its New Testament meaning are inconclusive.

[3]S. Barabas, "Conscience," *Zondervan Pictorial Bible Dictionary*, M. Tenney, ed. (Grand Rapids: Zondervan, 1963), p. 181.

[4]H. Osborne, "Σvνείδησις," *Journal of Theological Studies* XXXII (April 1932), p. 167.

[5]C. Maurer, "συνείδησις," *Theological Dictionary of the New Testament*, G. Friedrich, ed., G. Bromiley, trans. (Grand Rapids: Eerdmans, 1971), 7:917.

of the functions of conscience and of various types of conscience. Chapters 16 and 17 conclude this section with a look at the changes that can take place in the functioning of conscience in the act of regeneration.

CONSCIENCE IN THE OLD TESTAMENT

The Old Testament has no specific word for conscience. At first glance, this is surprising since the Old Testament devotes so much time to humanity's fall into sin and subsequent guilt. A closer analysis reveals, however, that the phenomenon of guilt and the functions of conscience are frequently described by Old Testament authors even though the Hebrew language has no direct equivalent to the word. The first experience of a guilty conscience is recorded in connection with the Fall, and Cain's attempted denial of responsibility for Abel's death[6] is one of the first evidences of a disordered conscience.

The Hebrew *lēb*, generally translated "heart," is periodically used to refer to the functions the New Testament attributes to conscience. David's *heart* troubled him[7] and he prayed for God to create a clean *heart*.[8] This use of *lēb* to refer to what we consider conscience is only one of many meanings communicated by this word, however, and we cannot think of "heart" as fully equivalent to conscience although both include (at times) some of the same functions. In fact, Robinson suggests that *nous* (mind) and *syneidēsis* (conscience) simply "represent sections cut out of the usage of leb and made prominent by a special terminology."[9]

The lack of a precise Old Testament equivalent to *conscience* is probably due to the fact that different views of human nature were held by the Greeks and Hebrews. The more holistic style of the Hebrew language and the Israelites' primary understanding of themselves in the context of the covenant relationship do not lend themselves to a specific faculty like conscience. The Israelites' fo-

[6]Gen. 4:3-11.
[7]1 Sam. 24:5; 2 Sam. 24:10.
[8]Ps. 51:10.
[9]H. Robinson, *The Christian Doctrine of Man* (Edinburgh: T. & T. Clark, 1958), p. 106.

cus was not on their relationship to conscience but rather on their covenant relationship with God. Brown put it this way:

> For the Israelites of the old covenant the problem of man's attitude to himself was less significant than that of his attitude to God. He was more concerned with his accountability before God than with exploring his self-consciousness. Confession was made to God whose law man sought to fulfill in obedience.[10]

Later, when we begin to draw together the biblical data relating to conscience, we will return to several key Old Testament passages that shed light on the origin, nature, and functioning of conscience, especially those in the first three chapters of Genesis. For now, however, I simply want to point out the Old Testament's periodical use of *heart* to refer to what we have come to know as conscience.

AN INITIAL DEFINITION

In Romans, Paul gives perhaps the clearest biblical statement of the role of conscience. He writes:

> For when Gentiles who do not have the Law do instinctively the things of the Law, these, not having the Law, are a Law to themselves, in that they show the work of the Law written in their hearts, their conscience bearing witness, and their thoughts alternately accusing or else defending them.[11]

In this passage,[12] Paul uses a limited definition of *conscience* that sees it as distinct from both the "law written on the heart" and

---

[10]C. Brown, "Conscience," C. Brown, ed., *The New International Dictionary of New Testament Theology*, vol. 1 (Grand Rapids: Zondervan, 1975), p. 349.

[11]Rom. 2:14-15.

[12]Traditionally, this passage has been interpreted to mean that even the Gentiles do the works of the Law because the law is written in their hearts. Although the validity of relating this passage to the non-Christian has been recently (and perhaps accurately) challanged by Cranfield ("A Critical and Exegetical Commentary on the Epistle to the Romans," *International Critical Commentary*, [Edinburgh: T. & T. Clark, 1975]), the light it sheds on Paul's understanding of conscience is not dimmed. (See B. Harris, "ΣΥΝΕΙΔΗΣΙΣ [conscience] in the Pauline Writings," *Westminster Theological Journal* vol. 24 [May 1962]; F. Godet, *Commentary on Romans* [Grand Rapids: Kregel, 1977]; and R. Lenski, *The Interpretation of St. Paul's Epistle to the Romans* [Minneapolis: Augsburg, 1961].)

"accusing thoughts." He speaks first of the works of the law written in the heart and then of conscience; finally, he speaks of thoughts that either accuse or defend. *If we take this as normative we must make some distinctions between the law written in the heart, the conscience, and the process of self-accusation and defense.*

If this rather carefully circumscribed definition of conscience embraced all of the New Testament uses of *syneidēsis*, our task would be simple. *Conscience* would simply be a designation for man's moral self-judgment and would bear witness both to our integrity and to our moral failures. Unfortunately, this is not the case. In 1 Corinthians,[13] when Paul speaks of a weak, easily defiled conscience, he uses *conscience* in a broader sense than witness bearing. He includes both an inner standard (in this case the belief that one should not eat meat offered to idols) and the guilty self-accusations as aspects of conscience. Similarly, John's reference to hearts that condemn[14] suggests a broader view of conscience. These passages show that conscience is sometimes used in Scripture to include both the standards by which we judge ourselves and the condemning thoughts (or feelings) in addition to the process of witness bearing or self-evaluation.

When we consider the functions of conscience in the next chapter we will see that it is difficult to limit the meaning of conscience to the narrow definition implied in Romans 2:14-15. For that reason I would like to offer an initial definition of conscience that includes a number of functions beyond witness bearing or testifying:

> *Conscience* (and at times, *heart*) is a term used to refer to a group of personality processes having to do with the evaluation of ourselves in light of certain standards or expectations.

In the following pages, I will attempt to expand this definition and clarify some common misunderstandings and misinterpretations of the biblical use of *conscience*. In doing this, I will suggest that (1) conscience should not be considered a separate faculty of the mind; (2) conscience is not entirely a God-given function; (3) the functions of conscience are not only fallible, but that some of

[13]1 Cor. 8:7-13.
[14]John 3:19-20.

them are designed to maintain, rather than alter, sinful behavior; and (4) there are close and important parallels between the functioning of conscience and the law.

THE FALLACY OF FACULTIES

Many lay persons assume that conscience refers to a concrete psychic entity existing within the personality. According to this understanding, conscience has its own existence within the personality and functions somewhat independently of other portions of the personality. Christians holding this view frequently see conscience as a separate endowment, or faculty, implanted by God in the personality. This can be exceedingly misleading. The term *conscience* is simply a shorthand way of referring to a group of processes or functions that are part of the total personality. Just as *heart* is used to refer to some of the innermost processes of the individual and *will* is used to refer to certain aspects of the process of decision making and commitment, *conscience* refers to the process of evaluating ourselves in light of certain standards and responding accordingly. We do not *have* a conscience any more than we *have* a heart or a will. We *are* holistic, willing, thinking, feeling, choosing individuals whose personality functioning can be described in shorthand by concepts like *conscience*, *will*, and *heart*.[15]

Although for convenience we may speak of conscience as an entity, it is imperative to keep in mind that it is not. To the degree that the word *conscience* serves as a vehicle for communicating a set of psychic processes, it is useful. But as soon as we begin to think of conscience as a separate faculty or psychic entity, we open ourselves to serious misunderstandings. We may, for example, miss the fact that conscience is inseparable from other intellectual and emotional processes. Research indicates that factors such as ego strength and overall mental health are as important

[15]"Conscience is a favorite Pauline word, but it usually stands for consciousness of having done either right or wrong, and can thus be qualified by an adjective, rather than, as in the more modern usage, for a faculty which acts as an inward guide to moral conduct" (G. H. Macgregor, "Conscience," *The Interpreter's Bible*, G. H. Buttrick et al., eds., vol. 2 [New York: Abingdon-Cokesbury, 1951], p. 297).

(if not more important) in determining moral behavior as conscience in the narrow sense with its accompanying sense of guilt. A series of the studies by Johnson, Ackerman, and Frank,[16] for example, showed that guilt feelings were unrelated to resistance to temptation, but that mental health was positively associated with resistance!

A second problem caused by viewing conscience as a separate entity is the tendency to see our conscience like something we *possess* (often in a passive way) rather than as a reference to our moral valuation processes. When we set up conscience this way we tend to enter into dialogue with it as though it is a separate self. This view can lead to neurotic means of relating to "conscience" that are, in effect, the same as relating to parental figures. If we responded to our parents' efforts at motivating us through shame, guilt, or pressure by giving up and becoming passive, we are likely to respond the same way to the pressures of our conscience. Or, if we rebelled because of our parents' guilt motivation, we are likely to respond to the pressures of conscience with even more rebellion. Many young adults struggle with this conflict. They seem impelled to rebel against their consciences' values in order to separate from and rebel against their parents. When we view our consciences as separate entities, we tend to encourage this process and avoid accepting full personal responsibility to both sides of our ambivalent wishes or feelings.

Individuals in therapy are often prone to this splitting off of portions of their personality. They say, "Part of me wants to do this but part of me doesn't." The implication is that they consist of a variety of discrete parts. Although this is an accurate reflection of their feelings or perception, it does not accurately reflect the reality of the situation. I sometimes respond to this type of statement with, "You mean you do and don't want to?" or "You mean you feel two ways?" My goal in suggesting this clarification is to help them see that they are whole people with a responsibility for *all* of their wishes, thoughts, and feelings rather than a person composed of "parts," some of which are alien. No matter how alien or

[16]R. Johnson, M. Ackerman, and H. Frank, "Resistance to Temptation, Guilt Following Yielding and Psychopathology," *Journal of Consulting and Clinical Psychology*, vol 32, no. 2, 1965, pp. 169-75.

external the sources of conscience once were, they are now functioning aspects of the individual's own personality. Acknowledging this both helps people gain a greater sense of wholeness and unity and accept greater responsibility for their own conflicts and struggles.

A third problem in viewing conscience as a discrete faculty is that we miss its dynamic, changing nature. When we conceive of conscience as an internal machine, or organ, we assume it functions (or should function) in the same way over the entire span of a person's life. In contrast to this, I would like to suggest that the functions of conscience need to be undergoing continual growth and change. Some functions may be appropriate in our lives in early childhood or prior to the time we are reconciled to Christ but inappropriate afterward. And all the functions that we know as "conscience" need to be maturing.

IS CONSCIENCE GOD-GIVEN?

Most conflicting understandings of conscience can be traced to the answer we give to one question, "Did God create man with a conscience that was designed to rule his moral life, or did the functions we know as conscience arise in another way?" If we see conscience as a gift of God, we will also tend to view the accusations arising from self-evaluations as God-given. But if conscience was not designed by God, we take an entirely different view. The workings of conscience will not be esteemed as highly and the emotions of guilt that it triggers will not necessarily be considered divine.

Baird expresses the widely-accepted Christian belief that conscience is a God-given faculty when he says that conscience is "the last remnant of his (humanity's) pristine magnificence."[17] In this view, conscience is the highest element of man's nature and the accusations arising from a guilty conscience are seen as God's means of motivating us to desirable behavior.

At first glance this viewpoint sounds extremely "Christian." Conscience shows us where we fail and inflicts a kind of psychic punishment designed to alter sinful attitudes and actions. It serves

[17]Thomas Baird, *Conscience* (Kilmarnock, Scotland: John Ritchie, n.d.), p. 12.

as an inner warning—a motivating pressure. But this understanding of conscience raises serious problems of scriptural interpretation. To begin with, it equates the guilt emotions triggered by the conscience with the voice of God. As we have seen in previous chapters, this is inconsistent with the New Testament view of motivation. Any view of conscience that sees psychological guilt (as contrasted to godly sorrow) as a godly motive is scripturally suspect.

A second problem in seeing the functions of conscience as God-given may be even more critical. This problem centers on the assumption that the functions we know as conscience existed before the Fall in approximately the same condition that they do today and that they somehow escaped the Fall essentially unscathed. This concept needs little discussion except to point out that it excludes some very basic aspects of human nature from the consequences of the Fall. The historical and current consensus of the church is that *all* aspects of the personality were negatively impacted by the Fall. There is absolutely no scriptural evidence to suggest that our intellects, our moral natures, and our choosing processes have been distorted through sin but that our consciences have not been distorted![18]

A third and even more telling criticism of this view of conscience is the teaching of Genesis 3:1-13 that some of the functions of conscience not only did not survive the Fall but actually had their beginnings—at least as we know them today—at the Fall. Far from portraying the operation of conscience as the *last* remnant of man's "pristine magnificence," Genesis portrays it as the *first* result of his sinful rebellion. In fact, Satan's appeal to Adam and Eve was that they would become as gods knowing good and evil. Before the Fall Adam and Eve's unity and their knowledge of good and evil came from their unity with God. Satan's temptation was for them to become their own center and to know good and evil apart from God. That is precisely what happened. In gaining the ability to know good and evil apart from God, Adam and Eve separated themselves from God and from their created selves. Their newly functioning conscience was not a vehicle for com-

[18]A slightly different view holds that God implanted the conscience *after* the Fall as a concession to humanity's fallen nature.

municating the goodness of God but rather a substitute for it. It was man's invention and desire. Bonhoeffer says:

> Conscience is concerned not with man's relations to God and to other men but with man's relation to himself. (Conscience) derives the relation to God and to men from the relation of man to himself. Conscience pretends to be the voice of God and the standard for the relation to other men. ... Bearing within himself the knowledge of good and evil, man has become judge over God and men, just as he is judge over himself.[19]

In becoming their own ultimate authority and judges, Adam and Eve plunged the human race into disunity and self-judgment and into attempts to hide and blame others to provide the illusion of innocence and remake their self-esteem.

These facts have led some[20] to conclude there was no conscience at all before the Fall. They see the entire process of self-judging as an act of autonomous man playing the role of God. Coming close to their view, Kuyper suggests that "judgment according to conscience was wholly foreign to Christ, who lived only to do the will of His Father."[21] Bonhoeffer espouses this view when he writes:

> Before the fall there was no conscience. Man has only been divided in himself since his division from the Creator. And indeed it is the function of the conscience to put man to flight from God. ... Conscience drives man from God into a secure hiding place. Here, distant from God, man plays the judge himself and just by this means he escapes God's judgment. ... *Conscience is not the voice of God to sinful man; it is man's defense against it* (italics mine).[22]

This view has considerable merit. It emphasizes the radical (and omnipotent) nature of humanity's fall into sin, the pride autonomous man takes in his powers of reason and accomplishments, the tendency of conscience to lead to the repression of

---

[19]D. Bonhoeffer, *Ethics* (New York: Macmillan, 1965), pp. 24-25.

[20]H. Bavinck, *Gereform Eerde Dogmatiek*, III (Kampen: Kok, 1898), and D. Bonhoeffer, *Creation and Fall* (New York: Macmillan, 1959).

[21]See G. Berkouwer, *Man: The Image of God* (Grand Rapids: Eerdmans, 1962), p. 177.

[22]Bonhoeffer, *Creation and Fall* (New York: Macmillan, 1959), p. 81.

guilt, the attempt to separate morality from a personal relationship with God (and make it into an inner psychic issue), and the radical nature of the solution (faith and a relationship of love so complete that our motivation for morality grows totally out of love). Humanity's conflicts of conscience do point to an ultimate cleavage within the personality and this split is neither part of God's design for humanity nor an experience of Christ. Whatever God's plan for bringing mankind into a full awareness of good and evil, it did not include a conscience that would autonomously evaluate and pass judgment on self, since these activities are substitutes for a life of faith. This view is not, however, fully satisfactory. Certain aspects of conscience (e.g., self-consciousness and our moral nature) existed prior to the Fall even though there was no division within the personality.

The view that appears to be consistent with Scripture, is that conscience as we know it is not a gift from God; it is not the last remnant of His pristine magnificence; and it is not a direct result of the Fall. While it is true that some of the functions of conscience were divine endowments built into the fabric of personality prior to the Fall, others are the direct result of our fall into sin. Even those pre-Fall endowments have now been distorted by sin and can in no way be seen as autonomously-reliable moral guides. Delitzsch put it this way:

> The existence of conscience, therefore, reaches beyond the fall, and has, in its manifestation of itself, run through a changeful history; it was one thing in its original position: it is another in its position under sin; it becomes another in its position under grace, through which it becomes renewed, together with our likeness.[23]

This understanding of conscience flies in the face of the understanding some Christians have of conscience. If some of the functions of conscience (e.g., autonomous self-judgment, god-like aspirations, and guilt feelings designed to atone for one's failures) are not the gift of God but rather a result of the Fall, they too are in need of redemption. They even need to be seen as central to

---

[23]F. Delitzsch, *A System of Biblical Psychology* (Grand Rapids: Baker, 1977), p. 168.

fallen humanity's autonomous efforts to rule our own lives. And if even the highest elements of our moral nature have been distorted by sin, we need to be extremely careful in equating qualms of conscience with the voice of God!

SUMMARY

In this chapter I have offered a general definition of conscience as a group of personality processes having to do with the evaluation of ourselves in light of certain standards or expectations. I have also suggested that the common tendency to view conscience as a separate faculty of the mind is unhelpful and that many functions of conscience, contrary to popular opinion, are not ordained of God. In fact, some of these functions reflect the essence of humanity's sinful nature. In the next three chapters we will attempt to refine this understanding of the nature and functioning of conscience by looking at the New Testament usage of *syneidēsis.*

Conscience and the Law

So far I have made two negative statements about the nature of conscience: that conscience as we know it today is not necessarily God-given, and that it is not a separate faculty or moral agency. Now we will consider some key New Testament passages that shed further light on the functioning of conscience. Just as some elements of conscience were present before the Fall and some result from the Fall, some of the functions are positive and God-given while others are unhelpful. We will begin with the positive works of conscience.

WITNESS BEARING

When Paul discussed conscience in relation to the law written on the heart and the accusing thoughts in Romans 2:14-15, he referred to the function of conscience as a witness bearer. Witness bearing is one of the main functions of conscience and consists of the process of evaluating ourselves in relation to some standard or ideal.

As we saw in our earlier discussion of this passage, Paul does not describe conscience as *containing* either the law or the accusing or excusing thoughts that come in response to witness bearing. The law, the conscience, and the thoughts work together, but at least in this passage are distinguished. Strong defines witness bearing as judgment and says it involves: "... applying this accepted law to individual and concrete cases in our own experience, and pronouncing our own acts or states either past, present, or prospective, to be right or wrong."[1]

The process presupposes both humanity's moral nature and the capacity to observe oneself objectively. Since we have already considered Romans 2:14-16, and since the witness-bearing function of conscience is rather clear, we will move on to the other two positive functions attributed to conscience in the New Testament.

ASSURANCE OF CONSISTENT LIVING

When Paul told the Sanhedrin he had lived "in all good conscience,"[2] and when he told Timothy that he served God with a clear conscience,[3] he referred to a function of conscience that grows logically out of witness bearing. When Paul evaluated himself and concluded he was living up to his ideals, he was assured that he was living consistently. In the same way, both believers and nonbelievers can evaluate the consistency of their lives by attending to the inner process of self-evaluation.[4] This type of assurance, resulting in what Scripture calls a clear conscience, is a prerequisite for a sense of integrity and, in the life of the believer, for confidence in witnessing. It should not, however, be simply equated with freedom from feelings of guilt. This clear conscience is more a function of the absence of regret or godly sorrow because one is living an integrated life.

CONSTRUCTIVE MOTIVATION

Conscience can also provide the motivation to live rightly. Although a narrow definition of conscience as simply a witness bearer excludes the process of motivation, passages like Romans 13:5 and Acts 24:16 seem to include a motivating force in conscience. In Acts 24:16 Paul says he strives to keep his conscience

---

[1]C. Strong, *Systematic Theology* (Old Tappan: Revell, 1907), p. 499.

[2]Acts 23:1.

[3]2 Timothy 1:3.

[4]Since we are fallen, this process is not entirely trustworthy; it needs to be supplemented by the corrective words of Scripture, and the leading of the Holy Spirit and other people.

clear and in Romans 13:5 he challenges us to submit to authorities for conscience sake. Both of these passages indicate that we are to act in ways that allow us to develop or maintain a certain state of conscience. Conscience, in other words, can serve as a positive motivating force to the degree it leads us to experience godly sorrow and live consistently from a motivation of love.

A NEW GOSPEL

Not all of the processes of conscience are as positive as bearing witness, assuring oneself of consistent living, and motivation for proper living. Paul's discussion of the weaker brother in 1 Corinthians portrays a conscience that inhibits unnecessarily. This activity goes beyond the motivation to live consistently, which is portrayed positively in Scripture.[5] It restrains us from engaging in any number of activities that are *not* sinful. Such unnecessary inhibition can actually be a source of neuroses. To avoid potentially debilitating guilt, some individuals under sway of such needless inhibitions carefully structure their lives according to a series of dos and don'ts. By rigidly carrying out "desirable" behaviors and avoiding "undesirable" ones, they attempt to maintain a sense of fidelity to God and avoid guilt feelings.

This process is essentially one of legalism. In fact, some commentators interpret conscience as an inner expression of the law. Thrall, for example, writes:

> In the world of Greek thought, conscience was spoken of metaphorically as a prosecutor, a judge, a stern accuser, and the like. It is an agent of condemnation. But this is precisely what the Law was, according to Paul. . . . The Law proves that all men are guilty. In 2 Corinthians 3:9 the ministry of Moses is called "the ministry of condemnation."[6]

[5]Rom. 13:5; Acts 24:16; 1 Peter 2:19; 3:14-16.

[6]M. Thrall, "The Pauline Use of ΣΥΝΕΙΔΗΣΙΣ," *New Testament Studies*, vol. 14, 1967-1968, p. 124. In a similar vein, C. K. Barrett comments: "The law has, as it were, left its stamp upon their minds; that stamp is their conscience." (*A Commentary of the Epistle to the Romans* (New York: Harper & Row, 1958), p. 124.

And Thielicke writes that conscience

> ... seeks in passionate acts of autotherapy to heal this wound and to attain rest. The means readily at hand for this purpose are those of the Law. They consist in good works and sacrifices. Their purpose is to free us from the accusation through attempts to attain moral and cultic righteousness. They do this by seriously trying to "make satisfaction," i.e., by trying to seize the initiative in the relationship between God and man.[7]

This attempt to secure approval and avoid guilt feelings by careful adherence to standards is ultimately rooted in legalism, idolatry, and omnipotence. It operates on the assumption that we can *do* something to merit acceptance or freedom from guilt and it also implicitly denies that Christ's death and resurrection destroyed all barriers between God and man. Placing conformity to any person, standard, or object between ourselves and God ensnares us in the trap of the weak Corinthian Christians who were, Paul suggests, engaging in a form of idolatry by abstaining from eating meat offered to idols.

> Therefore concerning the eating of things sacrificed to idols, we know that there is no such thing as an idol in the world, and that there is no God but one. ... However not all men have this knowledge; but some, being accustomed to the idol until now, eat food as if it were sacrificed to an idol; and their conscience being weak is defiled. But food will not commend us to God; we are neither the worse if we do not eat, nor the better if we do eat.[8]

In not eating meat, some Corinthian Christians were elevating idols to the status of gods and implying there was not simply one true God. While the term *idolatry* may be a bit strong for someone who is weak in the faith because of a lack of knowledge, Paul suggests that at its core this type of legalistic conformity is rooted in idolatry[9] and a lack of understanding that there is but one true God.

[7] H. Thielicke, *Theological Ethics*, W. Lazareth, ed. (Philadelphia: Fortress, 1966), p. 302.

[8] 1 Cor. 8:4, 7-8.

[9] Berkouwer suggests the same thing in his "Studies in Dogmatics": *Man: The Image of God* (Grand Rapids: Eerdmans, 1962).

In a similar way, by "keeping days and seasons" and attempting to maintain spirituality through avoiding taboos or performing desirable activities, we can also live as though these activities have the power to stand between ourselves and God or to earn access to Him. In other words, we worship our standards and our ability to fulfill them instead of worshiping God.[10] This process is often compounded by developmental experiences that reinforce our innate tendency to worship our ability to fulfill God's moral demands. Parents and others have taught us, for example, that attending movies, drinking, playing cards, smoking, or swimming on Sundays can remove us from fellowship with God. When these prohibitions and the underlying assumption that acceptance by God is conditional are carried into adulthood, people often assume they must do something to placate God, merit His favor, and avoid feeling guilty.

In some ways these people are victims of poor training or education. Yet they are not free from personal responsibility for their guilt and inhibitions. Because they feel safer, they continue choosing to inhibit themselves and attempting to earn the acceptance of their consciences, God, and others by their performance. Their hiding of their inner selves and focusing on external conformity is in effect rejecting Christ's death as the only basis for reconciliation with God. This is the path the Galatian Christians were beginning to take when Paul accused them of deserting Christ for a different gospel.[11] It is also a reflection of the autonomous effort of conscience to add something to the pure gospel of Christ.

THE CONDEMNATIONS OF CONSCIENCE

Closely related to the neurotic, inhibitory function of conscience is the process of self-condemnation. Feelings resulting from this process are deeply woven into most neurotic patterns—especially those of depressive and obsessive-compulsive personalities. I have briefly alluded to the process of self-condemnation above, but I shall develop this function a bit more. It is referred to by John

[10]See Rom. 3:9-31.
[11]Gal. 1:1-9.

when he writes, "We shall know by this that we are of the truth, and shall assure our heart before Him, in whatever our heart condemns us; for God is greater than our heart, and knows all things."[12]

John here makes it quite plain that we are not to exalt the condemnation of conscience. In fact, he appears to be linking the accusations of conscience to living "under the law." Just as Paul taught that the believer was free from the external condemnation that the law brings,[13] so John says we can overcome the inner condemnation of our hearts (consciences) through Christ. In commenting on this passage, Bill Counts writes:

> The conscience which judicially punishes us and tells us we are worthless and unlovable is denying the atoning work of Christ, opposing God and illegitimately using the law on us. Romans 8:1 states "There is therefore now no condemnation to those who are in Christ Jesus." Romans 3:24 states we are made acceptable to God, or justified, "by faith apart from works of law." If my conscience punishes me when God does not, then conscience is exalting itself over God.[14]

Probably the most serious misunderstandings of the role conscience plays in the life of the believer is seeing its condemnations as God-given, divinely-inspired, or in any way constructive functions. Unfortunately this is the view taken by C. A. Pierce in his widely quoted book on conscience. Pierce considers conscience an expression of the wrath of God at sin. Commenting on Paul's exhortation to the Roman Christians[15] to be subject to governmental authority, for conscience sake Pierce writes:

> Man by his nature and as an element both in society and in creation as a whole is liable to suffer, should he rebel against the limitations thereby involved, the Wrath, either external, or internal or both.

> *When the rebellion takes the form of a moral wrong that internal Wrath is what St. Paul understands by conscience.*

[12]1 John 3:19-20.
[13]Rom. 8:14.
[14]W. Counts, *Called to Be Free* (Old Tappan: Revell, 1980), p. 84.
[15]Rom. 13:1-7.

And both are parallel manifestations of God in action to main-tain the order of things; the one is the Wrath external and mediated by society, the other is its internal counterpart.[16]

If we accept this view of conscience we are back to square one in our understanding of guilt. Guilt is once again viewed as a form of self-punishment ordained of God to motivate desired behavior. But this continued punishment, even though it is self-inflicted, is no less inconsistent with the emphasis of Scripture on the complete efficacy of the Atonement. Either God's wrath was discharged and the penalty for sins paid at the Cross, or it was not. To make conscience an expression of the penal wrath of God is clearly (at least in the case of the believer) inconsistent with this broader biblical understanding. The awareness of our failures (the sense of guilt or knowledge of objective guilt) that comes from the witness bearing of conscience is a key to growth through discipline or chastisement but it should not be a stimulus to self-punishment. A more consistent interpretation of Romans 13:5 is offered by Dodd, who suggests:

> The Christian takes no part in the administration of a retributive system, but, insofar as it serves moral ends, he must submit to it. He himself lives by a higher principle, and he obeys the Government . . . not because he fears the retribution which follows on disobedience, but because his conscience bids him do so. The same motive justifies him in paying taxes to a pagan Government. . . . He pays them, not because he will be punished for non-payment, but because they help to maintain the moral order in a world which as yet does not know the order of grace.[17]

Here Dodd marks a clear distinction between fear and guilt motivation that accompany a secular (or a legalistic) approach to

---

[16]Pierce also says, "The meaning therefore of Romans 13:5 is 'it is your duty to God to be subject to the power; to rebel is not only illegal therefore; it is also morally wrong. It is not simply punishment by society that awaits the rebel, and the fear of which should deter him, it is also, for the law can be broken on occasion with impunity, the more terrible and less avoidable—for it is within him—pain of conscience'" (*Conscience in the New Testament* [London: SCM Press, 1955], p. 71).

[17]C. Dodd, *The Epistle of Paul to the Romans* (London: Hodder and Stoughton, 1932), p. 204.

motivation and the grace-oriented motivation propounded by Paul for believers. According to Dodd, conscience convinces us of our responsibility out of a motive of love, consistency, and loyalty rather than one of fear and feelings of guilt.

PARALLELS OF LAW AND CONSCIENCE

The parallels between the operation of conscience and the law can be instructive in our understanding of conscience. In fact, I believe that an understanding of how conscience functions as an inner legal process can do more than any other single thing to unravel and reconcile some of the apparently conflicting views of conscience. For purposes of comparison and contrast we can list four functions of the law:

1. To show us God's holiness (Exod. 2:1-21; Rom. 7:11).
2. To serve as a schoolmaster until Christ came (Gal. 3:24).
3. To give a moral structure to society (Exod. 21:1 – 31:18).
4. To show us our sin and lead us to despair and consequently to grace (Rom. 5:20-21).

The functions of conscience are parallel, since conscience also, first shows us God's holiness. Although the standards of conscience are badly warped and, according to Scripture, are far from trustworthy, they certainly contain at least a remnant of the law of God. Second, in the life of the non-Christian, conscience serves as a schoolmaster. Third, it gives moral structure to society. In the absence of a motivation of love growing from faith, the threats, punishments, and inhibitions of conscience serve a restraining function in society. Society must have some means of enforcing social order, and the demands of conscience are important ones. Just as the non-Christian may keep the law to avoid being caught by an officer of the law, so he may keep the law to avoid being caught and punished by his conscience. While we might wish for higher motivations, the fact is that without the fear of being apprehended and punished many more individuals would be violating essential social regulations.

The fourth function of conscience leads us to an extremely crucial insight. The conscience, just as the law, plays an important role in stirring up our sinful, rebellious tendencies, in showing us how we fall short, and in driving us to despair. Much like a "Wet-Paint—Do Not Touch!" sign evokes rebellion and demonstrates our sinful propensity, so the prohibitions of conscience can provoke our sinful natures. In this way, prior to salvation, our consciences can have an important role in driving us to faith by demonstrating what we cannot do ourselves!

This parallel use of conscience and the law also suggests that just as the believers' relationship to the law must be radically altered at the moment of faith, so must his or her relationship to conscience. The same law that served a divinely-given function before salvation is said by Paul to not be of faith but to be a vehicle of a curse. In the same way, *the conscience whose witness bearing prior to salvation led us to see ourselves and our inability to live up to whatever law we accepted and consequently helped move us to despair and, in turn, faith, can now be a vehicle for a curse. This curse comes when we continue to relate to conscience after salvation as we did before. That is, as long as we attempt to justify ourselves and avoid self-condemnation by meeting the demands of conscience, we are engaging in essentially the same process as were the Christians at Galatia whom Paul had to so severely rebuke when he told them, "A man is not justified by the works of the law but through faith in Christ Jesus."*[18]

SUMMARY

In this chapter we have surveyed the main functions of conscience. Positively, we have seen that conscience can bear witness or judge our lives, assure us of consistent living, and provide some constructive motivation. Humanity's powers of self-observation are elements of the divine image in man. Before the Fall, Adam and Eve were able to observe themselves and experience a high level of personal consciousness. Since the Fall, however, our self-consciousness has been separated from our consciousness of God. It became consciousness of one's *self* with a primary focus on one's *own* identity rather than one's identity in relationship to God. The Fall brought a fundamental shift in the focus of humanity's con-

[18]Gal. 2:16.

sciousness, which placed our own judgments and reasonings squarely in the center of the process of making moral judgments and displaced a love motivated dependency upon God.

With this shift came attempts to set our own standards of right and wrong and to make atonement for our sins through self-inflicted psychic punishment. Who could deny that many of our standards, goals, and expectations bear the stamp of our unique family environments or subcultures and our own psychological dynamics rather than the absolute values of a holy God?

Even more problematic than our self-styled standards and our self-atonement, is the origin and nature of the entire process of self-judgment. This process, generally held out as a unique and high human virtue, is usually assumed (by Christians) to be a divinely-given function. But a look at the Genesis record suggests this is not so. Before the Fall Adam and Eve engaged in no such process of self-judgment with judicial emphasis. They possessed a strong moral sense rooted in their love for and obedience to God. And they certainly had some knowledge of good and evil or they could not have been held accountable. But the very essence of Satan's temptation was that they should be *like God,* knowing good and evil. In other words, Satan's appeal was that Adam and Eve, in and of themselves, could make autonomous moral judgments and evaluations. This was not in God's design. For God, moral decisions were designed to be made on the basis of intimate fellowship and divine instruction. *Morality was an interpersonal process between God and man. It was not an intrapersonal process within the heart of man.*

Herein lies one of the major problems with the traditional Christian view of conscience and, interestingly enough, of Fromm's humanistic view as well. We sometimes live as though our consciences could continue to function somewhat adequately if God were to cease to exist tomorrow! The processes we have come to know as conscience are seen as capable of operating in both the Christian and the non-Christian as the voice of God, as a direct expression of His voice or as an adjunct to His voice. This neatly minimizes our need of God. Since we have come to trust our own ability to decide good and evil and to motivate ourselves through self-inflicted punishment, we have lessened our need of God. In a curious way, by viewing conscience as a reflection of the voice of God, we obscure our ongoing need to live our lives in intimate fellowship with Him. We have so glorified conscience that we are in danger of dethroning God in the natural outworkings of our lives and turning morality into an *intrapsychic* (desires and acts versus conscience) rather than an *interpersonal* (God and man) issue.

This misuse of conscience can be avoided by paralleling the work of the law and the function of conscience, and relating them both to the grace of God. By doing this, we can see that the functions of conscience (even though some are given by God) must be radically altered in the life of the believer just like the function of the law. Self-observation oriented to self-punishment, for example, becomes unnecessary since Christ means the end of the law and its attendant judicial system. All efforts at evaluating ourselves to pass out rewards or blessings are likewise unnecessary. Our focus moves from *self*-evaluation with the goal of punishment, propitiation, or reward to a focus on our love for God and our desire to obey His leading from a motive of love. Calvin described this process in his discussion of Christian liberty when he said:

> The first part is that consciences of believers, when seeking an assurance of their justification before God, should raise themselves above the law, and forget all the righteousness of the law.[19]

In another place, Calvin says:

> The second part of Christian liberty, which is dependent on the first, is that their consciences do not observe the law as being under any legal obligation, but that, *being liberated from the yoke of the law, they yield a voluntary obedience to the will of God.*[20]

This scriptural understanding radically alters the center of our moral consciousness. The right to establish standards, make judgments, and pass our punishments is given back to God so that our moral consciousness becomes less *self*-centered and more *God*-centered. This lifts a burden of responsibility from our shoul-

---

[19]J. Calvin, *Institute of Christian Religion* (Grand Rapids: Eerdmans, 1953), p. 131.

[20]Ibid., p. 132.

ders that we were never intended to bear. Just as Christ is the end of the law as a judicial system[21] for the believer, so He is the end of conscience as an expression of inner wrath or judgment.[22]

This biblical perspective also demonstrates that although conscience can be strongly shaped and influenced by our environment, at its core the phenomenon of psychological guilt arising from conscience is an act of autonomous self-propitiation. It is fallen humanity's attempt to pay for its own sins through self-inflicted punishment. In contrast, a love-oriented, constructive sorrow is a positive, God ordained form of motivation that can grow out of the functioning of conscience.

[21]I am using law here as a system involving earned blessings and incurred punishments, not as Scripture uses it as an expression of the will of God and as our divine standard for life.

[22]This understanding of conscience avoids the pitfalls of both the naturalization and glorification of conscience. It acknowledges (with some glorifiers of conscience) that man is a spiritual being created to be in fellowship with God and that his moral sensibilities are ultimately rooted in the fact that he is created in the image of God. It also acknowledges that problems of conscience testify clearly to the results of sin in the human race in general and a given individual in particular. At the same time this understanding of conscience (in agreement with the naturalizers) acknowledges that the demands and functions of conscience can be a serious source of emotional maladjustment.

15

Conscience, Works, and Faith

The use and misuse of conscience becomes even clearer when we see how Paul and other New Testament writers used descriptive terms like *clear, good, weak, strong, seared, defiled, evil, cleansed,* and *perfected* in referring to the conscience. An understanding of these terms also lays a foundation for the biblical resolution of the problems of conscience, which is tied up in an understanding of the relationship of conscience to faith and good works.

THE CLEAR CONSCIENCE

The most frequently mentioned conscience in the New Testament is a good, or clear, conscience, or one "void of offense toward God."[1] Although New Testament writers are strangely silent about what we today would consider a guilty, or guilt-ridden, conscience, they speak of a *good* or *clear* conscience on ten different occasions.[2] Paul says he lived his life "with a perfectly *good conscience* before God up to this day,"[3] and that deacons must hold "to the mystery of the faith with a *clear conscience.*"[4] In a similar vein Peter challenged Christians with these words: "Keep a *good conscience* so that in the thing in which you are slandered, those who revile your good behavior in Christ may be put to shame."[5]

---

[1]Acts 24:16.

[2]Other references to a good, or clear, conscience are: 1 Peter 2:19; 3:21; 1 Tim. 1:19; 2 Tim. 1:3; and Heb. 13:18. Paul also seems to have the same concept in mind in Rom. 13:5 where the believer is told to be in subjection to earthly rulers "for conscience sake."

[3]Acts 23:1.

[4]1 Tim. 3:9.

[5]1 Peter 3:14-16.

Paul's announcement that he had lived with a perfectly good conscience came in his address to the high priest Ananias and the Sanhedrin. Paul claimed that his conscience testified that he had been sincere in all his efforts to serve God. He had felt no sense of dishonesty or deceit.[6] It is interesting that Paul did not limit his "good conscience" to the time after his conversion. Apparently his zeal and sincerity *before* he become a Christian had also resulted in a clear conscience. He had been honestly following what he believed right and consequently he could state that even when he was persecuting Christians he had experienced a good conscience! *A good conscience, in other words, is not necessarily related to faith in Christ. Neither is it totally related to doing the absolute good. It is the result of sincere, consistent living in accordance with one's values, whether or not those values are correct.*

In 1 Timothy 3:8-9, Paul tells us that deacons must live upright lives at home and be consistent in faith. Here his use of *conscience* means that deacons must be without the sense of duplicity that comes from a double life, or lack of faith. He uses *good conscience* in the same way in 1 Timothy 1:5, where he places a good conscience hand in hand with a pure heart and sets both over against false teaching and hypocrisy.[7] As Barclay put it, "To have a good conscience is to be able to look at the knowledge which one shares with no one but oneself in the face, and not to be ashamed of anything in it."[8]

In each biblical use, the appeal to a good, or clear, conscience is an appeal to inner integrity, sincerity, and honesty. It relates to

---

[6]In commenting on Paul's assertion, "I have done what I believed to be right," Barnes writes: "This was a bold declaration ... yet it was strictly true. His persecutions of the Christians had been conducted conscientiously. ... Of his conscientiousness and fidelity in their (the Council's) service they could bear witness. Of his conscientiousness *since,* he could make a similar declaration. He doubtless meant to say that as he had been conscientious in persecutions, so he had been in his conversion and in his subsequent course" (A. Barnes, *Notes on the Acts of the Apostles* [Philadelphia: Westminster, 1960], p. 424).

[7]Similarly, Peter (1 Peter 3:16) encourages Christians to keep a clean conscience in order to shame their false accusers. The thought here focuses more on the effect a clear conscience will have on the believer's false accusers than it does on its value to the believer.

[8]W. Barclay, *The Letters to Timothy, Titus and Philemon* (Philadelphia: Westminster, 1960), p. 39.

boldness of witness,[9] a positive testimony,[10] and strength in suffering.[11] The failure to live a life characterized by a clean conscience results in a poor witness to the non-Christian and a sense of inner disloyalty or lack of integrity.[12]

What a good, or clean, conscience does not refer to is as important as what it does. Notice that Paul never relates the lack of a good or clear conscience to feelings of self-rejection or punishment. He doesn't warn his fellow Christians that failure to have a good conscience will result in a miserable, guilty, or depressed emotional state.[13] He doesn't, in other words, equate the lack of a clear conscience with feelings of guilt. His appeal for a good conscience is based on motives of love and consistency, which are aspects of godly sorrow but not psychological guilt.

This is important since guilt-troubled individuals frequently use these very passages to reinforce their guilt. They reason this way, "Since I am not living up to what I know, I cannot have a clear conscience. Therefore, my guilt is valid. I do not deserve to be free of it until I am living better." In one regard, they are correct. Sin in the believer's life does lead to an awareness of disharmony, psychic pain and the lack of confident expression of our Christian faith. But this is different from the punitive self-rejection of psychological guilt. To put it another way: sin should (and generally does) result in an inner awareness that we are not being true to ourselves, others (including God), and our Christian commitment. This is the opposite of a clear conscience and can be labeled a sense, or awareness, of guilt. If the awareness is accompanied by a genuine regret and desire to change the emotion, it is constructive or godly sorrow. In the life of a Christian, however, sin should

[9]Acts 23:1.

[10]1 Peter 3:14-16.

[11]1 Peter 2:19.

[12]The only use of *good conscience* that does not fit this meaning is 1 Peter 3:21, "And corresponding to that, baptism now saves you—not the removal of dirt from the flesh, but an appeal to God for a good conscience—through the resurrection of Jesus Christ." Here a good conscience is seen as resulting from the resurrection of Christ rather than a consistent life. This usage is closer to that of the author of Hebrews, which we will examine later.

[13]It is at this point that we part company with glorifiers of conscience who tend to see the condemnations and accusations of a guilty conscience as wholesome (or at least necessary) motivations.

not result in what we commonly call a guilty conscience with its attendant feelings of guilt and self-rejection and condemnation.

THE STRONG AND WEAK CONSCIENCE

The next most frequent Pauline use of conscience is found in 1 Corinthians. Nine times in chapters 8 and 10 Paul refers to conscience in addressing the issue of Christian liberty and the believer's relationship to others.[14] The specific issue was the rightness of eating meat that had been sacrificed to idols. In these passages, using the terms *weak* and *strong*, Paul makes reference to what we today might call a guilty conscience.

A conflict had arisen in the Corinthian church over eating meat that had been offered in sacrifice to idols. Some (those Paul called "strong") felt no qualms of conscience in eating this meat. Others, (here considered "weak") could not eat the same meat without feeling guilty. From the content of Paul's letter it seems that the strong (or liberated) Christians were abusing their freedom and causing problems for their weaker brothers.

Paul begins his discussion by saying there is absolutely nothing inherently wrong in eating meat that has been offered to idols. He writes:

> ... Concerning the eating of things sacrificed to idols, we know that there is no such thing as an idol in the world, and that there is no God but one. For even if there are so-called gods whether in heaven or on earth, as indeed there are many gods and many lords, yet for us there is but one God, the Father, from whom are all things, and we exist for Him; and one Lord, Jesus Christ, through whom are all things, and we exist through Him.[15]

And in chapter ten, he says:

> All things are lawful, but not all things are profitable. All things

---

[14]It seems likely that Paul took over and adopted the concept of conscience that was current in the Christian community of his day and adapted it to this situation. See Pierce, *Conscience in the New Testament* (London: SCM Press, 1955), and C. Maurer, "συνείδησις," *Theological Dictionary of the New Testament*, G. Friedrich, ed., G. Bromiley, trans. (Grand Rapids: Eerdmans, 1971).

[15]1 Cor. 8:4-6.

are lawful, but not all things edify. Let no one seek his own good, but that of his neighbor. Eat anything that is sold in the meat market, without asking questions for conscience sake; For the earth is the Lord's, and all it contains. If one of the unbelievers invites you, and you wish to go, eat anything that is set before you, without asking questions for conscience sake.[16]

"You are right," Paul says to the strong Christians, "in believing there is nothing wrong with eating meat that has been offered to idols. We know there is only one God and that the idols are not gods at all. They are simply the constructions of human hands." However, Paul says, "Not all men have this knowledge: but some, being accustomed to the idol until now, eat food as if it were sacrificed to an idol; and their conscience being weak is defiled."[17]

There were also a number of Christians at Corinth who had been saved out of idol worship. They had not matured to the point where they fully understood that there was only one true God. Consequently, says Paul:

If someone sees you who have knowledge, dining in an idol's temple, will not his conscience, if he is weak, be strengthened to eat things sacrificed to idols. For through your knowledge he who is weak is ruined, the brother for whose sake Christ died. And thus, by sinning against the brethren and wounding their conscience when it is weak, you sin against Christ. Therefore, if food causes my brother to stumble, I will never eat meat again, that I might not cause my brother to stumble.[18]

Paul tells the strong Corinthians that if one of their weak brothers sees them eating meat offered to idols he may be encouraged to do the same, and thus wound his conscience.

This wounding of a weak conscience is different from the absence of a clear conscience. This is no mere awareness of one's failures, no deep sensitivity to a life lacking in faith, sincerity, or consistency, and no experience of godly sorrow. This weak conscience can actually ruin or destroy a brother in Christ! *The opposite of a weak conscience, consequently, is not a clear conscience; it is a strong conscience. And the difference between a strong and*

[16]1 Cor. 10:23-27.
[17]1 Cor. 8:7.
[18]1 Cor. 8:10-13.

a weak conscience is the presence or absence of a knowledgeable, mature faith. The distinctions among clear, weak, and strong consciences can be stated this way. *A clear, or good, conscience is related to consistency in living. It is related to works growing out of love and sincerity. A strong conscience (and its opposite, the weak conscience) results from a mature and properly educated faith or a lack of it.* The weak conscience, because it is not informed by faith and forgiveness, can be exceedingly destructive. It doesn't result in godly sorrow as does the lack of a clear conscience. It leads to self-condemnation and destruction. The close relationship between faith and conscience is also reflected by the fact that when Paul discusses the same problem of the weaker brother and eating in Romans 14:1 he refers to them as "weak in the faith." In this passage, at least, he uses weak conscience and weak in faith interchangeably.

The confusion and despair the weak conscience engenders seems to come much closer to what we today call a guilty conscience. There is such a total sense of disloyalty and failure that the person is in danger of being ruined. Hodge writes:

> *A weak conscience is one which either regards as wrong what is not;* or one which is not clear and decided in its judgments. ... *The conscience is said to be defiled either when it approves or cherishes sin, or when it is burdened by a sense of guilt* (italics mine).[19]

The cause of the destructiveness of the weak conscience is extremely interesting and has major implications for the resolution of guilt. According to Paul, the act of eating meat was quite all right. The "gods" did not exist and the weak Corinthians could have been free to enjoy a good steak dinner. But they didn't know this. They assumed the gods were real and in eating meat offered to idols, they believed they were somehow giving allegiance to the gods. This, they assumed, would erect barriers between themselves and God and destroy the very essence of their relationship with Him. They believed eating meat offered to idols was standing between themselves and a relationship with God. In other words, they lacked faith in their position in Christ. Thielicke describes the problem this way:

[19]Hodge, *Commentary on the First Epistle to the Corinthians,* p. 146.

The conscience is thus unsettled by something which supposedly stands between God and us, occupying the place which
belongs to Christ alone—for it is He alone who gives peace of
conscience with His once-and-for-all redemption. Hence unrest
and alarm of conscience arise simply from the fact that the
comprehensiveness of Christ's lordship is not fully recognized.

As a result, unrest of conscience arises not through actual sin,
in face of which there can never be a "good" conscience, but
through failure to fix one's hope wholly and exclusively on
Jesus Christ as Lord. Accordingly, *the opposite of an unsettled
conscience is not a good conscience but a conscience which
is comforted and consoled, a conscience which is reconciled
to God.*[20]

Here we have a penetrating insight. *Problems of a disordered
or guilty conscience* (we are *not* now speaking of the lack of a
good, or clear, conscience that is accompanied by a godly sorrow)
*arise not from specific acts or thoughts of sin. They come from the
failure to recognize that there is only one God and that Christ has
fully paid the penalty for all of man's sins and reconciled man once
and for all to Himself.* They come from the belief that one's actions
may stand in the way of Christ and negate his reconciling work.
In short, they come from a lack of faith that results in an inability
or unwillingness to accept the efficacy of the atonement. In the
absence of faith (or in the presence of weak faith)[21] the individual
is left open to his or her own condemnations and confusion.[22]

We can see now that when we speak of a clear (or good)
conscience and a weak (or guilty) conscience we are not discussing two points on opposite ends of a continuum. We are actually
speaking of two different dimensions, one of which must precede
the other. When we speak of a weak conscience we are referring
to a person troubled with guilt. He is a person who, because of
a lack of faith, has not fully grasped the fact that through Christ

---

[20]H. Thielicke, *Theological Ethics* (Philadelphia: Fortress, 1966), p. 308.

[21]"But he who doubts is condemned if he eats, because his eating is not
from faith; and whatever is not from faith is sin" (Rom. 14:23).

[22]M. Thrall says, "He is a weak character in the present instance because his
faith is not sufficiently strong for him to believe wholeheartedly that the idols he
previously worshiped do not really exist" (*The First and Second Letters of Paul
to the Corinthians* [Cambridge: Cambridge University Press, 1965], p. 65).

our guilt is once and for all atoned and we are reconciled to God. Not grasping this truth this person continues feeling guilty over any number of things.

When we speak of a Christian with a clear conscience we refer to someone who has already settled the first and most fundamental issue of a guilty (or weak) conscience. He knows he is forgiven and that his sins cannot stand between himself and God. But out of this awareness and a responsive love to God he wants to live honestly, sincerely, and loyally so that he can say with a clear conscience that he has faithfully served the Lord. This latter motive is an issue of congruence or godly sorrow instead of guilt. The table in Figure 10 summarizes the differences between a clear and a strong conscience.

Figure 10

COMPARISON OF STRONG AND CLEAR CONSCIENCE

	STRONG	CLEAR (GOOD)
CHARACTERISTICS	Lack of guilt feelings and freedom to partake in "neutral" activities.	Sense of integrity
OPPOSITE	A weak conscience characterized by guilt feelings and needless inhibitions.	Sense of duplicity, dis-loyalty or lack of integrity.
SOURCE	Faith in the atonement and a comprehension of God's grace.	Consistent living (good works).

An interesting sidelight of Paul's discussion of the strong and weak Christian is that even a strong conscience is not portrayed as a sufficient moral guide. The strong Christians, knowing meat eating was not intrinsically sinful, were abusing their freedom and hurting their Christian brothers. They were also so proud of their liberty that Paul had to challenge them to not regard their brothers with contempt, "walk in love," and "be concerned with peace and the building up of one another" (Rom. 14:10, 15, 19).

THE SEARED AND THE DEFILED CONSCIENCE

In 1 Timothy, Paul mentions the seared conscience:

> But the Spirit explicitly says that in later times some will fall away from the faith, paying attention to deceitful spirits and doctrines of demons, by means of liars *seared in their own conscience as with a branding iron.*[23]

In Titus the defiled conscience is mentioned:

> To the pure, all things are pure; but to those who are defiled and unbelieving, nothing is pure, but both their mind and *their conscience are defiled.*[24]

These verses show other extremes in the functioning of conscience. It can become seared or defiled. Searing apparently refers either to a callousness or insensitivity similar to the functioning of conscience in the classical psychopathic personality, or to a branding or burning of one's crimes into their consciousness[25] that coexists with a "hypocritical show of sanctity."[26] In either case this conscience allows sinful attitudes or actions to go unchecked. In contrast to the weak conscience that inhibits unnecessarily, this conscience does not inhibit sufficiently.

[23]1 Tim. 4:1-2.

[24]Titus 1:15.

[25]Commenting on the meaning of "seared," Congdon writes, "The Greek word is kauteriazo, 'brand,' related to kauterion, 'branding iron'.... Does this imply that the conscience of such people is so perverse that they actually believe themselves doing right when they are working evil? Perhaps so. But the jealous and uncontained frenzy of evil which they exhibit will argue for a stronger motive than merely obedience to conscience. It seems probable enough that there is an inner conflict for them between the law of God (Romans 2:15) and their branded conscience in which they strive to make evil to be right and right, evil." (R. Congdon, "The Doctrine of Conscience," *Bibliotheca Sacra,* 102, 1945, 26ff., 470-89.)

[26]R. Jamieson, A. Fausset, D. Brown, *Commentary on the Whole Bible* (Grand Rapids: Zondervan, 1961), p. 1363.

Just like the person with a seared conscience, one with a defiled conscience is unable or unwilling to accurately evaluate his or her attitudes or actions and act rightly. Erdman suggests these people "have no power to discern right and wrong."[27] If Erdman is correct in suggesting the defiled refers to the failure to discern between right and wrong, then Paul's usage here is closely related to the process of bearing witness we discussed in chapter 14 and indicates a failure in that process of self-judgment.

CONSCIENCE IN HEBREWS NINE AND TEN

The only other New Testament uses of conscience relevant to our study are found in Hebrews.[28] Since we will return to these passages when we discuss the resolution of problems of conscience in the next chapter we will simply quote them here.

> *Hebrews 9:8-9:* The Holy Spirit is signifying this, that the way into the holy place has not yet been disclosed, while the outer tabernacle is still standing; which is a symbol for the time then present, according to which both gifts and sacrifices are offered which cannot make the worshiper perfect in conscience.

> *Hebrews 9:14:* How much more will the blood of Christ, who through the eternal Spirit offered Himself without blemish to God, cleanse your conscience from dead works to serve the living God?

> *Hebrews 10:2:* Otherwise, would they not have ceased to be offered, because the worshipers, having once been cleansed, would no longer have had consciousness of sins?

> *Hebrews 10:22:* Let us draw near with a sincere heart in full assurance of faith, having our hearts sprinkled clean from an evil conscience, and our body washed with pure water.

SUMMARY

This survey of the various New Testament uses of conscience elaborates and illustrates key features of our earlier definition. It shows

[27]C. Erdman, *The Pastoral Epistles of Paul* (Philadelphia: Westminster, 1925), p. 145.
[28]The only other New Testament references to conscience are 2 Cor. 4:2; 5:11. These passages, however, refer to the conscience of others and seem to add nothing distinctive to our understanding of its meaning.

that conscience involves the observation of ourselves, particularly in regard to the rightness or wrongness of our actions. It shows that conscience is fallible and open to educational influences. And it shows the close connection between conscience, faith, and law. Specifically, it shows how a positive evaluation of oneself results in confidence and assurance and that the conscience can be either strong or weak.

The strong conscience results from faith and knowledge, while the weak conscience results in destruction growing out of a belief that something is standing between oneself and God. This latter condition appears to result in what Tournier and others call false, or neurotic, guilt and what I am calling psychological guilt, or guilt feelings. The conscience can also be seared or defiled. This apparently relates to either a psychopathic or sociopathic lack of self-evaluation and to a lack of either constructive sorrow or feelings of guilt (or both).

16

Conscience and Justification

Now that we have traced the biblical picture of the origin and functions of conscience, we can turn to the scriptural solution to problems of conscience. In chapter 14 I suggested the key to this process lies in applying the grace of God to the functioning of conscience in much the same way we apply it to the law of God. Just as the grace of God frees the children of God from rigid adherence to external regulations and from fears of condemnation by God, it can also free us from pressured attempts to live up to impossible inner demands and from the fear of condemnation by our own consciences. In this chapter, I want to develop the comparison between the impact of the grace of God on these outer and inner legalistic systems and demonstrate how the doctrine of justification provides the foundation for resolving conflicts of conscience. To do this we will focus on chapters 9 and 10 of Hebrews.

CHRIST AND THE REUNIFICATION OF CONSCIENCE

In these chapters the author of Hebrews sets forth the contrast between the old covenant and the new. In chapter 9 he tells us the Old Testament tabernacle was

> a symbol for the present time. Accordingly *both gifts and sacrifices are offered which cannot make the worshiper perfect in conscience*, since they relate only to food and drink and various washings, regulations for the body imposed until a time of reformation (italics mine).[1]

[1]Heb. 9:9-10.

Before Christ the old covenant with its system of offerings could not perfect (complete) the conscience because the Law, which

> ... has only a shadow of the good things to come and not the very form of things, can never by the same sacrifices year by year, which they offer continually, make perfect those who draw near. Otherwise, would they not have ceased to be offered, because the worshipers, having once been cleansed, would no longer have had consciousness of sins? But in those sacrifices there is a reminder of sins year by year.[2]

There is something about conscience that could never be fully pacified by the Old Testament sacrificial system. Proper eating, drinking, washing, and fleshly ordinances could not satisfy the conscience. And even though the sacrificial system previewed the future, final atonement of Christ, the old covenant system could not perfect the conscience. Neither could it eradicate the split in man between what he is and what he ought or wants to be, nor could it solve the tendency for self-atonement and propitiation.[3]

Even though the old covenant communicated forgiveness, the very fact that repeated sacrifices had to be offered showed there was an ongoing awareness of sin. By contrast, Christ accomplished what the law could not.

> But Christ being come an high priest of good things to come, by a greater and more perfect tabernacle, not made with hands, that is to say, not of this building; neither by the blood of goats and calves, but by his own blood he entered in once into the holy place, having obtained eternal redemption for us. For if the blood of bulls and of goats, and the ashes of an heifer sprinkling the unclean, sanctifieth to the purifying of the flesh; *how much more shall the blood of Christ, who through the eternal Spirit offered Himself without spot to God, purge your conscience from dead works to serve the living god?*[4]

[2]Heb. 10:1-3.

[3]Kenneth Wuest writes, "These gifts and sacrifices could not make the worshiper perfect so far as his conscience was concerned. The word 'perfect' is *teleios* which does not mean sinless, but complete, finished. The word described that which needed nothing to make it what it should be, complete. The Levitical ritual as such did not touch the conscience. No ritual in itself ever does. There was nothing in it that could deal with conscience." K. Wuest, *Hebrews in the Greek New Testament* (Grand Rapids: Eerdmans, 1947), p. 155.

[4]Heb. 9:11-13.

Christ purges our consciences from dead works. Although we typically think of dead works as efforts to merit salvation, in this passage they are related to satisfying the consciences of the redeemed. Christ's blood, in addition to freeing us from the need to satisfy the demands of a righteous God, also frees us from meeting the demands of our consciences. It can purge us from repeated efforts to satisfy our own demands and complete or perfect our consciences.[5]

Applying these verses to our previous study of conscience, we reach a strategic understanding. *Conscience, in the broad sense that includes our moral standards, our processes of moral evaluation, our accusing and excusing thought, and an imperative to live in accordance with our standards, can never be satisfied or fully quieted by good works, by defenses that deny our sinfulness or by our own payments.* Since the Fall, conscience has functioned as an internal law with its own courtroom, its own prosecuting and defense attorneys, its own judge, and its own sentences. As autonomous individuals (even Christian individuals!), we select our standards, evaluate ourselves, bring ourselves to trial, judge ourselves, and pass sentence on ourselves. This process of self-administered justice can never fully quiet the conscience for it is based on our own efforts. This is the fundamental problem with glorifiers of conscience. They suggest the conscience is satisfied through works.

But what we cannot do through self-effort, an appropriation of Christ's life and death can accomplish. Since Christ paid the penalty for humanity's sins, we are once and for all perfected in the sight of God.[6] We can now allow the Word of God, the Spirit of God, and the people of God to convict us and show us where we need to grow. When Satan utilizes the processes of conscience to accuse us,[7] we say with Paul, "Who will bring a charge against God's elect? God is the one who justifies."[8] And when we are prone to punish and condemn ourselves for our failures, we must

---

[5]We are encouraged to "... draw near with a true heart in full assurance of faith, having our hearts sprinkled from an evil conscience, and our bodies washed with pure water" (Heb. 10:22, KJV).

[6]Heb. 10:8-14.

[7]Rev. 12:10.

[8]Rom. 8:33.

remember that we have no right to do so, for it is Christ "... who died, yes, rather who was raised, who is at the right hand of God, who intercedes for us."[9] In this way the functions of our consciences undergo a radical alteration. They move from self-atonement to His atonement. And in doing so they open us up to a love-oriented motivation of grace rather than the fear-and-guilt-oriented motive of law.

Just as we must undergo a radical change that acknowledges our total inability to earn *God's* favor and acceptance through our works, so our search for inner acceptance through the work of *conscience* must be abandoned. We can regain the inner unity lost in Adam's fall through Christ and Christ alone. It is only through His redemption that the entire process of self-judgment and punishment can be given up and that inner unity can be reestablished. We no longer have to try to be something we cannot be. And we no longer need to pay for our sins. Christ has made us acceptable to God and He has paid! Calvin wrote:

> Now if we ask in what way the conscience can be made quiet before God, we shall find the only way to be that unmerited righteousness be conferred upon us as a gift of God. Let us ever bear in mind Solomon's question: "Who will say, 'I have made my heart clean; I am pure from my sin'?" (Proverbs 20:9). ... Let even the most perfect man descend into his conscience and call his deeds to account, what then will be the outcome for him? Will he sweetly rest as if all things were well composed between him and God and not, rather, be torn by dire torments, since if he be judged by works, he will feel grounds for condemnation within himself? The conscience, if it looks to God, must either have sure peace with his judgment or be besieged by the terrors of hell.[10]

Bonhoeffer described the renewed sense of inner harmony that comes when we give up our efforts at appeasing conscience:

> We can now understand that the great change takes place at the moment when the unity of human existence ceases to con-

---

[9]Rom. 8:34.

[10]John Calvin, *Institutes of the Christian Religion*, J. T. McNeil, ed. (Philadelphia: Westminster, 1980), p. 765.

sist in its autonomy and is found, through the miracle of faith, beyond the man's own ego and its law, in Jesus Christ. . . .

When Christ, true God and true man, has become the point of unity of my existence, conscience will indeed still formally be the call of my actual being in unity with myself, but this unity cannot now be realized by means of a return to the autonomy which I derive from the law; it must be realized in fellowship with Jesus Christ. *Natural conscience, no matter how strict and rigorous it may be, is now seen to be the most ungodly self-justification, and it is overcome by the conscience which is set free in Jesus Christ and which summons me to unity with myself in Jesus Christ. Jesus Christ has become my conscience. This means that I can now find unity with myself only in the surrender of my ego to God and to men* (italics mine).[11]

And Thielicke suggests that the conscience needs to die to its old ways of functioning. He says:

Unrest of conscience cannot simply be done away by the offer of forgiveness. If it is to be pacified, *conscience must learn to understand itself in a wholly new way; it must "die," as it were.* Like the natural man himself, the unmortified conscience can only stand uncomprehending before the proffered forgiveness. Indeed, it senses in this very offer a threat which runs counter to its own instinct for self preservation.

Therefore, if conscience is to subject itself to the miracle of the remission of sins, it can do so only by declaring the dialogue between the accusing and excusing "thoughts" (Romans 2:15) to be unessential, indeed invalid. It can do so only by leaving, closing, and locking this whole courtroom, by forsaking its own fatherland, its own true home, and by going out into a foreign country—in short, by letting go altogether of what it once was (italics mine).[12]

The thing that "once was" that Thielicke here refers to is the whole operation of conscience in connection with the accusing and defending of Romans 2:15. It is the operation of conscience as a judicial system. To resolve problems of guilt and conscience,

[11]D. Bonhoeffer, *Ethics* (New York: Macmillan, 1965), p. 243.
[12]Thielicke, *Theological Ethics*, W. Lazareth, ed. (Philadelphia: Fortress, 1966), pp. 313-14.

we must acknowledge that the entire process of passing judgment on ourselves in order to make atonement through self-inflicted feelings of guilt or excuse ourselves by various self-efforts or defenses must come to an end. This system is a consequence of the Fall and has no place in the life of the believer. As an autonomous effort to provide peace in our own way, it is part of our sin nature and a rebellion against God's way of sanctification. All these attempts at self-reconciliation are expressions of fallen humanity's hostility to God. It is Christ (not ourselves) who has paid, and the Christian's only hope for peace of conscience is to give up the pattern of self-justification and atonement.

Once again, the parallel between law and conscience is significant. Just as the law brought condemnation,[13] so does the conscience not yet set free through Christ.[14] Just as Christ is the end of the law as a means of relating to God, so must faith in Christ lead to an end of conscience as a means of relating to oneself. Just as the law kept us in custody prior to faith,[15] and served as a tutor to lead us to Christ,[16] so the accusations of conscience and the inhibitions of conscience may have had a social value and been useful in bringing us to Christ and in being a tutor. "But now that faith has come, we are no longer under a tutor."[17] Just as the law is fulfilled by faith[18] so is the conscience completed by faith so that it need make no more self-punitive sacrifices.[19] Just as the sins of the believer freed from the law are no longer counted for condemnation,[20] so the believer whose conscience is altered by faith no longer condemns himself.[21] And just as grace makes the law (as a reflection of God's holiness, not as a system of works) clear to us and stimulates us to fulfill it in love, so do those whose consciences have been satisfied through Christ's

---

[13]Gal. 3:10-13.
[14]1 John 3:19-20.
[15]Gal. 3:23.
[16]Gal. 3:24.
[17]Gal. 3:25.
[18]Gal. 3:21-26.
[19]Heb. 10:14-22.
[20]Rom. 8:1.
[21]1 John 3:19-20.

death desire to fulfill the godly ideals of their consciences through love.[22] Martin Luther put it this way:

> So our conscience is bound to the law, under the old man; when he is slain by the Spirit, then the conscience is free; the one is released from the other; not that the conscience is to do nothing; but rather that it is now really free to cleave to Christ, the second husband, and bring forth the fruit of life.[23]

JUSTIFICATION AND INNER WHOLENESS

The psychological consequence of this process is the reversal of the disunited pattern of personality functioning set in motion at the Fall. No longer are we separated from God. Our unity with Him is reestablished because our sins have been atoned. No longer do we need to be separated from others because (since our sins and theirs are paid for) we can accept one another without judgment, blame, and condemnation. And we can now experience a deep inner reunification because we acknowledge our own inability to close the gap between who we are and who we should be and allow Christ to accomplish that. By accepting the fact that Christ has made us acceptable,[24] His atoning work becomes our point of inner reconciliation and allows us to give up our unrealistic goals, our efforts to satisfy our own judgments through performance and our efforts at self-atonement through guilt feelings. In short we give up our omnipotent, god-like strivings and let God be God.

In focusing on the legal aspects of the believer's pardon and reception of imputed righteousness, some Protestants have minimized the potentially radical impact the fact of justification can have on the entire personality. If we truly let the reality of our newly restored relationship with God soak into our lives, we can give up that whole process of self-accusation, self-justification, and self-atonement. Many Christians go through this experience at the time of conversion and/or at a later moment of spiritual commit-

[22]Eph. 5:1-8.
[23]M. Luther, *Commentary on Romans*, J. T. Mueller, trans. (Grand Rapids: Kregel, 1976), p. xxii.
[24]Eph. 1:6.

ment or restoration. When we recognize Christ has become our point of reconciliation, we experience a great sense of relief because we can give up our struggles to do well and make ourselves acceptable. This brings a radical shift in our attitude toward ourselves and others. By living in the awareness that we are forgiven by God we can move away from a works-oriented style of life, the repressions and denials prompted by guilt and the self-condemnations prompted by conscience. This shift from a self-atoning conscience also allows us to move from guilt feelings to godly sorrow. The conscience that is not altered through Christ continues to repress guilt, to work to avoid condemnation or to punish oneself in an effort to atone.

The redeemed and renewed conscience continues to observe our attitudes and behaviors (witness bearing) but this self-observation comes from a different motive. Its purpose is neither to accuse or excuse but to examine our own work[25] in light of Christ's commandment to love our neighbors as ourselves.[26] This self-evaluation growing out of love fulfills the law.[27] Faith, in other words, destroys the need for a self-justifying or self-condemning conscience.

SUMMARY

Many problems of guilt and conscience are based on turning the functions of conscience into an inner legalistic system that functions like the Pharisaism of Christ's day. We work to earn the approval of our consciences and we condemn ourselves when we fall short. Resolution of these problems comes only by acknowledging our inability to satisfy the demands of conscience through self-effort or self-atoning guilt feelings and through an appropriation of Christ's completely adequate payment for our sins.

[25]Col. 3:5-17.
[26]Matt. 22:39.
[27]John 14:15.

17

The Evolution of Conscience

Lying in the crib, newborn infants have no consciousness of concrete moral standards. They also have no developed sense of love, guilt, or constructive sorrow. Because of their as yet largely undifferentiated mental and emotional functioning, infants cannot even identify themselves as separate persons, let alone recognize their mother, father, or other people as separate individuals. This perceptual ability must develop before children can experience the mature, moral functioning we know as *conscience*, the feelings of self-condemnation and rejection we know as *guilt*, or the emotion of constructive sorrow.

The absence of these abilities and fully developed emotions is one reason many theorists explain the development of conscience on completely naturalistic grounds. Concluding the absence (or primitive nature) of these abilities means the infant is amoral, and being able to trace at least the broad outlines of the development of guilt and conscience from the later months of the first year of life, they see no need to hypothesize any innate source of morality. As we saw earlier, however, this naturalistic perspective poses several problems. It assumes each person enters life as an amoral individual, that all subsequent moral functioning is attributable to the socialization process, and that guilt is simply an internalized form of anxiety. It also fails to account for the universal presence of a sense of moral obligation or a moral imperative. These assumptions undermine the foundations of human dignity and neglect the fundamental moral nature of the human person. They also minimize personal responsibility and muddy the waters when we attempt to understand the complex functioning of guilt.

In contrast to the assumption that we are born morally neutral, Scripture tells us we are created as moral beings[1] but that we are also by nature "children of wrath,"[2] that we were "conceived in sin,"[3] and, although we cannot fully comprehend how it happens, that "through one man's (Adam's) disobedience many were made sinners."[4] Although the Bible is not at odds with all the viewpoints gained from naturalistic studies of conscience, it does reject some of them and it clearly places others into a different perspective.

In this chapter, I will attempt to sketch a picture of the development and functioning of conscience that encompasses both the natural developmental factors observed by theorists and biblical teachings regarding guilt and conscience. Because most of these factors have been discussed separately in early chapters, I will not fully explicate them here. Instead I will suggest how the many dynamics merge together to shape the functions of conscience and the emotions we know as *guilt*.

CONSCIENCE AND THE LEARNING PROCESS

During the first few months of life the infant's central nervous system develops rapidly. The perceptual processes mature to the point that infants are able to perceive others as distinct individuals and they gradually develop a rudimentary sense of selfhood. Initially this is basically a physical sense of self. But soon self-awareness expands to include viewing oneself as a thinking, feeling, willing person. As soon as this process begins, the infant is susceptible to moral influences from the environment.

Parents and others begin holding out standards of performance. They begin rewarding appropriate behavior and punishing disapproved attitudes and actions. This initiates the process of taking in the standards of one's environment and to the degree

[1]Rom. 2:15.
[2]Eph. 2:3.
[3]Ps. 51:5.
[4]Rom. 5:19.

the standards of conscience are the result of education and train-ing, explains the development of the ideals of conscience.

The exact processes by which the goals and expectations of the environment are taken in and adopted as one's own are sub-ject to a good bit of discussion and debate. Two general classes or means by which this happens can be isolated. The first includes simple imitation and the process of extrinsic rewards. Many val-ues are picked up in the natural process of living with and ob-serving others and on the basis of external rewards. Others are taken as one's own for more complicated reasons. In this later process, infants or young children take in the goals and expec-tations of the environment because they have a certain need or because they have a special value. Rather than simply modeling the behavior of another they desire to absorb others' values be-cause they are potentially very important. Ausubel and Kirk de-scribe these two ways of taking in the values of society as different methods of interiorization. They suggest:

> As an individual simply habituates to a given set of norms, values underlying these norms acquire an aura of axiomatic rightness and may be accepted as self-evidently valid. Here no particular needs of the individual are satisfied. A simple me-chanical type of imitation belongs in the same category; the expressed values of one person serve as a stimulus instigating acceptance of comparable values by another. However, when-ever such imitation involves a more active need to be like other persons or to conform to their expectations (apart from fear of punishment), it is more proper to speak of motivated interior-ization or identification. Identification, therefore, is a motivated form of imitation in which both the interpersonal relationship (direct or fantasized) between imitator and imitatee and the imitated act itself are highly significant for the learning that ensues.[5]

It seems to this writer that this latter means of taking in the standards and expectations of one's environment accounts for by far the largest share of the standards we "interiorize." In fact, it is difficult to picture any specific standard as being a truly moral one unless it is developed in the context of meaningful interper-

[5]D. Ausbel, *Ego Psychology and Mental Disorder: A Developmental Approach to Psychopathology,* D. Kirk, ed. (New York: Grune & Stratton, 1977), pp. 175-76.

sonal relationships, not simply on the basis of imitation or external rewards. For these reasons I will attempt to explore in greater detail the dynamics that account for children learning a set of moral standards that put the flesh on their inherent, though primitive, moral nature, and also the way children learn a set of self-corrective attitudes.

BIRTH OF THE IDEAL SELF

Psychologists typically use the term internalization to refer to the total process of taking in or internalizing the values, standards, and attitudes of one's parents and significant others. While psychoanalytic theorists[6] often make careful distinctions between various forms of internalization (such as incorporation, introjection, and identification), I will only discuss the broad outlines of the overall process here.

As soon as the infant's parents (or other authorities) begin holding out ideals and expectations (and approving or disapproving selected attitudes or actions) the process of internalization is set in motion. Children quickly learn that it is good to abide by their parents' wishes in order to avoid punishment.[7] But they also begin to take in their parents' expectations for reasons other than simply avoiding punishment. Being small, weak, and relatively helpless, children badly need the love and approval of their parents. Scoldings and disapproval send feelings of anxiety, isolation, and aloneness through young children. Contrary to mature adults who may stand for convictions in the face of great opposition and alienation, infants and young children are utterly dependent on their parents for emotional support. Being unable to cope with adult disapproval, they take the parents' standards as their own in the hopes of maintaining parental love and acceptance. If children can live up to parental ideals and expectations, they will not have to endure alienation and perceived rejection.

[6] R. Schafer, *Aspects of Internalization* (New York: International Universities Press, 1968).

[7] Kohlberg refers to this first level of moral development as the Pre-conventional Level ("Development of Moral Character and Moral Ideology," *Review of Child Development Research*, 1964).

Consequently, children's need for love is one of the most basic reasons they take in their parents' values as their own.

In addition to attempting to avoid punishment, gain rewards, and maintain the parents' love, a fourth motive plays a prominent role in children's desires to take in the goals and expectations of others. This is the desire to share in the parents' powers and wisdom and to eventually possess them independently. Being small and relatively helpless children are acutely aware of the power and wisdom of their parents. They see their parents' physical size and strength and their mental competence. They also see that parents have a great deal of freedom to make choices and run their own lives that children do not possess. Knowing that they lack these attributes, children attempt to become like their parents in as many ways as possible with the hope of eventually sharing that strength and knowledge. Parents see this dynamic played out repeatedly as children take on their parents' characteristics, playfully trying on their shoes, coat, or dress, and in general trying to be "like mommy" or "like daddy."

Based largely on these motives, parental ideals and expectations are gradually incorporated into children's lives. Along with the expectations of peers, religious leaders, significant others, and the media, they shape an image of what young children think they should become. These images have both positive and negative aspects. They include both a set of dos and a set of don'ts. These internalized standards merge with the growing child's own sense of things being right or wrong and his or her natural sensitivity to the breaches that come between parents and even very young children to form a set of ideals or goals. By late adolescence most individuals have developed a rather stable set of personal ideals or expectations. These goals, or "ego ideal," or "ideal self," as they are sometimes called, constitute the portion of the conscience that contains our standards and aspirations. They serve as a goal to motivate our actions and also as a standard by which we judge the acceptability of our attitudes and behavior.

THE DEVELOPMENT OF GUILT FEELINGS

At the same time children are developing a set of ideals, they are also taking in parental attitudes toward misbehavior and methods of punishment or correction. Just as children develop an ideal concept of what they think they should become, they also develop a set of corrective attitudes and actions. The young child spanking his own hands and saying, "No! No!" to himself is evidencing this process of internalization. He is inflicting upon himself the same type of punishment received from his parents.

Probably the most common result of misbehavior is some sort of parental punishment. When children disobey they learn to expect retribution. They are told, "Since you did that you should be punished." Gradually the experience of parental punishment instills an expectation of retribution. After this happens a few times, children feel anxious even when their parents are not present. They have developed a kind of internalized parent that speaks to them much like an actual parent.

A second parental response to misbehavior is a veiled threat of personal rejection. The mother of an adopted child told me of great difficulty controlling her new daughter. She had tried everything and finally found a way that worked. "I told her," she said proudly, "God doesn't love you when you are naughty!" Unfortunately, it isn't just these obvious expressions of parental anger and rejection that instill a fear of losing love. All human love is in some degree conditional, and most parents do love their children more when they are fulfilling their ideals and living up to their expectations. This sometimes subtle fact helps lay the basis for many children's later fears that if they don't live up to someone's expectations they won't be loved.

A third parental response to misbehavior is disapproval that tries to shame the child into more acceptable activities. Comparing one child to another, focusing repeatedly on a child's failures, or saying things like "Shame on you. You know better than that," or "Look what you've done now!" can all instill deep feelings of guilt and self-abasement in an impressionable child.

Over a period of years these three corrective parental responses are incorporated into young children's personalities and merge with their growing sense of empathy and concern for others. What originally came as external threats of punishment, rejection or disesteem are gradually changed into internal corrective attitudes. By taking these attitudes into their own personalities the children hope to accomplish two goals. The first is to avoid punishment. If children can scold or mentally punish themselves before their parents arrive on the scene perhaps they will not be punished by the parents. They assume (and sometimes quite correctly) that if they have already paid for their misdeeds the parents will exact no further payment! Children also take in parents' corrective attitudes in order to maintain their favor. They assume that they can gain parental approval and become like them by adopting their corrective attitudes just as they do their goals, standards, and expectations. These motives, coupled with the obvious modeling of the parent's corrective attitudes and actions appear to be the major factors behind the internalizing of the parents' standards. Combined with the child's own developing awareness of feelings of right and wrong and the process of projection we will look at later in this chapter, *these internalized fears of punishment, rejection, and disesteem comprise the three major ingredients of guilt.*

The attempt to earn parental love and grow up and become like them by taking in parental standards and corrective attitudes has major implications for the resolution of guilt. In fact, this process helps explain the seeming recalcitrance of many guilt feelings. In spite of the tremendous emotional damage they do, and in spite of the great psychic misery they cause, people are reluctant to give up either the unrealistic standards they inherited from parents, or their guilt-oriented corrective attitudes because they were developed to avoid further punishment and insure the continued love of the parents. *To the degree guilt emotions are influenced by parent-child interaction, they are both deeply ingrained by habitual interaction and provide a desired sense of security. It is partially because of this desire for security that even terribly guilt-ridden individuals cling tenaciously to self-defeating patterns of guilt and condemnation. They don't know any other way of controlling themselves and pleasing others.*

DEVELOPMENT OF CONSTRUCTIVE SORROW

All forms of discipline are not, of course, as potentially negative as fears of punishment, rejection, and lowered self-esteem. With a minimum amount of anger and frustration, parents can also (1) ignore their children's failures and let them profit from the consequences of their own behavior, (2) unconditionally love their children and reason with them about the effects of their action, or (3) lovingly yet firmly discipline them and help them see how they can do better. Just as children internalize their parent's negative corrective attitudes they also take in their positive ones. When these parental patterns are imitated and incorporated into a growing child's personality they merge with the child's developing sense of empathy and love and his or her rudimentary sense of things being "right" or "not right" to form another set of corrective attitudes that are very different from the punitive attitudes of guilt. These are loving rather than angry, patient rather than impulsive, and reasonable rather than demanding.

When these more loving self-corrective attitudes hold prominence over punitive ones, the person experiences a constructive form of sorrow, repentance, or regret. These attitudes also differ from those of the punitive guilt emotion in another critical respect. They are not attempts at effecting self-atonement! Since they are based on constructive, future-oriented discipline rather than punitive, past-oriented punishment, these attitudes are designed to improve one's future attitudes and actions, not to atone for one's past failures!

PERSONAL RESPONSIBILITY IN GUILT

In the previous section we have focused largely on the impact of parental treatment on the formation of the child's standards and corrective attitudes. Unfortunately, many theorists limit their analysis of the problem of guilt to these factors. They neglect both the child's primitive awareness of right and wrong and any other factors that might place upon the child some responsibility for the developmental direction the child's conscience takes. From this perspective, guilt is viewed entirely as the result of the child's taking in of parental and societal standards and methods of correction. A child's guilt is due to either unrealistically high expectations or to the harsh treatment received from others. Consequently, the child with problems of guilt and conscience is pictured as a victim. His guilt is simply a replica of the corrective responses leveled against him in childhood and his standards really aren't his own.

While this naturalistic view holds a good measure of truth, it fails to account for some important phenomena. It does not, for example, explain either the presence of a few apparently universal moral ideals or the sense of moral obligation or imperative. It also fails to explain why the ideals of some individuals are quite different from those of their parents and other socializing agents, or how guilt can be more severe for some people than the actual punishment received. Based simply on the internalization of parental ideals and corrective attitudes, we would expect both the child's ideals and corrective attitudes to be essentially replicas of their parents' ideals and attitudes. A biblical understanding of the nature of man and sin enlightens us on these issues. The presence of universal ideals and a sense of moral obligation is biblically seen as the expression of the image of God in man[8] and of the "law written in their hearts."[9] The tendency of many people to aim for unrealistic performance goals—even higher than their parents held out—is explained as a result of humanity's constant desire to be god-like (omnipotent). I believe this universal tendency is one of the most fundamental results of the Fall and a key insight for understanding the dynamics of conscience.

In addition to their striving for omnipotence, I see at least two other inner processes that lead inevitably to the formation of guilt regardless of parental treatment. Once a child matures to the place he can differentiate himself from his parents, he becomes aware that he is small, inferior, and, in certain ways, inadequate. At the same time, children also perceive their parents as all-powerful and all-knowing. Their parents' actual size and strength is magnified in comparison to the child's small size and limited knowledge and freedom. In fact, the parents take on the proportion of "gods" to small children who imagine their parents can do anything they conceivably wish. Since parents are typically three or four times the size of young children, they are perceived more like six-hundred-pound, eighteen-foot, omnipotent, giants than normal, finite human beings. This coupling of the child's feelings of weakness and his perception of his parents as all powerful and all knowing produces an important dynamic.

[8]Gen. 1:26.
[9]Rom. 2:15.

As the child decides he wants to become like his strong, intelligent, self-determining parents his perceptions are distorted by his small size and his as yet primitive perceptual process. Consequently, the ideal he sets for himself is not to become like a normal adult but like a huge, all-powerful, all-knowing parent! In other words, he wants to be like his parent "gods." This desire, which may be either a reflection of humanity's desires to be like God or simply a parallel process, casts a shadow over the entire process of the development of the functions we call conscience. Because of these processes the child's desire is not to grow up at his own pace into a reasonably healthy and wise adult. Instead he is always striving to be godlike. This desire programs him for repeated failure since he will never be as large or wise or as strong as he perceives his parents to be during the first few years of life.

Being aware of his actual limitations and the impossibility (at least for many years) of achieving his goal of becoming like his parents, let alone God, a child may turn to fantasy and personal idealization as a substitute for actual accomplishment. He begins to dream that he can accomplish amazing feats and pictures what he could ideally be. As he grows older he imagines himself a star athlete, a great intellect, or a person of unlimited wealth, prestige, beauty, or likeability. These aspirations are gradually added to the internalized expectations and ideals of parents and others and become a part of the ego ideal. From this time on the child experiences guilt feelings for falling short of these unrealistic ideals just as he does for failing to live up to the goals and standards taken over from his parents or his own inherent awareness of inner psychic disharmony. No longer is he simply feeling guilty for falling short of his parents' or others' expectations. No longer is he simply experiencing a rudimentary sense of things being wrong. And no longer is he simply the victim of others' unrealistic ideals. His innate tendency to run his own life has begun to solidify and take on concrete form, and his godlike desires are now coming back to haunt him. He so badly wants to be something (or someone) he is not, that he is willing to suffer the pain of guilt in order to maintain a false image of himself. Karen Horney gives an excellent description of this process in her discussion of the idealized self and the search for glory when she says:

When an individual shifts his center of gravity to his idealized self, he not only exalts himself but also is bound to look at his actual self—all that he is at a given time, body, mind, healthy and neurotic—from a wrong perspective. The glorified self becomes not only a phantom to be pursued; it also becomes a measuring rod with which to measure his actual being. And this actual is such an embarrassing sight when viewed from the perspective of a godlike perfection that he cannot but despise it. Moreover, what is dynamically more important, the human being which he actually is keeps interfering significantly with his flight to glory, and therefore he is bound to hate it, to hate himself. And since pride and self-hate are actually one entity, I suggest calling the sum total of the factors involved by a common name; *the pride system* (italics mine).[10]

Theologically considered, the net result of this entire process is self-worship, or idolatry. We refuse to accept ourselves as we are and cling to a picture of ourselves the way we think we could be. Guilt feelings, when seen in this light, are partly our own voice issuing condemnations for our failures to be sufficiently god-like. Horney continues:

All the drives for glory have in common the reaching out for greater knowledge, wisdom, virtue, or powers that are given to human beings; they all aim at the absolute, the unlimited, the infinite.... He is therefore the antithesis of the truly religious man. For the latter, only to God are all things possible; the neurotic's version is: nothing is impossible to *me*.... For his well-functioning, man needs both the vision of possibilities, the perspective of infinitude, and the realization of limitations, of necessities, of the concrete.[11]

The role of these god-like desires is not limited to the formation of unrealistic ideals. Similar dynamics also come to bear in the formation of our punitive guilt emotions. We have seen how children internalize their parents' corrective attitudes just as they do their standards and expectations. While this is true, it does not complete the picture of the origins of guilt feelings. When infants

[10]Karen Horney, *Neurosis and Human Growth* (New York: W. W. Norton & Co., Inc., 1950), pp. 110-11.
[11]Ibid., pp. 34-35.

(or children) do not get their way (we might call this having their omnipotence frustrated) they typically respond with anger. They believe (in a god-like sort of way) that they should always have their way, and are resentful when they don't. Their anger, however, distorts their perception of the parent who frustrated their wishes. On the basis of the mechanism of projection, children assume that their parents are angry also. Much like an adult (only much more so because of the relatively under-developed and undifferentiated nature of the child's psychic system) who is angry with another person and assumes that person is angry with him, the children believe that their parents are angry with them.

When children take in their parents' corrective attitudes they do not, therefore, take them in as they are in reality. Instead, they take in *their perceptions* of their parents' corrective attitudes. In short, they project their own intense anger onto their parents, add the great strength they have attributed to their parents to the anger they projected onto them, and then internalize their parents' corrective actions and attitudes as they believe them to be. *In this way the child's conscience becomes more punitive than his parents were in reality. Whatever angry punishment the parent actually meted out is compounded by the child's perception of his parents as omnipotent and the child's projection of his own hostility onto the parent.*

This dynamic helps explain the severe harshness conscience can take. Even children with basically well-adjusted parents who do not rely on fear motivation can develop harsh consciences because of the anger within themselves. Anytime a child's wishes are not met (whenever a child's omnipotence is frustrated), he reacts in anger.

In addition to projecting anger onto the parents, children may also want to push away (reject) parents who do not give them what they want or devalue them and see them as bad for not fulfilling their wishes. Just as happens with anger, these feelings of rejection and disesteem are also projected onto the parents, furthering the distortion. Consequently, when children take in their parents' corrective attitudes, they are actually reaping the results of their own rage and rejection and disesteem of their parents for frustrating their desires. Each of these, of course, influences the development of the three components of guilt feelings: self-rejection, self-punishment, and a loss of self-esteem. While children with harsh parents are much more prone to developing punitive consciences, the frustration of omnipotent desires and the projectively distorted perception of the child's parents are at least as important a cause of guilt as actual parental mistreatment.

INTRINSIC AND INTERNALIZED GUILT

By now the significance of the interaction of a child's inner psychic processes and his interpersonal relationships for the development of conscience and feelings of guilt should be clearer. There is an intricate process of inter-personal and intra-personal interaction involving one's own wishes and desires, the wishes of others, and the emotions of respect, love, envy, fear, and anger that together shape the child's conscience and proneness to guilt. Two aspects of this process deserve a further word of clarification. The first has to do with the difference between intrinsic and internalized guilt.

As I have attempted to demonstrate throughout these pages, the development of guilt feelings cannot be satisfactorily explained simply by the process of internalizing the judgments of others. Neither can they be explained solely as an innate process of conviction and moral judgment. Both intrinsic and internalized processes are involved in the dynamics of guilt feelings. Without an inherent moral nature and sensitivity to right and wrong, humans could be socialized to no greater degree than animals. But without the impact of parents and significant others, mature morality also could not develop.

This twofold source of both positive morality (constructive sorrow) and feelings of guilt opens up another way of looking at the problem of guilt. Just as we can distinguish between guilt feelings and godly sorrow on the basis of the cognitive and affective *components* of these experiences, we can distinguish between intrinsic and internalized guilt feelings (or godly sorrow, for that matter) on the basis of their *origins*.

Since we are social beings who develop our values and motivations in the context of relationships with others we obviously cannot fully separate either our standards or our corrective attitudes into intrinsic or internalized. Nevertheless it is often helpful to ferret out which of our values reflect the law written in our hearts and which are the imposed or internalized values of others. Many people suffer intense guilt for failing to be what their parents or others thought they should be even though they didn't have the God-given gifts to do that. And others experience guilt or godly sorrow for failing to be what God created them to be because they denied His inner design and instead pressured themselves to be what others wanted.

Similarly, some of our punitive guilt feelings are the result of the pressures and condemnations we received from parents and educators while others come from our own frustrated wishes and self-atoning propensities. When we look at the development of malfunctions of conscience in the appendix and the resolution of guilt feelings in part 5 we will look further at this distinction between intrinsic and internalized guilt feelings.

AMBIVALENCE IN GUILT

The final developmental dynamic of guilt is the effect of children's ambivalent feelings toward their parents in the formation of guilt. Very briefly, it is because children both love and resent their parents that guilt feelings develop. Without loving attachments children would have no reason to idealize the parents, take in their values, and attempt to be like them. But without anger children would not distort their parents, fear them, and internalize such punitive self-corrective attitudes. Without love, in other words, children would have no vested interest in taking in the parents' values. Yet without anger and resentment (the child's and the parents') no one would develop punitive emotions of guilt.

In the formation of a child's conscience, we see the result of both the idealization and the resentment of the parent. Children's ideals function as an inner representative of envied and loved parents. Children admire their parents' (and later their own) lofty ideals and expectations even though they can't measure up to them. At the same time they resent their parents (and later themselves) because of the unreachable ideals. They both love and resent their parents' and later on their own set of ideals!

AN INTEGRATIVE VIEW OF CONSCIENCE DEVELOPMENT

Based on our God-given moral nature, the law written on our heart, our basic sinfulness, our universal sense of moral obligation, our primitive inner awareness of guilt as something gone wrong, and the internalization of the projectively distorted ideals and corrective attitudes of parents and others, we all enter adulthood with a rather well-developed moral system. While the content and nature of this moral system varies greatly from person to person, the psychological mechanics involved are essentially the same in every person. This moral system can be diagrammed as in Figure 11.

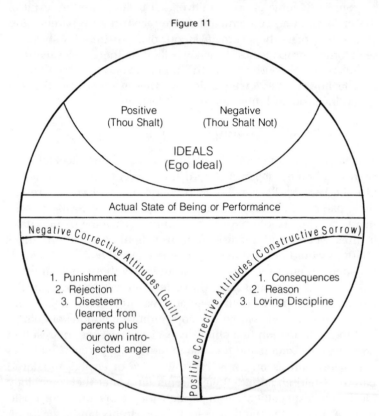

Figure 11

Whenever we fall short of our ideals (whatever their origin), we experience some type of corrective response. This corrective response (either guilt or constructive sorrow) is based on the attitudes developed in early life. To the degree we were angry when we didn't get our own way, and to the degree we internalized angry, punitive images, we experience guilt feelings.

When guilt is experienced for violating a negative prohibition (thou shalt not), we tend to experience self-inflicted punishment (or what we might call guilt proper). When guilt is triggered by our failure to live up to a *positive* ideal (thou shalt) we are more likely to experience shame or a loss of self-esteem. Self-punishment, in other words, is triggered more by aggressive acts or thoughts (fantasies) that violate our inner prohibitions, whereas feelings of shame or disesteem result from our failures to reach inner goals or expectations. To the degree that we develop positive corrective images in our formative years, we experience constructive sorrow. This love-motivated desire to change is based on our concern for all parties involved rather than on our desires to avoid self-punishment or rejection.

Having now discussed the major dynamics in the development of guilt and conscience, I would like to tie these in with our earlier discussion of the relationship of sin and psychopathology and guilt. In brief, this is the way I see the intertwining of normal developmental experiences and our own sinfulness in producing feelings of guilt. After each process I note whether it grows largely out of the individual's own internal world (intrinsic) or from the impact of the environment (internalized).

1. Every person is born as a moral being yet in a fallen condition. As such we have an inherent potential for disunity with ourselves, God, and others (Intrinsic).

2. One aspect of our fallenness is the desire to have our own way and to rebel against God, parents, and others (Intrinsic).

3. As fallen persons in a fallen world, infants experience a rudimentary form of anxiety based upon the failure of the people in the environment to fulfill their God-given needs (Intrinsic).

4. As fallen beings, infants also experience a rudimentary form of guilt when they are angry, frustrated, or upset about not having their wishes met (Intrinsic).

5. When we violate our relations with God, ourselves, and others, (even in early childhood), we have at least a rudimentary awareness that something is wrong in our lives. As we mature, this awareness differentiates into a clearcut sense of right and wrong (Intrinsic).

6. Throughout childhood we take in the values of parents and others and incorporate these into our developing set of ideals (ego ideal or ideal self).

These values are built upon the child's basic moral nature as a bearer of the image of God and provide much of the specific content of his/her moral standards (Intrinsic *and* internalized).

7. We also develop desires to grow up and be like our strong, intelligent parents. These ideals, however, are distorted by the child's perceptual immaturity. Combining with our inherent desires to be god-like, they result in the formation of some very unrealistic goals and expectations (Intrinsic).

8. At the same time that we internalize our parents' values and standards, we also take in their corrective attitudes (either loving or punitive) (Internalized).

9. The punitive corrective attitudes of parents combine with our own projected anger and our rejection and condemnation of our parents for not giving us what we wanted and are experienced as feelings of guilt (Intrinsic and internalized).

10. Our parents' loving corrections combine with our own intrinsic relational desires and positive feelings to develop feelings of constructive sorrow (Intrinsic and internalized).

11. When we fall short of either our God-given standards, the standards of others, or our own grandiose expectations, we experience an *awareness* or *sense* of guilt. One of the functions of the Holy Spirit is to bring our failures to awareness and create this *sense* of guilt (Intrinsic).

12. This sense of guilt leads to punitive psychological guilt to the degree that we developed punitive attitudes during our formative years and to the degree that we have an innate desire to autonomously atone for our own sins and effect reconciliation through our own efforts (as did Adam and Eve) (Intrinsic and internalized).

13. Guilt feelings are essentially attempts to please ourselves, others, or God through atoning for our perceived moral failures with self-inflicted psychic pain (Intrinsic and internalized).

14. To the degree that we have not internalized punitive guilt feelings in childhood, and to the degree that we have given up our efforts at self-atonement, we are able to lovingly correct ourselves—the foundation of godly or constructive sorrow (Intrinsic and internalized).

SUMMARY

In this chapter I have attempted to bring together the understanding we have of guilt and conscience through naturalistic observations with a biblical understanding of the nature of man, sin, and guilt. Although this is a complex process, I believe we have sufficient understanding to see that both a naturalistic view that ignores humanity's intrinsic moral nature and the role of sin in the development of guilt feelings and a religious view that ignores the impact of internalization processes in the formation of guilt feelings are inadequate. A comprehensive understanding of the dynamics of guilt requires attention to both the intrinsic and internalized components of this complex experience. Readers interested in the development of specific pathologies of conscience are referred to in appendix 2.

Therapy of Guilt

Many psychotherapists claim counseling should be free of all moral (and value) judgments and that biblical standards and insights have no place in the counseling process. Part 5 argues that all therapists, either overtly or covertly, bring their values and assumptions into counseling. I also suggest that a biblical understanding of guilt and conscience should strongly impact the Christian counselor's therapy but that the way this impact is worked out in counseling is a function of the counselee's need, the therapeutic modality we are operating from, and the counselor's own personality.

18

Common Therapeutic Ingredients

Figure 12 calls attention to four potential sources of maladjustment of conscience. The first is the set of aspirations labeled the ego ideal or the ideal self. The second is our level of performance. The third is the set of corrective attitudes utilized to motivate acceptable attitudes and behavior, and the fourth is our set of self-evaluative processes. In these final chapters, I would like to flesh out the therapeutic implications of this understanding of guilt feelings.

Figure 12

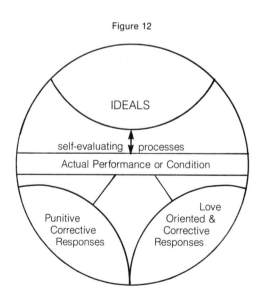

In this chapter we will begin by looking at the key ingredients common to all effective therapies of guilt. In Chapter 19 we will look at two therapeutic approaches to guilt that despite some crucial insights, are inadequate as models of counseling. In concluding chapters we will look at how we can utilize the biblical understanding of guilt in the counseling process.

THE UNCOVERING PROCESS

When Adam and Eve hid in the trees of the garden God called them out of the guilt-induced hiding place by asking, "Where are you?" And when they justified their hiding because of their nakedness, He replied, "Who told you you were naked? Have you eaten from the tree of which I commanded you not to eat?" Demonstrating His total comprehension of the dynamics of Adam and Eve's guilt, God called them firmly from their hiding place.

All therapy of guilt must similarly pick up on the behavioral clues that indicate a person is hiding, explore the guilt that motivates the hiding, and ultimately confront the real offense at the root of the guilty emotions.

Until the defenses warding off repressed guilt are explored there is no way individuals can see the true source of their guilt feelings and begin resolving neurotic patterns. Their defenses will continue hiding their inner fears of punishment and rejection and the real and imagined offenses that lie at their root. In discussing the necessity of analyzing guilt, Angyal wrote:

> Guilt is always present but it is never in the open. *When manifest guilt feelings are minimal or absent, the therapist's first task is to bring them to the patient's awareness by utilizing the indirect indications that both reveal and disguise guilt.* On the other hand, conscious guilt feelings may be present and even prominent, but on the surface they rarely refer to the actions or attitudes that caused the real guilt. This guilt, of which the patient is aware only dimly or not at all, is usually camouflaged by the manifest guilt feelings, often exaggerated or irrational (italics mine).[1]

---

[1] A. Angyal, *Neurosis and Treatment: A Holistic Theory* (New York: John Wiley & Sons, 1965), pp. 234-35. Angyal continues, "Some of the most common disguises are certain brands of fear, symptoms or behavior patterns that have the function of 'undoing' the acts leading to guilt, protestations of perfect goodness and innocence, distortions of reality systemically aimed at minimizing one's guilt, or lack of emotional response to instances of obvious factual guilt."

David is a good example of the effects of hidden guilt.[2] As long as he denied his sin, he experienced emotional oppression. But once he acknowledged and confessed his sin, he experienced forgiveness. The way God revealed David's guilt also illustrates the necessity of confrontation in the therapeutic process. Being sent by God to convict David of his sin of adultery with Bathsheba, Nathan told David a story of a rich man who stole a poor man's only lamb. Burning with anger David said "surely the man who has done this deserves to die. And he must make restitution for the lamb fourfold." Then Nathan firmly but in love for his good friend David, announced, "You are the man!"[3] Nathan didn't wait until David saw it all for himself. Under the leading of the Lord he confronted David with his sin and with the consequences of it.

Such careful, consistent, and loving uncovering of our coun-selee's sinfulness is a prerequisite both for the resolution of un-necessary guilt feelings and for the development of a sense of inner wholeness and constructive sorrow. As long as we are either denying our sinfulness to avoid feeling guilty or punishing ourselves to avoid rejection or punishment from others, we have little time or energy to devote to constructive sorrow or true repentance. We are so tied up in our own self-serving mechanisms that we are not free to be concerned with others—the essence of godly sorrow. But, like David, once we see the true extent of our sin we can ask forgiveness and experience godly sorrow and true repentance. David summed this up beautifully when he wrote:

> Deliver me from bloodguiltiness, O God, Thou God of my salvation; then my tongue will joyfully sing of Thy righteousness. O Lord, open my lips, that my mouth may declare Thy praise. For Thou dost not delight in sacrifice, otherwise I would give it; Thou art not pleased with burnt offering. The sacrifices of God are a broken spirit; a broken and a contrite heart, O God, Thou wilt not despise.[4]

Samuel's handling of Saul's disobedience to God regarding the Amalekites is another good illustration of how defenses must sometimes be cut through decisively. The Lord told Saul to destroy all the Amalekites and their possessions, but Saul took the

---

[2]Ps. 51.
[3]2 Sam. 12:5-7.
[4]Ps. 51:14-17.

king alive and also spared sheep, oxen, fatlings, and lambs.[5] When
Saul saw Samuel he piously proclaimed, "Blessed be thou of the
Lord: I have performed the commandment of the Lord."[6] Calling
Saul on his deceit, Samuel replied, "What meaneth then this bleat-
ing of the sheep in mine ears and the lowing of the oxen which
I hear?"[7] Therapists can well relate to such obvious attempts at
hiding the truth when we recall clients with clenched fists claim-
ing, "I'm not angry!" or blushing and saying, "I'm not embarrassed!"
But like many clients Saul continued his efforts to proclaim his
innocence. He quickly replied: "*They* have brought them from the
Amalekites, for *the people* spared the best of the sheep and oxen,
to sacrifice to the Lord your God; but the rest *we* have utterly
destroyed."

Notice how Saul accuses the people for the disobedience, but
takes credit for the partial obedience. He says, "*They* brought them
. . . and the rest *we* destroyed." Samuel ignored that ploy and once
again repeated the Lord's command and Saul's disobedience[8] but
Saul again proclaimed his innocence:

> I did obey the voice of the Lord, and went on the mission on
> which the Lord sent me, and have brought back Agag the King
> of Amalek, and have utterly destroyed the Amalekites. But the
> people took some of the spoil, sheep and oxen, the choicest of
> the things devoted to destruction to sacrifice to the Lord your
> God at Gilgal.[9]

Not to be sidetracked, Samuel again cut right through Saul's defenses and said: "Rebellion is as the sin of witchcraft, and stub-
bornness is as iniquity and idolatry. . . . Because thou hast rejected
the word of the Lord, he hath also rejected thee from being king."[10]

Only after all of that does Saul finally admit, "I have sinned."[11]
Samuel's persistent pursuit of Saul's defenses is a good model for
psychotherapists. Until the hidden guilt is faced by clearing away

[5]1 Sam. 15:1-15.
[6]1 Sam. 15:13.
[7]1 Sam. 15:14 (KJV).
[8]1 Sam. 15:15 (KJV).
[9]1 Sam. 15:20-21.
[10]1 Sam. 15:23 (KJV).
[11]1 Sam. 15:24 (KJV).

disguises and defenses there can be no true repentance, constructive sorrow, or remorse.

ANALYZING UNREALISTIC EXPECTATIONS

A second component of effective guilt therapy is an analysis of unrealistic personal ideals or standards. As we saw in chapter 18, it is easy for the developing child to internalize unrealistic expectations. He can be taught, "You should *never* be angry," "You should *always* be nice," "You *must* do better," and "You *ought* to do as well as your brother." Interaction with demanding or critical parents, competition with siblings and peers, legalistic religious training, and broadly held societal expectations can all lead to the internalization of impossible expectations and ideals.

As these influences are ferreted out in therapy, counselees begin to see which of these values are healthy and which are not. They can see which were realistic and which were not. And they can see which are consistent with divine revelation and which are not. Secular therapists, of course, will not be concerned with helping counselees align their value system with Scripture. But they will help counselees evaluate the socializing influences that impacted their lives and assist them in giving up ideals that appear to be neurotic, unrealistic, and/or at odds with an honest appraisal of the individual's capacities and potentials.

When we look at the unique Christian contributions to the therapy of guilt in chapter 22, we will see that Christian counselors have an added resource in helping counselees give up unrealistic goals and rearranging their ideals and expectations. For the time being, however, I simply want to suggest that any therapy that is effective in reducing guilt must give serious attention to the sources of unrealistic ideals and help counselees begin to throw off the shackles of these impossible expectations. This is true for both one's intrinsic expectations and the internalized expectations of others.

RESOLVING AMBIVALENCE

Closely related to altering unrealistic ideals is the necessity of working through ambivalent attitudes toward oneself and significant others. Guilt feelings always involve a mixture of love and anger since, if we have no concern for others, we experience no guilt for injuring them. In a similar way, if we have no investment in our own ideals—if they are not loved or prized by us—we experience no guilt when we fail to fulfill them. Guilt feelings only arise when we offend someone we love or when we violate our valued inner ideals.

The fear of facing ambivalent attitudes is one reason therapy with guilt-laden people can be painfully slow. It is not unusual for neurotically depressed people to begin therapy with strong feelings of *self*-hatred but with overtly positive attitudes towards parents, spouses, or significant others. If the therapist suggests the presence of negative attitudes toward these key people he or she is frequently met by a sincere denial of anger or some type of response that both excuses the other people and lays the blame at the counselee's own feet. Sue, a thirty-five-year-old minister's wife, had an almost irresistible tendency to do this. She was suffering from serious depression and had entertained thoughts of suicide for several years. She showed up for one appointment looking terribly depressed. When I inquired about the reason for her depression she related an incidence with her husband from the past week.

Sue's husband pastored a small church and held an evening job to make ends meet. They had three young children, rented a small home, and lived on an extremely tight budget. From the beginning of their married life, they had lived in rented apartments or homes and never had a place of their own. This, coupled with her husband's busy schedule, her need for more emotional support, and a variety of intrapsychic dynamics had stirred up a lot of resentment toward her husband. But because of her depressive style, Sue had great difficulty acknowledging her anger or expressing it to her husband.

During the week, Sue purchased material for new drapes for one room of the house. She had shopped carefully and knew she could make some attractive drapes at a reasonable price. Unfortunately she spent a few dollars over their budgeted amount. When her husband came home, he was furious over her "breaking" the budget. When I asked how she felt when her husband attacked her for spending too much money on the drapes, Sue replied,

"Terrible! It was a stupid thing to do!" Seeing how she had quickly turned the blame to herself, I tried to get at her anger toward her husband by asking, "How did you feel toward Ray when he became angry at you?" Immediately she replied, "Horrible! I feel sorry for him. He pastors all day and works an evening job to try to meet our needs and I louse it up. I'm always doing stupid things like that! I was trying to be helpful but I should have been more careful!"

I tried two or three other ways of getting her to face her resentment but each time she quickly turned the blame upon herself. Finally I said, "If you were not a Christian, and were doing your very best to fix up your home and your husband came home and bawled you out for spending ten dollars over the budget, and you were totally uninhibited and could say anything you felt, what would you tell your husband?" Immediately, and with anger in her voice, she said, "I'd tell him, 'I hate your guts!' "

Sue's reaction is typical of depressed individuals. From early childhood they have learned to repress anger because they feared reprisal, disapproval, or loss of love. Whenever they began to blame their parents or others they were rebuffed or in some way had the blame laid back on their shoulders. Consequently, instead of remaining in touch with their anger toward *others* they began to assume that *they* were the ones at fault. Although painful, this "solution" does have the advantage of maintaining peace in the family and not stirring up parental anger or emotional withdrawal. Depression and self-hatred, however, are the prices people pay for maintaining parents' conditional love and approval. In the case of Sue, her tendency to repress anger was reinforced by her Christian subculture and her concept of what a minister's wife should be. Clearly, if feelings of guilt are to be resolved, this kind of repressed anger must be uncovered. As long as hostility toward others is hidden, we will continue to turn that anger on ourselves in the form of guilt.

We can see how introverted anger becomes guilt by looking at the process of internalization. As we saw in chapter 17, children take in both their parents' standards and their corrective attitudes. If, however, we have resentment to our parents, especially resentment over the standards they held out for us, we will hold the same attitudes toward these standards and ourselves *after* we internalize them as we did before. If we resented our parents' pressuring us to become perfectionists, for example, we may take in their perfectionistic standards and pressure ourselves much as our parents used to do. See Figure 13.

Figure 13

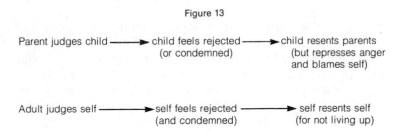

Parent judges child ⟶ child feels rejected ⟶ child resents parents
(or condemned) (but represses anger
and blames self)

Adult judges self ⟶ self feels rejected ⟶ self resents self
(and condemned) (for not living up)

In other words, what began as an ambivalent (love and hate) attitude toward our parents has become love and hatred of ourselves. We both love and admire our lofty standards but resent them and ourselves because of our inability to fulfill them!

As counselees face ambivalent attitudes to parents and understand how these mixed feelings contribute to their guilt they are able to start throwing off both the unrealistic standards and their own feelings of self-condemnation for not fulfilling them.

THE THERAPEUTIC RELATIONSHIP

Theorists of all orientations (with the possible exception of strong glorifiers of conscience or a few cognitively oriented therapists) agree that the quality of the therapeutic relationship is a central (if not *the* central) issue in all effective psychotherapy. To the degree that guilt is a relational process growing from the soil of interaction with parents and significant others, it is clear that effective guilt reduction must be a relational process.

Beginning with the now well-known study of the therapeutic relationship by Fiedler,[12] research findings have consistently indicated that the personality of the therapist and the quality of the therapeutic relationship are among the most important variables in effective psychotherapy. Fiedler found that experienced psychoanalysts, nondirective therapists, and Adlerian therapists conceptualized the ideal therapeutic relationship much more similarly to each other than they did to less well-trained therapists of their own theoretical persuasion. Experienced psychoanalysts, in other words, were more like experienced nondirective and Adlerian therapists in their understanding of and interaction in the therapeutic process than they were like less-experienced psychoanalysts.

More recently Jerome Frank, in assessing the state of research in psychotherapy, concludes:

> The results of outcome research strongly suggest that more of the determinates of therapeutic success lie in the personal qualities of the patient and the therapist and in their interactions than in the therapeutic method.[13]

In the words of Charles Truax and Robert Carkhuff, helpful therapists must be empathetic, warm (but nonpossessive) and authentic.[14]

Two aspects of the therapeutic relationship that are central to the resolution of guilt are acceptance and nonpunitiveness. Since at its deepest level guilt is both self-rejection and self-punishment, we must provide another option if our counselees

[12]F. Fiedler, "The Concept of An Ideal Therapeutic Relationship," *Journal of Consulting Psychology,* 1950, vol. 14, pp. 244.

[13]J. Frank, "The Present Status of Outcome Studies," *Journal of Consulting and Clinical Psychology,* 1979, vol. 47, no. 2, pp. 311.

[14]Charles Truax and Robert Carkhuff, *Toward Effective Counseling and Psychotherapy* (New York: Aldine, 1967), Hans Strupp, based on several thorough research studies, divides therapists' attitudes into two general categories. "On the one hand, it is a basic attitude of understanding, respect, and compassion— what Albert Schweitzer calls 'reverence for life.' It is the ability to listen without preoccupation, prejudgment, or condemnation. It is the ability to pierce the neurotic distortions, the socially unacceptable attitudes and acts, the more unsavory aspects of the personality, and to see behind it a confused, bewildered, and helpless individual trying to shape his destiny, hampered and hindered by his neurotic conflicts and maladaptions. On the other hand, it is an attitude of coldness, calculation, 'clinical evaluation,' distance, 'objectivity,' aloofness, moral judgment and condemnation." (Hans Strupp, *Psychotherapists in Action* (New York: Grune, 1960), p. 99.

are to grow out of their self-defeating cycles of guilt. Rogers put it this way:

> Our hypothesis is that the client moves from the experiencing of himself as an unworthy, unacceptable, and unloveable person to the realization that he is accepted, respected, and loved, in the limited relationship with the therapist.[15]

Although of a very different nature than Rogers's acceptance, Christ's relationship with the woman taken in adultery is an example of the healing power of acceptance and forgiveness. When the religious leaders were about to stone her, Christ stepped forward to say, "Let him who is without sin cast the first stone."[16] Later, after the crowd left, he assured the woman that he did not condemn her. Then he challenged her to "go and sin no more."

An interesting aspect of this story is that although Christ did not condemn the woman he did instruct her to "sin no more." Some therapists hesitate to label anything sin or offer any moral suggestions for fear of creating more guilt or condemnation. Client-centered therapists, for example, place great stress on the avoidance of any judgment or evaluation. But Christ made no arbitrary equation of sin with condemnation. He was able to call sin sin while still communicating a noncondemning attitude. This ability to "speak the truth in love"[17] is one distinctive of Christian counselors. Since we can offer acceptance based on God's forgiveness, we do not need to avoid confronting clients with sinful patterns in order to communicate acceptance. Once clients see our interventions and confrontations in the light of God's forgiveness they can begin making the important distinction between a love-motivated correction or interpretation and a judgmental one.

A therapeutic relationship characterized by honesty, acceptance, and nonpunitiveness impacts each of the four sources of guilt suggested by Figure 12. It softens self-punitive attitudes by modeling a healthy, love-oriented correcting attitude. It encourages frank self-evaluation because the counselee does not have to be afraid of condemnation and it encourages counselees to give

---

[15]Carl Rogers, *Client Centered Therapy,* p. 159.
[16]John 8:7.
[17]Eph. 4:15.

up unrealistic goals and expectations by showing they can be accepted as they are. Feeling accepted they are freer to explore the unreasonableness of some of their standards and have less need to cling to unrealistic ideals as sources of security. Finally, the increasing self-acceptance that grows out of the acceptance of a therapist frees counselees to act in accordance with their increasing self-esteem.

SUMMARY

The fundamental ingredients of effective therapy discussed in this chapter relate directly to the four focal points of the development of guilt outlined in chapter 17. The analysis of unrealistic ideals is designed to loosen unnecessarily rigid, stringent, neurotic, or godlike goals. A focus on the conflicts and sinfulness hidden beneath defensive patterns encourages a mature self-evaluative process that leads to facing the origins of neurotic guilt, an increasing sense of authenticity, and a healthy remorse or godly sorrow. And an analysis of the ambivalence underlying guilt helps alter punitive self-corrective attitudes. None of these tasks, however, will be effective if undertaken in a simply cognitive manner. They must be worked out in the context of an ongoing relationship with a person who models self-acceptance, nonpunitiveness, and authenticity and who makes it possible to work through both the intrinsic and internalized sources of guilt feelings.

Inadequate Models of Therapy

Having looked at some therapeutic processes common to all effective therapy of guilt I would now like to look briefly at two prevalent but inadequate therapeutic approaches. These approaches, while containing significant kernels of truth, are limited because they downplay one or more of the four major aspects of the guilt process. The first of these approaches is built on the belief that guilt feelings can be resolved largely through lowering unrealistic ideals.

LOWERING THE IDEALS OF THE CONSCIENCE

If guilt is triggered by a gap between what we are and what we think we should be, it is natural to assume that, by lowering our expectations, guilt feelings will lessen. This is the approach some counselors take to resolve guilt. They encourage clients to throw off their rigid sexual "inhibitions" and their "outmoded religious beliefs" in order to gain freedom from guilt. This approach, however, has generally not been articulated clearly in the literature of psychology. One notable exception is Albert Ellis. The basic assumption of Ellis's "rational emotive therapy" (RET) is that "fundamental irrational premises lead to emotional disturbances." One of these emotional premises is ". . . the idea that one should be thoroughly competent, adequate, and achieving in all possible respects if one is to consider oneself worthwhile."[1]

Consequently, a key activity of RET is challenging the client's

---

[1]Albert Ellis, *Humanistic Psychotherapy* (New York: McGraw-Hill, 1974), p. 37.

irrational beliefs.[2] The following excerpt from one of Ellis's therapy sessions illustrates this approach.

> Your problem actually is the fact that you have a lot of what I call "shoulds," "oughts," and "musts," which unfortunately you were taught when you were very young. You were taught these by your father, your mother, your church. . . . But if you didn't have this concept of ought which unfortunately is nicely defeating your own ends, then you wouldn't believe this—you wouldn't be disturbed.[3]

In some ways Ellis's goal of ridding oneself of irrational premises is a positive goal. To the degree one's ideals reflect omnipotent, God-like desires for perfection or are the result of socialization processes that caused repression of one's true self (the self as God designed it to be), they must be altered if therapy is to be effective. As long as we live under the false assumption that we can somehow merit the approval of ourselves and others by living up to unrealistic, perfectionistic ideals we can never throw off the shackles of guilt. Only the acknowledgment that we are finite creatures with real limitations who are in need of forgiveness provides the foundation for healthy self-acceptance and release from guilt.

Similarly, if we have internalized unrealistic standards or goals that forced us into socially or parentally acceptable roles at the expense of our own individuality, we must give up our allegiance to these goals to find freedom from guilt. The child who has been pressured to work for top grades and enter college even though he had minimal verbal gifts and is obviously talented in mechanics needs to throw off (or at least alter) his parents' expectations in order to feel free to use his God-given gift. In similar ways young adults who have been repeatedly encouraged to become physicians, teachers, ministers, or to "take over the family business" may struggle with intense guilt until they realize that vocational choices need to be based on an evaluation of their God-given gifts

---

[2]In RET the altering of supposedly unrealistic ideals and self-expectations is not the sole focus of therapy. In other places Ellis speaks of altering both one's behavior and one's self-corrective attitudes. The challenging of unrealistically high ideals, however, is a major focus.

[3]Albert Ellis, AAP Tape Library, vol. 1, "Loretta" (New York: Institute for Rational Living, n.d.).

and the leading of the Holy Spirit rather than parental or societal expectations.

Unfortunately, methods of therapy such as Ellis's frequently have a strong bias against authority in general and religious training in particular. Ellis believes that therapists should directly attack their patients' religious beliefs in order to be free from their "irrational premises." In one lecture he said:

> So will the therapist, if he himself is not too sick or gutless, attack his patient's religiosity. Not only will he show this patient that he is religious—meaning as we previously noted, that he is masochistic, other directed, intolerant, unable to accept uncertainty, unscientific, needlessly inhibited, self abasing, and fanatic—the therapist will quite vigorously and forcefully question, challenge and attack the patient's irrational beliefs that support these disturbed traits.[4]

In addition to the tendency of some therapists to attack their patients' religious beliefs and moral values, methods of therapy focusing largely on the lowering of ideals are less effective than we might assume for other reasons. To begin with, they postulate too strong a correlation between the width of the gap between one's performance and ideals and the amount of guilt experienced. These therapeutic approaches are based on the assumption that greater deviations from one's ideals result in greater degrees of guilt and that lesser deviations cause lesser amounts of guilt. As logical as this sounds, this simple formula is rarely true. Many people with exemplary behavior that closely approximates their ideals are riddled with neurotic guilt, while others with huge gaps between their ideals and their performance (at least at a conscious level) experience little guilt. *The intensity of guilt is not proportionate to the degree that our achievements fall short of our ideals.* It is more a function of the corrective attitudes embedded in the personality. Slight behavioral deviations associated with highly punitive corrective attitudes produce great guilt while large deviations committed by a person with few punitive attitudes produce very little guilt.

A second reason for the limited success of therapeutic ap-

---

[4]Albert Ellis, AAP Tape Library, vol. 1, "The Case Against Religion" (New York: Institute for Rational Living, n.d.)

proaches directed largely toward lowering ideals is that they are often based on a moral relativism. Therapists operating from this orientation may assume that counselees are suffering from guilt feelings for violating unrealistic ideals, when these ideals are actually God-given reflections of the law "written on the heart" of every person. While we might endlessly debate the exact origin and content of this inner law, the Scripture clearly teaches the existence of some universal moral standard, or awareness, that is not susceptible to ready removal by external means. Attempts to gain relief from guilt feelings by lowering one's standards neither eliminates the inner awareness of something gone amiss nor the nagging sense of guilt and the need for constructive sorrow or remorse. The awareness of our condition of sin may be repressed or in other ways disguised, but it will not be satisfactorily resolved so long as there is an unbridged gap between God-given moral values and one's inner attitudes and behaviors.

A third difficulty facing therapists attempting to reduce guilt simply by the lowering of standards is the unconscious nature and origin of many of our ideals. The conscious adoption of a new set of standards is insufficient to effect a dynamic change in guilt feelings unless the shift in values extends to the deeply ingrained and frequently unconscious values adopted during early childhood. Take the rebellious young adult as an example; after living for years in what he considers a restrictive, guilt-inducing religious family (or subculture), he decides that he has had all the guilt he can handle. He has tried "being good," and it hasn't worked. Consequently, he will throw off his rigid parental standards and adopt a new morality. For a moment he feels free. His new found peer support helps combat some of his rigid values. But before long that old sense of guilt returns. This time, however, it is disguised through repression, reaction formation, projection, or rationalization. Sometimes the person does not recognize the new forms that guilt has taken but his driven behavior, condemnation of those on his religious or political right, depression, or other symptoms tell us the painful accusations are present just the same.

These guilt feelings persist because of the lengthy and loving significance of the parental relationships that provided the soil for the development of the person's ideals. Fifteen or twenty years of internalizing parental values and standards do not easily give way to a sudden philosophical change or a different set of conscious values. Even though the parent-child relationship may not have been ideal, it was still the closest and most significant human experience our hypothetical young adult has ever known. The habits, values, and attitudes learned there are exceedingly change-resistant. He can rebel against them apart from the context of a loving interpersonal relation but to give them up without a similarly meaningful new love relationship is practically impossible. This means that although altering unrealistic ideals is an important part of therapy, it generally cannot be accomplished simply by exhortation, education, or a change of philosophy. In truly guilt-ridden individuals it comes over a lengthy period of time as new and healthier ideals are internalized through the intimate interaction of deep friendships or effective therapy.

A fourth problem in solving guilt problems by lowering one's standards is the fact that the neurotic person frequently does not *want* to lower his grandiose self-expectations. Many a beginning counselor has been puzzled by how tightly people cling to the standards that result in their self-devaluation. The source of this rigid clinging lies in the sense of pride and security the individual receives from these standards. Even though he doesn't live up to his standards, he harbors pride for holding such exalted goals. His pride is not over his god-like performance but over his god-like demands! Horney put it this way:

> A neurotic person's very high standards make him feel that he is a moral wonder to be proud of, regardless of how he actually is and behaves. He may have recognized in analysis his ravaging hunger for prestige, his poor sense of truth, his vindictiveness; but all of that does not make him any more humble or make him feel any less a superior moral being. To him these actual flaws do not count. His pride is not in being moral, but in knowing how he should be. ... Is not his suffering another proof of his superior moral sensibilities? Hence to sustain this pride seems worth the price.[5]

The gain (in terms of false security and pride) he receives from clinging to unrealistic aspirations appears to the neurotic to be

---

[5]Karen Horney, *Neuroses and Human Growth* (New York: W. W. Norton, 1950), p. 93.

worth the price (of guilt and self-condemnation) he has to pay. A good number of therapeutic impasses have grown out of the therapist's failure to realize that his or her counselee's fragile identity is bound up in this kind of logic. To give up these unrealistic ideals would mean forfeiting the whole foundation of the shaky identity. Consequently clients resist giving up the very aspirations that are central to their maladjustment.

This survey of the limitations of therapeutic approaches that focus on the lowering of ideals is not meant to suggest that attention to the standards of the ego ideal is unimportant. It is. The limitations of this therapeutic emphasis comes more from the tendency to believe that ideals can be altered simply by cognitive or rational processes, the assumption that smaller gaps between one's aspirations and performance result in lesser amounts of guilt, the tendency to neglect the need for the development of a healthy attitude of self-acceptance based on a meaningful therapeutic relationship, and the failure to recognize the client's strong resistance to altering ideals.

RAISING PERFORMANCE

The second inadequate model of guilt reduction is common to glorifiers of conscience. If people feel guilty because they fall short of their standards, it seems logical to improve their behavior and conform to their standards in order to reduce guilt. Consider, for example, the previously cited quotation from Glasser:

> To be worthwhile we must maintain a satisfactory standard of behavior. To do so we must learn to correct ourselves when we do wrong and to credit ourselves when we do right. If we do not evaluate our own behavior, or, having evaluated it, if we do not act to improve our conduct where it is below our standards, we will not fulfill our needs to be worthwhile and will suffer as acutely as when we fail to love or be loved.[6]

And Adams states:

> *The counselee's behavior is wrong; there is nothing wrong with his emotions.* His conscience, i.e., his ability to make judge-

[6]Glasser, *Reality Therapy* (New York: Harper & Row, 1965), p. 10.

ments about his own behavior (accuse or excuse), may trigger
all sorts of pleasant or unpleasant emotions it is true. *Sinful
behavior leads to unpleasant emotional experiences. But the
way to get relief from these is not by attacking the emotions,
but by changing (repenting of) the behavior* (italics mine).[7]

As we saw earlier, this approach to guilt and self-esteem runs
contrary to a New Testament view of motivation that sees actions
flowing out of inner attitudes and right behavior resulting from
the fact that we are loved, accepted, and forgiven by God. We are
to work *from* our acceptance and forgiveness, not *for* our acceptance and forgiveness. In addition to the problem of a reverse (legalistic) form of motivation, the attempt to solve problems of guilt
by increased performance runs into the same problems that attempts to lower one's standard do. The Bible indicates that it is
not the degree of deviation from the ideal that constitutes man's
objective guilt and leads ultimately to feelings of guilt, but rather
the very presence of our failures. James writes: . . . "For whosoever
shall keep the whole law, and yet offend in one point, he is guilty
of all."[8] And Paul wrote: "For as many as are of the works of the
Law are under a curse; for it is written, 'Cursed is everyone who
does not abide by all things written in the Book of the Law, to
perform them.' "[9]

Therapeutic experience consistently supports the biblical
teaching that it is not the *extent* of one's objective guilt that de-
termines his or her experience of psychological guilt but the very
fact that we fall short of any of God's ideals for our lives.

A third weakness of the works view of guilt reduction is its
relative neglect of punitive guilt feelings. Attempts to reduce guilt
by improving behavior miss the same crucial issue as efforts to
reduce guilt by lowering standards. They both overlook the fact
that to reduce guilt, punitive guilt motivations must be replaced
by loving, self-corrective attitudes. The ability to alter one's attitudes and behavior is a crucial ingredient of personal adjustment,
but this change should flow from the fact that one is accepted
and forgiven rather than be a means of earning self-acceptance
and freedom from guilt.

[7]Adams, *Competent to Counsel* (Nutley, N.J.: Presbyterian and Reformed,
1972), p. 110.
[8]James 2:10 (KJV).
[9]Gal. 3:16.

SUMMARY

In this chapter we have looked at two inadequate approaches to resolving guilt. Although effective therapy will generally include both a reevaluation of one's goals and altered behavior, overemphasis on either of these is fraught with therapeutic pitfalls. Attempts to reduce guilt by lowering one's standards may neglect both the fundamental moral nature of personality and the fact that guilt feelings are not necessarily proportionate to the degree of deviation from one's goals. In a similar fashion, attempts to reduce guilt by improving one's behavior are built on the false assumption that guilt feelings are highly correlated with the failure to fulfill one's ideals.

Thinking back to Carter's concept of an identity-based morality, we can also see that these two approaches to guilt reduction represent two alternate expressions of the flesh. The attempt to reduce guilt by lowering standards encourages acting out of sinful impulses while attempts at improving behavior reinforce legalistic, fleshly conformity. In both cases we are trying to seize the initiative to do something about our condition instead of accepting Christ's reconciliation.

20

The Myth of Value-free Therapy

Now we will examine the unique contributions that a biblical understanding of guilt can make to counseling. But to do that we must first answer the question, How, if at all, should we bring our Christian understanding of the nature of guilt into therapy?

During the late 1940s and the 1950s a rather strong consensus developed among psychotherapeutic practitioners that professional therapists were ethically bound to avoid bringing their religious and philosophical values and ideals into the therapeutic process. Partly as a result of the prevailing opinion that individuals with psychological adjustment problems were more sick than sinful, therapists concluded that bringing moral issues into therapy (by the therapist) was irrelevant at best and a violation of the patient's rights at worst. Supported on the one hand by psychoanalytically oriented therapists who viewed the therapist's neutrality as a necessary condition for the development of transference and on the other hand by therapists operating from humanistic and existential perspectives stressing the primacy of personal autonomy, this viewpoint quickly attained the status of dogma in the mental health establishment. Young therapists were admonished (sometimes in very authoritarian ways!) to avoid communicating their values to counselees. One of the cardinal "sins" a therapist could engage in was bringing one's own values into therapy. Therapists who did this encountered strict disapproval and responded with as much guilt as they would have had for violating a religious norm! Although this disapproval took a sophisticated form, individuals who engaged in this type of activity were nevertheless strongly condemned. They were not labeled "sinners," but they were called "rigid," "authoritarian," or "insufficiently analyzed." Only immature therapists would stoop to the low level of bringing their own values into therapy. Rogers, for example, wrote that the therapist "... can be only as 'nondirective' as he has achieved respect for others in his own personality organization."[1] By implication, therapists who are not nondirective have probably not achieved respect for others!

While advice giving *can* communicate a lack of respect, the assumption was that it *must*. Few paused to reflect on the possibility that (1) the decision to attempt to *not* bring values into therapy was in itself a value decision, (2) it might be impossible *not* to bring one's values into therapy, (3) it might be *profitable* to bring values into the counseling process, and (4) values could be brought into therapy in a nonjudgmental way that would not violate a healthy level of personal autonomy.

FALSE ASSUMPTIONS

In recent years psychologists have begun to question the assumptions of value-free therapy. The most obvious weak link in this chain of assumptions is the belief that the decision to conduct "value-free" therapy is not in itself a value. By now most well-known proponents of value-free therapy, for example, Carl Rogers, are well aware of the philosophical underpinnings of their views. Unfortunately many students have adopted their master's philosophical stances and unthinkingly assumed that they were based on scientific considerations. They have even entered into heated debate over the impropriety of bringing values—especially religious ones—into therapy without being willing to scrutinize their own philosophical givens. Reflecting on his experiences with this phenomena during his graduate and postgraduate training with Albert Bandura, Carl Rogers, and Robert Sears (and later with B. F. Skinner, Joseph Wolpe, and others), Allen Bergin writes:

> These were good experiences with great men for whom I continue to have deep respect and warmth; but I gradually found our views on values issues to be quite different. I had expected their work to be "objective" science, but *it became clear that*

[1]Rogers, *Client Centered Therapy* (Boston: Houghton Mifflin, 1965), p. 21.

> *these leaders' research, theories, and techniques were implicit
> expressions of humanistic and naturalistic belief systems that
> dominated both psychology and American universities, gener-
> ally.* Since their professional work was an expression of such
> views, I felt constrained from full expression of my values by
> their assumptions or faiths and the prevailing, sometimes coer-
> cive, ideologies of secular universities.[2]

Bergin's experience parallels that of many Christian graduate students in psychology who have either had their religious beliefs
attacked or ridiculed directly or who have felt it necessary to "go
underground" with their faith until they received their degree!
Fortunately this is beginning to change as psychologists are becoming more philosophically sophisticated and realizing that
therapy is as much a moral enterprise as it is a psychological one.

The second assumption—that it is possible to avoid bringing
one's values into therapy—is also now beginning to fade in popu-
larity. In addition to the logical impossibility of interacting deeply
with another human being without communicating some values,
research has demonstrated this simply does not happen. Truax,
for example, performed an analysis of one of Carl Rogers's successful counseling cases and concluded that Rogers differentially
reinforced client responses by systemically using empathy, acceptance, and (believe it or not) directiveness! He found that Rogers
reinforced the patient's learning of discriminations, the patient's
insights, and the similarity of the patient's style of expression to
that of the therapist, by the use of empathy and acceptance. He
did not reinforce the patient's ambiguity with empathy or acceptance. Instead, he tended to respond to ambiguity with directiveness! Rogers obviously valued the first three client responses and
reinforced them. If Rogers, the father of nondirective counseling
cannot avoid letting his values dictate his therapeutic responses,
it is highly unlikely other therapists are able to accomplish this
idealistic feat!

Once it became apparent that it is impossible to keep values
out of therapy, some theorists began focusing attention on the

---

[2]Allen Bergin, "Psychotherapy and Religious Values," *Journal of Consulting
and Clinical Psychology*, 1980, vol. 48, pp. 95-105.

possibility of using values in psychotherapy. London, for example, suggests,

> When conflicts revolve around moral issues, how is it possible to help without becoming directly involved in the moral issue? How is it even possible, for that matter, to decide whether a conflict is realistic without moral involvement? It is specious to argue, as some therapists do, that moral concerns are simply manifestations of "resistance" and that the underlying dynamics of the client's situation never relate to moral problems. It seems viciously irresponsible for the therapist to argue that, at such times, he must formally remove himself from the discussion by telling the client that the therapy session can be helpful for discussing "personal, emotional problems, not moral ones."
>
> This kind of concern may be one of the things that brought him to a psychotherapist in the first place, and however independent a soul he may be, one of the main things that keeps him there is the hope that he can be helped to guide himself along lines of behavior that will make his life more meaningful and satisfying.[3]

The fourth assumption, that it is impossible to bring values into therapy in a noncondemning way or in a manner that does not violate the patient's autonomy, is equally faulty. This concept is based on the faulty equation of morality with moralism. Although it must be admitted that many people (including some counselors) do communicate values in a moralistic, condemning way, this is not necessary. The central concept of ego morality (and of Fromm's humanistic conscience) is the assumption that values can be selected because they are helpful rather than because one would feel guilty if he did not endorse them. Similarly the entire biblical message of forgiveness says that we do not have to stand under condemnation for our sins. It is precisely at this point that the Christian counselor can promote a greater freedom of self-exploration. As our counselees realize the full extent of Christ's atonement and the fact that they are totally free from condemnation, they are freed to explore their sins and failures with less self-condemnation.

[3] P. London, *Modes and Morals of Psychotherapy* (New York: Holt, Rinehart, and Winston, 1964), pp. 7-9.

THE BIBLE IN COUNSELING

In spite of recent clarification regarding the inadequate assumptions of value-free therapy by both researchers and theoreticians, Christian therapists are still divided over the appropriateness of bringing values into counseling. My own experience with graduate students in psychology suggests that even many Christian students hesitate to utilize their spiritual resources in their clinical work. Whether this is a function of their undergraduate education, cultural influences, or supervisory input, I do not know. I am aware, however, that many students seem to believe they should be operating on the now largely discredited value-free assumptions, and that they initially experience a great deal of guilt if and when they become more up front with their own values.

Some Christians take the position that Christian counseling must not be significantly different from non-Christian counseling or else we will stop being therapeutic and begin indoctrination rather than therapy. From this perspective, any uniquely Christian contributions come from our conceptualizing of the therapeutic process, our increased sensitivity to the struggles of Christian clients, our respect for their values, and our silent witness. Others assume that by definition, if counseling is to be Christian it must use Scripture.

Thomas Oden, until recently[4] an articulate spokesperson for the first view, formulated a Christian understanding of therapy as a clarification of the ultimate ground of humanity's acceptance. In relating a theology of revelation (following Barth) to a therapy of insight (following Rogers), Oden suggested there was essentially no need for an explicit discussion of biblical revelation in the therapeutic process. Because this is a well-articulated and rather frequently-followed therapeutic perspective, we will look at it in some detail.

Oden begins by suggesting that the acceptance offered by all

---

[4]Oden has recently made a significant shift in his theological understanding as reflected in his *Agenda for Theology* (New York: Harper & Row, 1979). Although I am not aware of his writing anything on therapy since 1979, I suspect that his increasingly orthodox theology will challenge him to reconsider his past perspective.

therapists (Christian and non-Christian) points to a greater acceptance beyond the person of the therapist.

> Since all human action is based on some self-understanding involving implicit metaphysical, ontological, and cosmological assumptions ... we can say that all human action has philosophical and theological presuppositions. ... The action of the therapist is not different from any other human action in that it presupposes a certain understanding of existence. It is evident that the only understanding of existence that makes sense out of the activity of the psychotherapist is the assumption that man ought not to be neurotically guilty, anxious, hostile, and under the power of destructive compulsions. The therapist accepts the client in the midst of his guilt and compulsions not on the narrow assumption that he is just privately acceptable to the therapist as a human being but on the much more basic assumption that he is acceptable as a human being by the cosmos or the universe or by being itself and that he is intended for authentic life. *The counselor is not the source of acceptance; he only points to an acceptance that has its source beyond himself.*[5]

Then Oden locates the source of that acceptance:

> *This implicit assumption is precisely what is made explicit by God's self-disclosure in Jesus Christ.* The Christian kerygma seeks to state clearly and decisively that God has made himself known as one who accepts us unconditionally, that the One who gives us life is *for* us (italic mine).[6]

Summarizing his perspective, Oden writes:

> A simple syllogism captures the core of our proposal: *(a) If, in order to be effective, psychotherapy must meditate an accepting reality which is grounded in being itself; (b) if the accepting reality in being itself has disclosed itself in an event to which the Christian proclamation explicitly witnesses; then (c) the implicit ontological assumption of all effective psychotherapy is made explicit in the Christian proclamation.*[7]

[5]Thomas Oden, *Kerygma and Counseling* (Philadelphia: Westminster, 1966), pp. 21-22.
[6]Ibid., p. 23.
[7]Ibid., p. 24.

In other words, according to Oden, even non-Christian therapists are implicitly communicating God's unconditional acceptance and representative ministry.

This assumption raises a question about the need for an explicit communication of the Christian message in therapy. If all therapy is *implicitly* communicating God's unconditional acceptance, is it necessary or helpful to make this communication *explicit*? Oden addresses the issue as follows:

> The nub of this issue is whether divine acceptance must be mediated *verbally*, or whether it can be authentically mediated unverbally through an interpersonal *relationship*. *Our argument hinges on the assumption that liberating divine acceptance can be mediated concretely through interpersonal relationship without overt witness to its ground and source.*
>
> Admittedly the helping person who understands himself under the analogy of God's help may from time to time point the client directly to the source of the accepting reality, but the moment he does, he ceases being a counselor and becomes a preacher. If in rare circumstances such a witness is deeply meaningful, even in so-called secular psychotherapy, the therapist on such occasions should be keenly aware that he is shifting his role radically and may find it exceedingly difficult to shift back into a listening, clarifying, accepting relationship, since the intent of the kerygma is so easily distorted by the neurotic mind. More so, he should never forget that this liberating Word can be effectually embodied in relationships in which language is not even necessary. The cross, for example, is a language event, a word that is spoken (nonverbally, relationally) in an occurrence (italics of second sentence mine).[8]

Oden's view of all therapy as an expression of "the love of God hiddenly present through interpersonal relationships" fits with a universalist concept of salvation. If it is true that all humanity stands accepted by God, then an explicit proclamation of the gospel is not imperative. If, on the other hand (and in agreement with the historical position of the church) we believe Scripture speaks a word of judgment to those who are outside of Christ as well as a word of forgiveness to those who have been reconciled

---

[8]Ibid., pp. 28-29.

through personal appropriation of Christ's death, this is an unsatisfactory solution. A mirroring of God's love and valuing of the person is a necessary, but not a sufficient, ingredient of effective psychotherapy. Christ's death may have been (as Oden suggests) a language event but it was accompanied by verbal communication. At the beginning of His ministry, Jesus read from the Prophet Isaiah and spoke of its fulfillment.

> The Spirit of the Lord is upon Me
> Because He anointed Me to preach the gospel to the poor.
> He has sent Me to proclaim release to the captives,
> And recovery of sight to the blind.
> To set free those who are downtrodden.
> To proclaim the favorable year of the Lord.[9]

At the end of his earthly ministry, while on the Cross, Christ promised one of the criminals, "Today you shall be with Me in Paradise."[10] He also cried out, "My God, My God why hast Thou forsaken Me?"[11] The Cross was not simply a nonverbal "language event." It was a living out of the Good News that was preached to "set the captives free."

Oden's concern over confusing the work of preaching with the work of counseling is understandable. These differences in roles and functions have sometimes been obscured. But removing all verbal witness from the counseling process seems to me an artificial and arbitrary way of attempting to preserve the "purity" of psychotherapy. If we are to treat our counselees as holistic individuals, we must be willing to address their needs both implicitly and explicitly. Paul Tournier put it well:

> We are the instruments of healing grace when we prescribe the remedies God has given us, when we handle the lancet, when we use the forces of nature over which He has given man dominion (Genesis 1:28), and when we work for the development of science to which He Himself has called man (Genesis 2:19). We are again the instruments of His grace when the sick in mind find release through our psychological techniques.

[9]Luke 4:18-19.
[10]Luke 23:43.
[11]Mark 15:34.

But should we remain silent when it is a question of man's supreme malady, his great human anguish, his existential sickness—when it is a question of the sense of guilt, with which all our unbelieving colleagues are concerned today, moved as they are by their compassion and their great pity for human suffering? Should we conceal God's great answer because theologians accuse us of exceeding our role as doctors and of encroaching upon their territory? No! . . . we cannot enter the field of psychology without sooner or later coming imperceptibly and inexorably, even before we have realized it, upon human problems, those concerning the meaning of life, perdition and salvation, despair and hope, the sense of moral guilt and the forgiveness of God.[12]

THE USE OF SCRIPTURE IN THERAPY

I believe a counselor's use of Scripture in counseling parallels the differing Christian understandings of witnessing or evangelism; it also reflects the counselor's personality style and theoretical orientation. Most of us, for example, are probably not entirely comfortable with the type of street corner evangelism that confronts a total stranger with the question, "Brother, are you saved?" On the other hand, many of us are also not content to carry out our Christian witness at strictly a nonverbal level. While we may stress the importance of our quality of life and daily Christian witness, we at least want to be prepared to give "a reason for the hope that is in us"[13] and many go beyond this. These differing approaches to evangelism grow out of our theological (or denominational) heritages, our own unique personalities, our understanding of God's working in our lives, and our understanding of the needs of the person we happen to be in contact with. These same factors need to be considered in discussing the use of Scripture in the counseling process.

Some therapeutic approaches also lend themselves more naturally to an explicit Christian witness than others. A Christian counselor offering vocational and educational guidance may find it quite appropriate to bring biblical principles of stewardship of

[12]Tournier, *Guilt and Grace*, p. 198.
[13]1 Peter 3:15.

life and divine leading into the counseling process. On the other hand, a Christian therapist practicing orthodox psychoanalysis would not be able to find a place for an explicit Christian therapy if he wished! The therapeutic use of transference and the necessity of the therapist to remain as neutral as possible make any kind of direction inconsistent with this therapeutic modality. Other therapeutic approaches similarly lend themselves in varying degrees to the verbal use of Scripture in counseling.

I have found Wolberg's division of therapeutic approaches into *supportive, reeducative,* and *reconstructive* models a useful way of conceptualizing some of the similarities and differences among psychotherapies as well as their suitability for the direct use of Scripture.[14] Supportive therapies are directed largely to helping the counselee adapt to the environment or cope with problems of living without undergoing any "depth" changes or restructuring of the personality. These therapies aim at restoring equilibrium in crisis situations, solving situational problems, and relieving bothersome symptoms. They are not designed to resolve long-standing personality patterns or unconscious conflicts. Supportive therapies make primary use of direction, guidance, advice giving, catharsis, reassurance, prestige suggestion, environmental manipulation, and somatic treatment.

These therapeutic approaches readily lend themselves to the direct use of scriptural principles and concepts. Prayer, Bible study, memorization of Scripture, and spiritual guidance can be used effectively to help individuals organize their values and belief system and receive needed support and direction. A direct sharing of scriptural concepts of forgiveness and resolution of guilt also fits naturally into these modalities as do assigned readings on selected topics.

Reeducative therapies hold out somewhat more extensive goals than supportive therapies. Wolberg defines the goals of reeducative therapy as:

> the modification of behavior directly through positive and negative reinforcers and/or interpersonal relationships, with deliberate efforts at environmental readjustment, goal modification,

[14]L. Wolberg, *The Technique of Psychotherapy,* Pt. 1, 3rd ed. (New York: Grune and Stratton, 1977), pp. 14-15.

liberation of existing creative potentialities, and hopefully, promotion of greater self growth. No deliberate attempt is made to probe for unconscious conflict. Nevertheless, the individual achieves sufficient command of his problem to enable him to (1) check acting-out tendencies, to rectify remediable environmental distortions or to adjust to irremediable ones, (2) to organize his life goals more rationally and to execute them in a facile manner, (3) to consolidate some adaptive defenses and to alter others that are less adaptive.[15]

Among the more common reeducative therapies, Wolberg sees behavioral therapies, client-centered therapy, rational-emotive psychotherapies, psychiatric interviewing, reeducative group therapy, marital therapy, and philosophical and religious approaches to adjustment.

A look at these therapeutic approaches shows that most of them also lend themselves to an explicit use of biblical principles and concepts. In fact, Wolberg discusses the effect of religious experience as a reeducative phenomena. He writes:

There is no doubt that dramatic relief from neurotic suffering is possible after religious conversion. Through conversion the individual may harmonize himself with the order of the universe, and feel a oneness with the world or a union with God. Riddled by anxiety, tortured by self-doubt, the person in anguish is susceptible to the help held out to him through salvation by the evangelist. A reeducational experience develops as he moves in his conversion from defeatism to hope. By confessing his wickedness, he attains both forgiveness and the means to a blessed existence. Feelings of insignificance are replaced with a sense of distinction as one of God's instruments. Competitive strivings are abandoned; hate changes to love, tolerance and compassion. Remarkable shifts in attitudes and behavior may follow.[16]

Cognitive, behavioral, and rational emotive therapies seem to be ideal therapeutic modalities for an implicit use of Scripture. In fact, Lawrence Crabb's "biblical counseling" is in many respects a reinterpretation and integration of these therapeutic modalities

[15]Ibid., p. 101.
[16]Ibid., p. 155.

with Scripture. Consequently, his therapy focuses on changing faulty thought patterns. He writes:

> My belief should be obvious that the critical change in helping a person live effectively involves altering his Basic Assumption, the third element in this model. Every problem in the model can be avoided completely if the basic assumption is in line with revealed truth. The truly well-adjusted person is one who depends on God alone (and what He chooses to provide, which includes the Christian community) to make him significant and secure. Despair, frustration, resentment, anxiety, guilt, a sense of emptiness, neurotic symptoms—every problem can be traced directly to a wrong assumption about how to meet personal needs. The primary problem with people today is misplaced dependency. We depend on everything but God to meet our fundamental needs. *What then do we try to change? How a person thinks, what he is depending on, what he believes he must have if he is to feel truly worthwhile. We must change his mind* (italics mine).[17]

Based upon his understanding of the cause of personality malfunctioning (wrong assumptions) and the solutions (correct assumptions), Crabb offers the following summary of his therapeutic approach:[18]

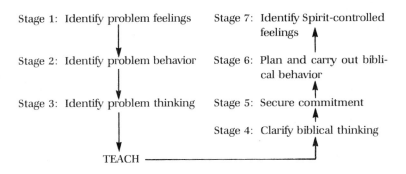

Stage 1: Identify problem feelings

Stage 2: Identify problem behavior

Stage 3: Identify problem thinking

Stage 7: Identify Spirit-controlled feelings

Stage 6: Plan and carry out biblical behavior

Stage 5: Secure commitment

Stage 4: Clarify biblical thinking

TEACH

---

[17]L. Crabb, *Effective Biblical Counseling* (Grand Rapids: Zondervan, 1977), p. 139.

[18]Ibid., p. 160.

Notice the emphasis on teaching. The content of teaching for Crabb is biblical truth designed to correct one's faulty assumptions. While some counselors would take issue with the highly cognitive nature of Crabb's understanding of therapy, his views do indicate how biblical principles can easily be brought into reeducative counseling.

In somewhat less didactic ways, other forms of reeducative therapy lend themselves to a sharing of scriptural principles and insights. The large amount of biblical revelation dealing with marriage, family, and interpersonal relationships, for example, makes most marital therapy an ideal modality for an explicitly Christian discussion of personal growth and adjustment. Similarly, the many Scriptures that speak to problems of guilt and self-esteem lend themselves to most forms of reeducative counseling. The counselor can naturally respond to clients' self-condemnations and accusations with sensitive acceptance, insightful exploration, and a clarification of the difference between punitive guilt feelings and constructive sorrow. Sharing of biblical passages like Romans 8:1 and 1 John 3:19-20 can provide a cognitive foundation for the resolution of feelings of guilt.

Reconstructive therapies are directed toward a more radical change in the personality structure of the counselee. Although these therapies attend to situational issues and symptoms, their primary focus is on effecting major changes in long-standing personality structures and styles. Consequently reconstructive therapies focus a great deal on repressed feelings, desires, and conflicts, as well as past developmental experiences that have shaped the personality structure. They also give special attention to the defenses counselees use to ward off anxiety and guilt and to the therapeutic relationship. Wolberg places all of the varieties of psychoanalysis and psychoanalytically-oriented therapy as well as transactional methods of therapy in this reconstructive category.

These therapies lend themselves to the explicit use of Scripture in varying degrees. Therapists can incorporate scriptural principles into transactional models and some of the more interpersonally-oriented approaches to counseling in much the same way as in reeducational therapies. Reconstructive therapies that are built largely around the transference relationship and the attempt to work through repressed feelings of dependency, hostility, and fear, however, do not lend themselves as readily to an explicit use of Scripture. There are at least two reasons for this. To begin with, these therapies believe that a great deal of the cure of pathology comes from the resolution of past conflicts with parents and significant others as relived in the therapeutic relationship. To revive these conflicts, the therapist adopts a neutral therapeutic stance. This neutral stance, the frequency of the therapeutic sessions (two to five times per week), and sometimes the patient's reclining on the couch, all promote a controlled regression in which patients begin to experience the same feelings toward the therapist that they experienced toward parents and others in early life.

Although this neutrality involves a warm and sensitive concern for the welfare of the client, any advice or sharing of the therapist's values or beliefs interferes with the client's ability to transfer the attitudes he holds to key people in his life onto the therapist and consequently short circuits the therapeutic process. It makes it difficult for the counselee to react to the therapist like other key people in his past or present environment because the therapist has taken on a strong stance of his own. The therapist, in other words, is no longer a neutral person. Although we now realize that there is no such thing as a completely neutral therapist, psychoanalysts still try to remain as neutral as possible and to avoid any kind of direction or advice that would interfere with the process of transference.

A second reason some reconstructive therapies do not lend themselves to a sharing of scriptural insights has to do with the resolution of feelings of dependency and hostility. Therapists of this orientation assume that any form of advice or offering of solutions tends to reinforce the counselee's dependency and interfere with the analysis of the patient's conflicts over feelings of helplessness and consequent resentment.[19]

For the above reasons, Christian therapists following reconstructive models of therapy tend to bring their Christian understanding of guilt and other problems to bear on their *conceptualization* of the counselee's needs and the counseling process more than in their specific *verbalizations.* Consequently

---

[19]Client-centered therapists face this same dilemma.

many engage in little if any explicit introducing of biblical material into the counseling process. They feel free to discuss spiritual or biblical issues if the counselee brings them up, but they will not initiate the process and will not offer advice of any kind.

A PERSONAL PERSPECTIVE

Since this is not primarily a book on psychotherapeutic technique, I will not go into any more depth on the possible ways of using Scripture in the counseling process. Before leaving the topic, however, I would like to share my own viewpoint. I do this with some hesitancy because I am aware that some will probably find my viewpoint to be too weak on the use of Scripture and others may find it too strong. If my personal perspective helps stimulate serious dialogue on either the appropriateness of using Scripture in therapy or on specific ways of bringing biblical concepts into counseling, however, I will be rewarded.

After fifteen years of counseling, including supportive, reeducative, and reconstructive therapy, I am convinced that effective therapy includes (1) a quality relationship between the counselor and the counselee, (2) the counselee's learning to face truth, especially the truth about himself, in a nondefensive manner, and (3) the resolution of the client's tension (anxiety and/or guilt) between who he is and who he wants or ought to be. As long as we lack a safe and caring relationship, the courage to really know ourselves, or a resolution to the distance between our ideals and our concrete reality, there can be little growth. If these are the crucial ingredients of therapy we will do all we can to be individuals who provide these needed therapeutic conditions and we will also be committed to helping counselees find the truth about themselves. Since Scripture is a significant source of truth about ourselves I would like individuals that I work with in therapy to be familiar with the truths of Scripture that speak to their needs. If a counselee already has a knowledge of biblical truth relating to his problem, I do not attempt to cover that same ground again. Instead, when issues of biblical revelation arise (such as the distinction between guilt and constructive sorrow or the fact that the believer is no longer under condemnation), I attempt to help them deal with why they seem unable or unwilling to appropriate the biblical truth they already know intellectually.

On the other hand, if a counselee is not aware of some biblical data that is relevant to his or her problem I introduce that material as I do any other helpful information. I am committed to helping counselees learn to face reality and see the truth about themselves, and they cannot do this if we ignore such a significant source of reality as the Scripture. Just as all therapists' interventions are guided by basic theoretical assumptions about the nature of man, the nature of and conditions for growth and healing, so are mine. I see no fundamental reason for a Christian therapist to be any more hesitant to bring scriptural resources to bear on a counselee's needs than a psychoanalyst is in relying on his understanding of the Oedipus complex, a client-centered therapist's understanding of the organismic valuing system and the client's supposed ability to trust himself fully, or a rational-emotive therapist's challenging of what he views as irrational ideas (including the belief in God)!

If secular theorists do not hesitate to be guided in their therapy by their theory, certainly we Christians need not hesitate to do the same. Frankly, I think a lot of Christian counselors have been sold a "bill of goods." We have been told by secular therapists that it is unethical to allow our values and scriptural understandings to influence our therapy, while at the same time these therapists have gone merrily on their way indoctrinating clients with their own beliefs in humanity's basic goodness, the belief that problems are largely environmentally induced, the belief that there either is no God or, if there is, that He is irrelevant to their problems, and with the belief that if they are really disturbed they are sick, not sinful. It is high time we started challenging these assumptions explicitly in our therapy, and the therapy of guilt is one of the most obvious places to begin. In our final chapter we will look at some specific scriptural principles that can be incorporated into our counseling practice with individuals experiencing feelings of guilt.

SUMMARY

For over thirty years mental health professionals have assumed that values and moral or religious issues should not be brought into therapy. An evaluation of this perspective, however, reveals that it is impossible to avoid bringing values into therapy and that in many ways psychotherapy is a moral enterprise. Although all counselors (including Christians) need to avoid authoritarian interactions and need to encourage client exploration and responsibility, it is not only appropriate but extremely helpful to bring scriptural insights into counseling. We do this with a sensitivity to our own personalities, the leading of the Holy Spirit and the needs of our own counselees.

 21

Psychotherapy, Guilt, and Grace

In chapter 18 we discussed principles of guilt reduction that are common to all effective counseling. The biblical principles discussed there, since they are similar to insights of secular psychologists, could be labeled *compatible*. These insights include the need for an accepting, noncondemning relationship, an uncovering of repressed guilt, and the relinquishing of unrealistic ideals. Since these contributions are not unique to Christianity and since we have discussed them previously, we will only briefly note them here. I would like to remind the reader, however, that we should not neglect their presence in biblical revelation.

Long before the insights of modern psychology, people were being healed because of the proper functioning of the body of Christ and the application of these biblical truths. In studying the contributions of psychological research and theory to our understanding of personality we need to remember that all of these insights did not originate in the twentieth century! The fact that non-Christians have come to some scriptural insights is a testimony to God's revealing Himself both through His Word and through His creation. Since God is the creator of the personality and the endower of our intellectual gifts, it is natural that non-Christians (using the intellect God gave them) will discover many dynamics of the functioning of personality. In fact, to the degree that guilt feelings grow out of natural developmental processes and experiences we should expect non-Christians to be able to comprehend them.

When we critiqued the naturalizers, humanizers, and glorifiers of conscience, we drew on a second category of biblical insights. This category of contributions includes the insights Scripture offers that contradict or correct secular theories and assumptions. Just as the Bible supports the importance of accepting relationships and the uncovering of repressed guilt common to many secular theorists, for example, it also leads us to reject such views as the belief that guilt feelings are simply the result of environmental factors. It also rejects attempts at reducing guilt through improving behavior or lowering one's standards. Although this category of contributions is also not totally distinctive it does help crystalize a more accurate and comprehensive view of the dynamics of guilt. Since these contributions were discussed when we reviewed the naturalizers, humanizers, and glorifiers of conscience, we will simply list several of these contradictory insights in summary form.

1. The knowledge that approaches to guilt reduction based on improved behavior are inadequate.
2. The awareness that views tracing the origin of guilt solely to the environment are inadequate.
3. The knowledge that lowering one's standards will not in itself resolve guilt feelings.
4. The awareness that children are not born innately good or morally neutral and that this has implications for our understanding of guilt.

In this chapter I want to consider a third, more explicit category of biblical contributions for understanding guilt. If we label the first category of biblical contributions *compatible* because they are essentially the same as those of good psychology, and the second category *contradictory* because they contrast with some secular viewpoints, we could label this third group of insights *complementary*. This category includes the unique contributions that the Bible makes to our understanding of guilt that go beyond secular thinking but are consistent with all true insights and therefore complement the accurate insights of secular psychological views. These insights go beyond what we know of guilt from naturalistic study, put the knowledge we gain from naturalistic study in a broader perspective, and explain the ultimate origin and solution of problems of guilt. In this way they tend to address guilt feelings that are intrinsic in their origin rather than those that are internalized. We have already mentioned most of these contributions as we have attempted to lay out a biblical view of guilt in earlier chapters. At this point, however, I would like to pull these key biblical concepts together to demonstrate the important role they can play in the therapy of guilt. In doing this I will not be writing a treatise on counseling technique but rather on basic truths or principles that can be incorporated when working with people from a variety of therapeutic styles or approaches.

THE REALITY OF OBJECTIVE GUILT

The most fundamental contribution the Bible makes to our understanding of guilt is the realization that guilt feelings are ultimately rooted in objective guilt. Feelings of self-condemnation and punishment, no matter how subjective and neurotic, witness to an important reality—the reality that we are objectively guilty. We are not functioning the way we were created to function. We are sinful and our sinfulness is both a violation of our created natures and an offense toward God.

The guilt that Adam and Eve experienced when they sinned was not the result of an inadequate socialization process. It was the result of a major shift in their personalities that came with the autonomous assertion of their wills against God. Rather than accepting their position as created beings and finding their identity in their relationship with God, they took upon themselves the task of building their own autonomous identity. The moment this happened they ceased to function as integrated persons. They experienced a horrendous gap between who they were and who they were created to be. And they immediately set upon an effort to close this gap and the gap between themselves and God. Although the sins of parents and others strongly impact the development of guilt feelings they do not account for either this basic split in man or the self-atoning nature of guilt feelings. We must be careful not to view (or let clients view) this condition of guilt as simply a static legal condition they are in. Our condition of guilt is not simply a state of guilt before God. It is an ongoing, active process in which we continue trying to carry out Adam and Eve's autonomous approach to life.

With Christian counselees, the reality of objective guilt may be self-evident and little therapeutic time may need to be spent on this fact. In my experience, however, even professing Christians with a rather thorough knowledge of the concepts of sin, guilt, and salvation frequently fail to apply these concepts to their own psychic functioning, especially their experience of psychological guilt. They may readily attribute their problems (including guilt) to sin, but they don't know *how* or *why* guilty feelings relate to sin. They don't understand the nature of the split in their personality that leads them both to try to earn peace of conscience through self-effort and pay for their failures through guilt. Since they feel more guilty than most people, they also tend to single themselves out as being especially bad or sinful.

Depending on my client's dynamics, the type of therapy I am doing, and the point at which we are working in therapy, I sometimes say things like, "The tension you are describing seems to be part of the human struggle between what we were created to be and what we are." or "Your guilt feelings seem to grow out of a struggle that comes with being aware we are not all we could be (or were created to be)." All I am attempting to do at this point is orient my client and begin to put his or her guilt feelings into a broader perspective. Later in therapy we will move beyond this general concept to some of the specific dynamics, especially the workings of my client's omnipotent desires and self-atoning dynamics.

With non-Christian counselees, the setting we are working in and the way we hold ourselves out to the public will influence the way we bring biblical concepts into therapy. If we are pastors or counselors, work in a church clinic, or hold ourselves out as Christian therapists, it is easy to initiate a discussion of biblical principles. When a new client is struggling with guilt feelings I occasionally say something like, "As you know, I'm a Christian counselor. As I understand the Bible, your guilt feelings would seem to have some basis in fact. Perhaps the reason you're feeling guilty is that you *are* guilty." Then I mention some of their apparent moral failures or sinful attitudes that appear to be related to their guilt. In each instance I am suggesting a connection between my clients' guilt feelings and their behavior or attitudes. If a client is open to this viewpoint, I will either pursue it further (to the point of sharing the forgiveness available through Christ) or wait until a more appropriate time and do so.

If a client rejects or sees the concept of objective guilt as irrelevant I simply move on to whatever other issues concern the client. To the degree that their guilt feelings are the result of less than healthy parent-child interaction, I can still offer a great deal of help with their guilt. If my client is open, however, I want to help him or her face this piece of reality in order to grow toward emotional health and wholeness and to become open to the grace and acceptance of God. I do not do this in an authoritarian and manipulative way that violates a counselee's free choice, but I do share it. Depending on our own therapeutic approach and individuality, we may share this insight by way of personal testimony, through suggested readings, through a reading or sharing of Scripture or through a combination of these and other means. I believe we have a responsibility to attempt to lead our counselees to the ultimate source of their guilt, since not to do so implies that we believe naturalistic factors are a sufficient explanation. To me, this is intellectually dishonest as well as being less than thorough psychotherapy. It is failing to confront a counselee with a very important piece of reality. It also misses an opportunity to lay a foundation for introducing a person to his maker.

GOD-PLAYING AND GUILT FEELINGS

Although a number of theoretical perspectives stress the importance of analyzing and modifying unrealistic ideals, no secular theory can provide an ultimate explanation of the process. In pointing out the impact of unrealistic parental standards and of grandiose childhood fantasies, secular theories provide some crucial therapeutic guidance. But in helping clients see that beyond these unrealistic expectations lies an even deeper instinct of self-worship, we give them a much deeper understanding of their guilt and a greater sense of personal responsibility for their unrealistic goals. We help them see that their grandiose standards are actually the opposite of humility and reflect an attempt to lift themselves above others in pride.

A biblical understanding of the nature of God-playing also helps explain why some people are so reluctant to give up their grandiose standards. It is not simply the security function these omnipotent processes provide by attempting to maintain the love of significant others. It is also our prideful desire to be number one. We simply do not want to acknowledge the real limitations we have as human beings. I find that when clients begin to grasp this insight they experience a significant sense of relief and hope because they realize they are not simply the victims of others' unrealistic standards and pressures. They experience an increased sense of dignity and inner strength as they begin to see how their own pride contributes to their feelings of guilt.

I have also found the timing of this insight to be crucial. To tell counselees early in therapy in the throes of deep depression and self-condemnation that they are really rejecting Christ's atonement and trying to be like God may drive them deeper into depression. It can also come across as simply more condemnation or as more of the same old thing: "Your problem is that you are sinful!" But when counselees begin to experience caring and acceptance and to work through some of the anger at those who held out unrealistic standards, they are generally ready to look at their own responsibility without such intense self-condemnation. I have helped some clients look at this dynamic by saying something like, "We have talked a lot about the pressure your parents (or teacher or church) put on you as a child but I sense there's more to it than that. It seems that even though their expectations didn't fit you, you really wanted to believe you could fill them. In fact, I'm of the impression that even if your parents *hadn't* held out any unrealistic goals, you would have developed some on your own!" This observation typically opens up the whole area of my counselee's own goals and wishes and god-like aspirations.

An analysis of the desire to cling to unrealistic expectations may also lead to the topic of humility. Since biblical humility is rooted in a realistic self-evaluation that takes into consideration both our significance as bearers of the image of God and our finiteness and fallenness as created beings,[1] the giving up of god-like aspirations helps clients move naturally in this direction. Biblical humility, rather than reinforcing neurotic self-degradation, leads to a balanced and healthy self-esteem that allows us to see ourselves as God sees us. This acceptance of our actual condition reduces the likelihood of further guilt because we are not striving to be something we are not. It also leads to constructive sorrow when we see that we fall short of God's desires.

[1]Rom. 12:3-8.

THE SOURCE OF GUILT FEELINGS

At the same time we want counselees to realize their guilt feelings ultimately stem from their sinful condition and their attempt to unify their lives on the basis of self-effort, it is also helpful for them to know that guilt feelings do not come from God. This is important because so many Christians equate guilt feelings with divine conviction and end up seeing God as the author of psychological guilt. Consequently they assume guilt feelings reflect a kind of divine justice and believe the solution lies simply in confession and altered behavior that will make God realize that you have suffered enough and stop convicting you. Because these people see their guilt feelings as coming from God, they tend to (1) make no distinction between godly (or constructive) sorrow and psychological guilt, (2) be unaware of the influence of developmental factors on the functioning of guilt and conscience, (3) overlook the fundamental nature of guilt as self-atonement or self-punishment, (4) be unaware of the fallibility of conscience, (5) see guilt reduction as an instantaneous process, and (6) conclude that since they experience more guilt than others they must be more sinful.

Some Christian counselees receive great relief when they understand that their guilt feelings do not come from God. When a counselee has grown up in a legalistic or guilt-inducing environment, I may simply say, "You know, you talk a lot about your sins and guilt as though you think you *should* be feeling guilty. Are you aware that the word *guilt* is never used as an emotion in the New Testament and that Christians are *never* commanded to feel guilty?" The counselee's response to this question usually opens up an opportunity to explore his or her theological misconceptions. The knowledge that guilt feelings are not the God-given result of divine conviction allows our counselees to begin exploring both the environmental sources of their guilt and their own omnipotent efforts at self-atonement. As this happens clients can begin to move beyond the superficial belief that guilt feelings are the direct result of specific personal sins to an understanding of how guilt develops both from being sinned against (by parents and others) and from our own grandiose expectations and self-punishments. This broadens the counselee's understanding of the source and nature of guilt and opens up avenues for change.

CONFESSION AND REPENTANCE

Another way of expressing these concepts is to say that until counselees move beyond simple confession of specific sins to true repentance over god-playing and self-atoning behavior, and to an understanding of the developmental origins of their guilt, they will never have full release from guilt. I am of the impression that one reason some Christian therapists hesitate to share biblical insights into the healing of guilt lies precisely here. They are aware that the repeated confession of sin and the quoting of 1 John 1:9 has for some clients become simply a religious ritual that obscures rather than reveals deeper conflicts and guilt. Not wanting to promote repression, ignore the deeper disturbances, or offer what may be seen as a superficial solution they ignore the Bible's potential contributions to the therapy of guilt and turn almost exclusively to naturalistic psychological perspectives in their attempts to be helpful.

The understanding of guilt I have attempted to present here allows us to go beyond basic biblical truths such as the reality of objective guilt and the need for confession to the fact that guilt feelings do not come from God, to the developmental processes that contribute to guilt feelings and to the deep instincts of pride and self-atonement lying at the core of guilt. They allow us to resolve repression rather than reinforce it. And they explain why much confession doesn't work. The reason is many people simply confess specific known *sins* in order to gain forgiveness rather than admitting that their entire nature is oriented to doing what *they* want and that they need a radical change in the way they approach their identity and self-acceptance. Their confessions, in other words, can be a way of manipulating God and of avoiding facing deeper sin. These confessions are temporary ways of "getting God off our backs," rather than really changing our behavior because they do not involve deep repentance that admits our total inability to meet God's holy standards and the futility of trying to merit either God's acceptance or our own. Only this level of repentance and change can begin to break up the self-glorifying functioning of conscience.

JUSTIFICATION AND REGENERATION

Most of our discussions of the Bible's contributions to the resolution of guilt are based on the fact of Christ's atoning death.
Christ's atonement and our appropriation of God's forgiveness
through salvation are clearly the central biblical concepts relating
to guilt. For starters, the atonement removes the external threat
of condemnation that is a realistic source of fear in the life of the
person outside the circle of faith. "There is therefore now no condemnation to them that are in Christ Jesus,"[2] and Christ is the
"propitiation (satisfaction) for our sins."[3] This radical change in
our standing before God often has an immediate and direct impact not only on fear but also on the reduction of guilt feelings.
If God does not condemn us, we need not condemn ourselves. I
recall one counselee who had been in therapy for several weeks.
She walked in and excitedly told me what her pastor had said the
previous Sunday. Preaching in Romans, he had made the simple
statement, "*God* is not ashamed of *you*." Somehow that struck her
deeply as she relayed, "I've *always* thought God would be ashamed
of me!" While this young lady had many other issues to work
through, that insight was a turning point in her attitude toward
herself. Although she knew all about the doctrine of justification
theologically, it had never struck her in a personal way.

An often neglected dynamic growing out of the atonement is
the inner shift, or reorientation, of the self that happens at the
moment of regeneration or rebirth. Although we cannot fully comprehend this change, it is clear that the spiritual new birth involves
much more than a change in our judicial condition. Too often
Protestant Christianity, in stressing the doctrine of justification
and reacting to the Roman Catholic view of justification, has neglected the fact that human nature is indeed changed at the moment of spiritual birth. M. R. Gordon, for example, in his discussion
of regeneration in *The New Bible Dictionary*, claims, "It would be
safe to say that there is no change in the personality itself; the

[2]Rom. 8:1 (KJV).
[3] John 2:2 (KJV).

person is the same."[4]

Although Gordon goes on to say the person is controlled differently since the new birth (the Holy Spirit instead of sin), this seems to miss the point both biblically and psychologically. The Bible sees the process of regeneration as so important that we are labelled new creatures.[5] Although the outward evidence of this change is not always as radical as we would like, I am of the impression that if there has not been a fundamental inner change in the personality, there has been no regeneration. Just as in physical birth, spiritual birth has both a major continuity and a fundamental discontinuity. In most regards, the newly born person (physical or spiritual) is the same. Our physical attributes are not altered and our temperaments are generally not significantly different. But inwardly a fundamental change has taken place that can begin to effect major alterations in the personality.

I believe the core of this change has to do with a new attitude toward ourselves that grows out of our acknowledging God's omnipotence and our creatureliness. Prior to conversion, we each live our lives in god-like fashion. We operate on the assumption that our lives are what we make of them. Living on this assumption puts the responsibility for healing our inner sense of division or disunity squarely on our own shoulders. *We* are responsible for living up to our own standards and if *we* fall short *we* are the ones who pay. Unfortunately, the only means we have for achieving this task are those of the law or autonomous self-effort.

In the process of regeneration we acknowledge our sinfulness and separation from God and our inability to close either the gap between ourselves and God or between the people we are and what we aspire to be. This lays a foundation for a radical change that can effect the total personality and especially feelings of guilt. We say for the first time, "I cannot be what I want or ought to be on my own." This acceptance of our finitude and sinfulness includes yielding to God both the definition of who we are (or would like to be) and the right to inflict punishment on ourselves when we fall short. In other words, by giving up our grandiose self-

[4]M. R. Gordon, "Regeneration," in *The New Bible Dictionary*, J. D. Douglas, ed. (Grand Rapids: Eerdmans, 1962), p. 1081.

[5]2 Cor. 5:17.

expectations and our attempts at atoning for our own sin through self-inflicted punishments we experience a radical shift in our inner life and a lifting of the burden of psychological guilt.

Although it is impossible to fully comprehend, the vast majority of Christians can attest to the fact that while their lives are not all they would like them to be (or perhaps in some instances little of what they should be!) there is an awareness of who they are in relation to God that did not exist before regeneration. I believe that awareness grows out of the fundamental core of regeneration and reflects the knowledge that we are inwardly different. We know who we are (as spiritual children) in relationship to our heavenly Father. This fact, and our awareness of it, has a humbling effect and is the ultimate foundation for giving up the entire process of alternately hiding and paying for our sins and for accepting the truth about ourselves in a balanced, constructive manner.

Although some people receive drastic relief from *internalized* feelings of guilt through therapy that does not involve an explicit Christian witness, there is a limitation to how far this relief can go. Even though we may free people from many punitive internalized guilt feelings, we cannot eliminate sin. And as long as we have unredeemed sin in an unreconciled individual, we will have a person who has to struggle with *intrinsically* derived feelings of guilt. The non-Christian may analyze his internalized perfectionistic standards and self-punitive attitudes. And he may take in both more realistic standards and more loving, corrective attitudes by identifying with a loving and accepting counselor. But he can never experience the depth of freedom that comes from accepting God's unconditional, unmerited acceptance, which totally removes the need to perform in order to be accepted or suffer to atone. At a deep level every human being knows we're not what we should be. We also have an awareness that we are judged for our failure and that sin should be paid for. Only an acceptance of Christ's work resolves that intrinsic problem.

Since many guilt feelings are caused partly by the reinternalizing of our own hostility, learning to handle our anger in a constructive biblical manner also helps resolve guilt. While it is beyond our current scope to discuss the scriptural contributions to handling anger, I would like to briefly mention two key biblical concepts involving anger. The first is the necessity of overcoming our repressions and honestly admitting to and facing our anger. The second is the principle of recognizing the sovereignty of God and the fact that "Vengeance is Mine, I will repay, says the Lord" (Rom. 12:19). As we are increasingly honest with ourselves and God and see life from this perspective, we can learn to face and resolve our anger in a way that does not reinforce our feelings of guilt.

Unfortunately many Christians are not experiencing the fruit of their regeneration and justification. They may know the doctrines, and they may even have overcome their fear of the judgments of God through a knowledge of their position as forgiven children. But theirs is an *interpersonal* reconciliation. They have not carried over the results of justification into their inner lives and consequently are still troubled by feelings of guilt. The solution to this only comes with an *intrapersonal* realization that we can no more satisfy our consciences than we can satisfy a holy God. We must give up trying to merit self-acceptance or self-atonement just the way we gave up trying to earn God's acceptance. We must, in other words, *apply* the doctrine of justification to our inner lives and our intrinsic guilt. Jesus Christ has paid for our sins so we are free from the need to work, defend, or atone, no matter what our failures.

GUILT AND GODLY SORROW

During the course of effective therapy many counselees go through an apparently paradoxical experience of becoming *more* aware of their sins and failures yet feeling *less* guilty. This increased awareness of sinfulness and decreased feeling of guilt, however, generally does not take place in isolation. It is accompanied by an increase of godly sorrow. Without this, therapy would be promoting a movement toward sociopathic or psychopathic functioning. We would see our failures but not be troubled by them; we could continue to act out our sinful desires. Instead of this, however, clients undergoing effective therapy tend to develop an increased measure of godly sorrow that replaces their previous guilt emotion. Their appreciation to their therapists for loving patience, acceptance, and confrontation, their increased sensitivity to the needs and rights of others, and their deepened comprehension of the grace and love of God help them become more loving and committed to a life of integrity and responsibility. Figure 13 illustrates the shift from guilt motivation to an identity based morality operating from godly sorrow that should occur in counseling. The solid line represents feelings of godly sorrow and the broken line feelings of guilt.

Since after therapy we are still sinners, the analysis and resolution of guilt are only a beginning. The resolution of guilt accompanying the end of therapy turns out to be the beginning of a path of loving constructive sorrow. That is not a continuous feeling but it is an experience we have when we undergo divine conviction.

Figure 14

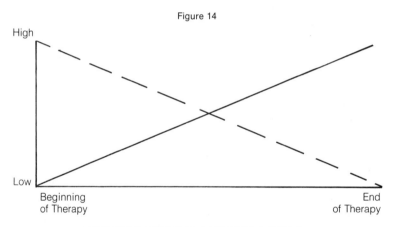

| High | | |
| Low | Beginning of Therapy | End of Therapy |

A FOUNDATION FOR PERSONAL WORTH

In early chapters I attempted to demonstrate how problems of inadequate self-esteem grow out of the judgments of conscience and can be considered one of the main ingredients of psychological guilt. Although our focus here is not largely on solutions to inadequate self-esteem we must address this issue if we are to be most helpful to those struggling with guilt.

Although I am less than satisfied with Oden's understanding of the therapeutic processes as simply a living out of God's unconditional valuing of the individual, I am in hearty agreement with his stress on the ultimate ground of humanity's sense of dignity and worth and the centrality of communicating that sense of worth in the therapeutic process. In fact, the ability of many secular therapists to be therapeutically helpful lies in this very fact. This success perplexes some Christians (so much that some even deny their success!) because they cannot understand how an emotional healing process can be stimulated by non-Christian therapists. This concern is based on a misunderstanding of the therapeutic process that overvalues its cognitive ingredients and ends up with precisely the opposite dilemma that Oden's emphasis on an "implicit" communication of God's unconditional acceptance creates. Christians who believe non-Christian counselors cannot be helpful are implying that there is no meaningful sense of worth or acceptance communicated apart from an explicit proclamation of the gospel. This view minimizes the relational aspect of therapy and the impact of common grace just as Oden's view minimizes the importance of a cognitive awareness and the sharing of the content of special revelation.

One distinct advantage of utilizing scriptural resources in therapy lies in our ability to formulate the ultimate ground or source of our counselees' right to a sense of worth or value. Both in our own understanding of the worth of the individual and in our verbal communication we can have a sense of consistency since we see every individual as created in the image of God and as an object of God's redemptive plan. The non-Christian may offer acceptance and communicate a valuing of the individual but this valuing is not based on as stable or as consistent a foundation. It can be built on the view that the counselee is "privately acceptable to the therapist as a human being,"[6] or on a philosophical view that attempts to place a high value on the human person even though we are seen as chance beings who are the result of an accidental collocation of atoms. But it cannot communicate nearly as deep a sense of dignity as the biblical view of personhood. Ultimately a solid sense of identity comes from knowing who one is in the eyes of his or her Creator!

[6]Oden, *Kerygma and Counseling* (Philadelphia: Westminster, 1966), p. 22.

Conclusion

In the opening chapter I shared the struggle I had as a young Christian psychologist in relating my psychological and biblical understandings of guilt. I had been reared to believe that most (if not all) guilt feelings came from God. But my psychological training and experience in counseling suggested that most (if not all) guilt feelings were unhealthy and counterproductive! To resolve that conflict I undertook this biblical and psychological study of guilt.

I began my study with the confidence that since God is the source of all knowledge and that truth cannot ultimately conflict, there must be a way of deepening or correcting either my biblical or psychological understanding to resolve this apparent conflict. That assurance has been fully met by an understanding of the scriptural distinction between objective guilt, guilt feelings, and godly sorrow, and by deepened insight into the self-atoning nature of guilt feelings, the dynamics of early infancy that are the soil of later developed guilt feelings, and the potentially dynamic impact of Christ's atonement in resolving the anxiety and guilt we experience over being less than we were created to be. For me this has been a rich and meaningful study.

In this day of personal lostness and alienation we cannot afford to neglect the deep problems people face, to abdicate depth therapy to those limited by their naturalistic assumptions about life, or to offer superficial spiritual solutions. We must be willing to grapple deeply with both the needs of the human soul and the concrete ways that faith in Christ confronts those needs. I will be greatly rewarded if this book serves as a stimulus for others to explore the riches of God's Word for the in-depth transformation of the personality.

Appendix 1: Beyond Guilt in Parenting and Preaching

In spite of the teaching of the Bible on guilt and conscience, many Christians continue to believe guilt feelings come from God and many parents, pastors, and teachers make regular use of guilt motivation to stimulate others to desired behavior. In this appendix I would like to look at few implications of the scriptural understanding of guilt and conscience for motivation—especially as it relates to the work of parents and pastors. I do this because I am convinced that many educators, parents, and Christian leaders have some serious distortions of the biblical view of motivation and unwittingly place people under a burden of guilt and condemnation. In failing to grasp the omnipotent processes of self-atonement underlying guilt they reinforce rather than resolve problems of conscience. To see how this can be avoided I will briefly mention six general principles that grow out of biblical view of guilt and conscience. Then we will look in greater detail at alternatives to guilt in parenting and preaching.

BASIC PRINCIPLES

Since some of the processes of conscience reflect fallen humanity's efforts to satisfy itself through works and self-atonement, we must avoid glorifying the work of conscience and reinforcing humanity's tendency to turn to his own solution to inner disunity and guilt.

For pastors, teachers, counselors, and parents this means ways must be found to hold out biblical ideals and motivate growth without implying that the fulfillment of these ideals is a way of resolving guilt or providing a sense of inner unity. Although we are called to motivate others to maturity, we must be careful not to suggest that behavioral change is a biblical means of resolving guilt or building self-esteem. We need to follow a motivational approach that communicates the fact that acceptance, forgiveness, and self-regard are the rights of every person who trusts in Christ and that proper behavior flows *from* these inner attitudes rather than by a means of earning them.

> *Since the ideals of conscience can be developed and influenced by others (1 Cor. 8-10), and since some of our ideals come from man's goal of becoming like God (Gen. 1-3), we need to help people ferret out which of their aspirations are God-given and which are not.*

Perfectionistic persons with impossible, neurotic expectations are often laboring under the false assumption that their goals are divinely given, while depressed and dependent people often live under unbearable guilt because of their inability to measure up to the standards of parents, society, or a Christian subculture. Tragically, these standards frequently do not represent the voice of God at all! And even Christians highly absorbed in doing God's will and becoming Christ-like are sometimes unknowingly trying to reach a perfectionist ideal that denies their humanity and contradicts the fact that Christian maturity doesn't happen overnight. Spiritual teachings that emphasize the importance of one or more crisis encounters or a once-and-for-all spiritual experience over an ongoing growth process are especially likely to reinforce this tendency.

> *Since the knowing function of conscience can be seriously distorted through either excusing thoughts (Rom. 2:15) or the searing of conscience (1 Tim. 4:2), helpful parents, pastors, teachers, and counselors will help unmask the distorted thinking and defensive patterns people use to avoid seeing the nature and extent of their sinfulness and their failure to live up to the biblical standards.*

Some people believe they can free others from neurotic guilt feelings by not preaching or teaching on sin. But precisely the opposite is true. Until people experience conviction that helps them see their sinful patterns they will experience the negative results of unconscious guilt. Only when hidden sinful attitudes and actions are brought to light can we receive release from guilt.

Since the conscience may be educated (or miseducated) we may need to help people become aware of the significant influences in their personal history.

Since distorted functions of conscience were typically learned in intimate parent-child relationships, they probably will not be unlearned without insight into these relationships and without significant new, more positive personal relationships. People who have learned unbiblical expectations from parents, and those who have internalized condemning corrective attitudes can gain freedom when they understand the developmental influences on their punitive or overly strict consciences. This is an area where the fellowship of the body of Christ in loving and forgiving one another helps incorporate spiritual truth. It is also one of the most significant healing processes in effective psychotherapy.

We need to help people develop a biblical alternative to punitive feelings of psychological guilt and the self-atoning processes of conscience.

In all of our counseling, teaching, and parenting we need to communicate to those troubled by psychological guilt that their feelings are self-destructive and that there are better ways of being motivated to desired behavior. We need to model loving, self-corrective attitudes and lead others to see the difference between the two.

GUILT IN PARENTING

Recently I was watching our daughter play a Saturday morning soccer game. Standing near the goal I overheard two twelve-year-old girls on the other team discussing their coach. "I think I'll quit!" the first girl said. "All she ever does is yell!" "Me too," the other girl chimed in. "She *never* tells us when we do *anything* right!"

Listening to their coach I quickly understood what the girls meant. She was throwing out a constant round of commands and condemnations. "What's the matter, Sheri?" she would yell. "Wake up and get in the game!" "That's your fault, Kari; you should have been in position," or "I don't believe it, Jill; can't you do anything right?" Not surprisingly, the morale of that entire team was low.

Then I started paying attention to our daughter's coach. He, too, was yelling constantly. "Nice pass, Debbie," he yelled at our daughter. "Good teamwork, Kim." "Way to hustle, Rachael." "Keep at it, Carol; you'll get it next time." And when our girls came off the field at half time, our coach had an encouraging word for every child! What a difference! One team enjoyed themselves and knew their coach was for them, win or lose. The other was discouraged and defeated. Their coach didn't know how to encourage them; so all she did was criticize.

This coach displayed four key ingredients of guilt motivation. By constantly criticizing and telling her girls what to do she held out *unrealistic expectations*. Twelve-year-old girls cannot be expected to *always* stay in position or to *never* miss a kick. The coach's *anger* was another potential source of guilt. Children who live with this kind of threat and motivation generally incorporate these hostile attitudes into their own self-corrective system. This coach was also *shaming* and *condemning* her players. She was in effect telling them, "You are inadequate!" And her tone of voice clearly communicated that she felt they should be punished. All of these reactions tend to connect with the child's inherent tendencies to self-punishment and create serious feelings of guilt.

Parents wishing to rear children with a minimal amount of guilt will attempt to react precisely opposite to this coach. They will hold out realistic expectations that are consistent with their children's God-given talents and developmental levels. They will correct their children in love instead of anger. And they will not shame and condemn them. In essence, they will learn to discipline their children by grace instead of law. Under law acceptance is conditional to our behavior, blessings must be earned and punishment comes with failure. Under grace acceptance is unconditional, blessings are freely bestowed, and there is loving discipline instead of punishment.

Since most of us become angry and resort to guilt motivation when our children disobey or fail to carry out their responsibilities, one of the best ways of avoiding guilt motivation is to learn to discipline firmly and consistently. Since this is not a book on child rearing we will not go into specifics. I would suggest, however, that parents must come up with alternatives to repeatedly nagging children: "Feed the dog," "Brush your teeth," or "Make your bed," and to finally punishing or threatening them in anger. These comments instill self-doubt and create resentment and guilt. To overcome this style of parent-child interaction, we need to learn to encourage our children, to help them develop a regular schedule of responsibilities with clear consequences for failure to carry them out. Always talk respectfully with children. If a policy is set, for example, that children do not eat breakfast unless (or until) their morning chores are completed, most children will quickly learn to carry out their responsibilities without the nagging pressures or condemnations that stir anxiety, resentment, and guilt. And since a set consequence has already been established, we are less likely to respond in anger and condemnation.

The following guidelines can help parents avoid instilling unnecessary feelings of guilt in their children.

1. Set realistic standards appropriate for the child's developmental level, unique gifts, and personality.
2. Communicate respect.
3. Discipline consistently.
4. Correct in love instead of anger.
5. Accept responsibility for our part in family conflicts instead of blaming the children.
6. Avoid shaming or condemnation, which usually only occurs when we are angry.
7. Be encouraging and supportive.
8. Model openness, honesty, and godly sorrow.

GUILT IN PREACHING

When I was a child in Sunday school we used to sing:

> Oh, be careful little feet where you go,
> Oh, be careful little feet where you go.
> For the Father up above
> Is looking down in love,
> So be careful little feet where you go.

Then we sang additional verses of, "Be careful little hands what you do," and "Be careful little eyes what you see." As a sensitive child I remember the image of God those verses helped create. I pictured God up in heaven watching every move I made. I knew he loved me but the clear message was, "You better be very, very careful of everything you see and do and everywhere you go or God will be upset with you!" By themselves, verses like these are harmless—or potentially even helpful. They don't necessarily instill serious feelings of guilt or fear because some children pick up more on the fact that God is looking on us *in love* than that he is rigidly scrutinizing our every step. But for sensitive children, especially those who are the recipients of much parental anger and guilt motivation and for those who sit under some fear or guilt-inducing teaching, songs like this can clearly contribute to the development of fear and guilt.

Certainly as adults many of us have sat through sermons, offerings (especially those for starving orphans or for the building fund that is seriously behind schedule), or missionary challenges that left us feeling guilty or condemned. One of my clients, for example, told me how a youth pastor tried to motivate him to take a leadership role in the church. Although my client was already over his head in studies and other responsibilities, the pastor told him, "You will quench the Holy Spirit and the blood of the people will be on your head!" Although most guilt motivation is less subtle than this, many Christians receive periodical messages implying, "You are basically failing, and you ought to feel guilty if you don't do better."

Years ago my wife and I joined a church near our home. We liked the pastor and the people and the church had a good program for our children. We become involved and were soon teaching a class. After several months, however, we both started feeling a bit disappointed and discouraged about our church. We couldn't put our finger on it but just knew that we weren't leaving church spiritually and personally refreshed. As we looked at both our own lives and our experience at church we finally realized what was troubling us. Although our pastor was a very likeable and dedicated person who was also a good speaker, he was scolding the congregation in every message. It wasn't obvious because he wasn't an angry man and he didn't use huge emotional appeals. But nearly every message said, "Here is something else you have done wrong and need to change. You aren't the kind of Christian you ought to be."

In itself, this is not necessarily a problem. All of us need to be challenged and corrected. But the preaching was seriously out of balance. There was little emphasis on what God had done for us. There was practically no loving encouragement or support. And there was very little practical emphasis on the grace of God. The end result of this was to make us feel guilty for our failures and responsible for doing better but essentially on our own to do it. I am convinced that many people are sitting under this type of ministry and experiencing rather strong feelings of failure or inadequacy without the hope, encouragement, and grace they need to change.

Some speakers have become masters at evoking guilt. They preach a strong message condemning a certain vice or lifestyle and then ask everybody who wants to "rededicate their life to the Lord" to stand up. If you are left sitting (even if you have never had a problem in that area and the Lord hasn't spoken to you) you can really feel awkward! There is the pressure of what others will think and the tendency to feel guilty if you aren't on your feet conforming to the pastor's wishes.

Other people stir up guilt by indirectly (or sometimes directly) implying that if you have different thoughts than the pastor, the church leader, or the Christian subculture, there must be something wrong with you. The high school biology student who starts wondering if evolution might be preferred over immediate creationism, the wife who is entertaining thoughts of separating from a husband who abuses her, or the person who questions "the way we've always done it" can very quickly come under the scornful eye of others in the church—particularly of leaders who want to carefully control their flock.

A friend told me of the anxiety he felt when he spoke out against building a recreation center for their church because he thought they should either be doing more for missions or erecting more Christian education space. His church supposedly operates on a democratic congregational system but after the pastor and board had decided they needed a recreation center, then told how the Lord had clearly led them and how the members now had to exercise faith, anybody who spoke in opposition was suspected of being unspiritual or uncooperative. And sure enough, as soon as he raised other options another member quickly stood up and essentially said, "I think we ought to trust our leaders and not ask questions." After the meeting several people told my friend they shared his opinions but were afraid to voice them. Their fears of rejection and guilt had kept them silent. Later, however the church had difficulty funding the building because many people did not see the need for it.

Another friend told me how in a church business meeting dealing with a deficit that was growing $5,000 to $10,000 monthly and could push the church near bankruptcy, a number of people, rather than being willing to cut expenses, simply accused those who suggested that option of lacking faith. In using these illustrations I am not attempting to take a position on church governmental processes or difficult issues of faith and works. I am attempting to illustrate, however, how leaders can use their influence to intimidate others out of fear or guilt to gain conformity.

Another common contributor to the development of guilt feelings is the implication some teachers and Christian workers communicate that there is only one way to be spiritually mature. We tell people if they will witness regularly, have devotions every morning, abstain from a few selected forms of entertainment or gratification, and practice one or more spiritual formulas they will experience joy in their Christian lives. And if they try all of our suggestions and find they do not work they are left with only one conclusion: they have failed again. Something is wrong with them. They are guilty.

Although well-intended, this style of preaching and teaching misses several important facts. It ignores the fact that people are very different. Some people couldn't read the funny papers or sports section for a half hour each morning, let alone the Bible! And some people, being extremely shy and socially withdrawn, find any social interaction difficult, let alone witnessing to a stranger. Yet we imply that everybody ought to do it our way and that if they don't, they should feel guilty. This approach to Christian living minimizes the process of growth in the Christian life and suggests that we should rather quickly reach a healthy spiritual plateau by following someone else's formula. Once again, this programs people to fail, holds out unrealistic expectations, and encourages guilt.

Since time doesn't allow us to try to track down all of the possible sources of guilt in preaching and teaching, I would like to move on to a look at why most of us find it easier to motivate others by guilt than by more constructive means. Then we will take a look at a biblical example of positive motivation and a few specific guidelines for avoiding guilt motivation.

THE DYNAMICS OF GUILT MOTIVATION

As we have seen in earlier chapters, guilt functions in our own lives both as a method of control and a means of punishment or atonement. In feeling guilty we are either trying to motivate ourselves to change or atoning for our failures. Since most of us at least occasionally motivate ourselves by guilt it is only natural that we do the same to others. And if we were motivated by guilt as children we will tend to motivate others the same way. Typically we initially try motivating people by encouragement or love, but if that doesn't work we turn to pressure, threats, or guilt. As parents, for example, if our children have ignored our past reminders, we may become furious and lash out saying, "I'm sick and tired of your irresponsibility. You *never* do *anything* we tell you." Or as teachers we may attack and scold our class for being disinterested, lazy, irresponsible, or spiritually immature.

Just as our own guilt feelings reflect our omnipotent, god-like desires to pressure ourselves into conformity with our ideals or atone when we fall short, so our guilt motivation of others reflects these same two dynamics. In motivating others by guilt we are either attempting to control people or to punish them for not conforming to our wishes. Underneath the attempt to motivate others by guilt, in other words, is the desire to be omnipotent or god-like in their lives. *We* want to motivate people to behave the way *we* want them to behave. And *we* want them to suffer feelings of guilt when they don't conform to *our* desires.

The child psychologist who shames his children in public and tells them, "You'll make me look like a fool!" or angrily asks, "What will people think?" and the pastor or building chairman who pressures the congregation with comments about their lack of faith or the poor testimony of their unfinished building, are both trying to coerce and control people through guilt. Typically these guilt motivators have not stopped to consider that (1) they have not trained their children well or (2) the new building was the pastor's dream and went beyond the people's needs and means and may be a reflection of his (or a few others') own pride. In other words, by making others feel guilty, they avoid looking at their own potential guilt! They also attempt to control others.

Frankly, some parents and leaders do not want to give up either control of others or their scapegoating. They (in a god-like fashion) want to control others' lives, pass out punishment when they can't control others, and avoid looking at their own failures. To stop motivating others by guilt would leave them feeling impotent, helpless, or guilty! How else could one motivate children or employees or parishioners to accomplish what we believe they should do? Motivating by love sounds like good theory but sometimes we are either unwilling or too impatient to see if it works. We may also be lacking a model of how to motivate through love.

A BIBLICAL EXAMPLE OF MOTIVATION

The last two chapters of Hebrews contain an excellent example of biblical motivation. Although the author clearly confronts his readers, he does not do it on the basis of guilt feelings. After taking ten chapters to point out the superiority of Christ to the law and warning any pseudo-believers that there is firm judgment for those outside of Christ, the author spends the entire eleventh chapter reciting many Old Testament examples of faith. He then begins chapter twelve with:

> *Therefore*, since we have so great a cloud of witnesses surrounding us, let us also lay aside every encumbrance, and the sin which so easily entangles us, and let us run with endurance the race that is set before us, *fixing our eyes on Jesus, the author and perfecter of faith*, who for the joy set before Him endured the cross, despising the shame, and has sat down at the right hand of the throne of God.[1]

[1]Heb. 12:1-2.

The challenge here is that in light of all that Christ has done for us and all that God has done for His saints of other ages, we mature and live godly lives. The "therefore" ties the coming challenge to everything the author has been teaching us. Then our attention is called to the fact that our eyes should be on Jesus, the author and finisher of our faith. We are not told to focus either on our failures or our successful efforts. Our sins are already atoned because of the Cross. Then in chapter 13, we are told to "love the brethren" (v. 1), "be hospitable" (v. 2), be sensitive to the "ill treated" (v. 3), avoid fornication (v. 4), and "be free from the love of money" (v. 5) *because* Christ has said, "I will never desert you, nor will I ever forsake you" (v. 5). After further challenges to sound doctrine we are reminded that Jesus died to "sanctify the people" (v. 12), that we are seeking "a city to come," (v. 14), and that God is pleased with our sacrifice of service (v. 16).

Not once in the entire challenge does the author attack or condemn his readers. And not once are they motivated by guilt. The entire appeal is based on what Christ has done, is doing, and will do for us. Then, the section concludes with the benediction:

> Now the God of peace, who brought up from the dead the great Shepherd of the sheep through the blood of the eternal covenant, even Jesus our Lord, equip you in every good thing to do His will, working in us that which is pleasing in His sight, through Jesus Christ, to whom be the glory forever and ever. Amen.[2]

Once again, the focus is on Christ. It is he who paid and who is working in us.

Although the topic of motivation in preaching is an extensive one that I certainly do not feel competent to write on fully, I would suggest several guidelines that can help pastors and others who teach and speak to avoid creating unnecessary guilt in our hearers.

1. Set realistic standards for parishioners.
2. Minister to meet the needs of the congregation.
3. Stress our position in Christ and what He has done for us.
4. Involve people in planning programs and projects.

[2]Heb. 13:20-21.

5. Balance conviction with encouragement and forgiveness.

6. Distinguish between God's firm but living correction of His children and the wrathful punishment those who reject Christ are under.

7. Do not scold or preach in anger but "Speak the truth in love."[3]

8. Evaluate our own attitudes as speakers to see that we are not attempting to manipulate our hearers.

9. Try to offer concrete steps to regular growth instead of vague formulas and challenges.

10. Model a humble acknowledgment of our own failures.

SUMMARY

Although the conservative church has stressed that the only way of finding acceptance by God for salvation is through Christ, we have sometimes implied that people must live up to certain standards to be fully accepted by themselves or by God on a daily basis. In fact, in motivating others by guilt, we undermine our parishioners' and children's belief that they are fully acceptable to God through Christ. Put differently, while teaching that we are saved by grace, we have sometimes taught (or at least lived as though) the grace of God is not enough to motivate us to be sanctified. Consequently we have resorted to fear and guilt to motivate our children and parishioners to change in order to avoid feelings of guilt and condemnation.

Only an application of the scriptural truth that we are once and for all acceptable to God through Christ and that our entire motivation for godly living must come as a response to his love will enable us to positively encourage others toward biblical maturity.

[3]Eph. 4:15.

Appendix 2: Development of the Pathological Conscience

One of the most perplexing questions for students of personality is why one person can be overwhelmed by the debilitating accusations of a guilty conscience while another (perhaps even from the same family!) engages in all sorts of antisocial or sinful behaviors without an apparent twinge of guilt. This appendix suggests key factors in the development of major malfunctions of conscience.

In part 4 we have discussed three sets of processes influencing the functioning of conscience and feelings of guilt. The first involves the formation of the child's ego ideal or the ideal self. The next has to do with the development of our corrective attitudes of guilt or constructive sorrow. And the final relates to the child's perceptual development and capacity for self-evaluation. An understanding of the interaction of environmental and intrinsic processes affecting these three sets enables us to understand why people have such different types of conscience and why some develop malfunctioning consciences.

THE NEUROTIC INHIBITING CONSCIENCE

All counselors and pastors are acquainted with individuals who are highly rigid, fearful, and constricted. These people are afraid of stepping out and trying new things. They are not spontaneous and sensitive emotionally. Their moral codes tend to be narrow and restricting. If they are Christians, they probably have a careful set of dos and don'ts that guide their behavior. People with these overly restrictive consciences have usually had problems in the development of their ideals and aspirations. Rather than growing up open to new experiences and willing to initiate and try new things, these people reached adulthood with an overly high value on conformity and control. This inhibitory style of life grows either from their own early goals and wishes, or from the expectations held out for them by parents and significant others.

When the parent-child relationship is characterized by conditional love and excessive pressure to conform to external guidelines, children who badly need parental love and acceptance are often willing to deny expression to many of their wishes and feelings in order to earn their parents' acceptance. When this happens children expend great amounts of energy becoming what their parents desire them to be. They work hard to be a top student, a good athlete, a dedicated Christian, or an extremely polite person so that they will merit their parents' approval. They also avoid activities and reactions that might merit parental disapproval. If these children's parents believed some form of entertainment was sinful they incorporated these prohibitions into their developing ideal. If the parents were strongly committed to a political ideology these children incorporated that into their ideals. And if the parents were ardent followers of a particular Christian belief or denomination the children included those commitments in their developing ideals.

Although parents should communicate values to children, problems come when we attempt to force values on our children (especially extrabiblical ones) in a way that leaves little room for them to think for themselves or in a way that ties our love to their conformity. A child's moral, religious, economic, political, and social beliefs can become so determined by the parents that they have little or no room left for creative expression or independent judgment.

Other persons suffering restrictive, inhibiting consciences are struggling not with the internalized standards of parents and other authorities but with their own potentially sinful wishes or goals. They may, for example, have strong lustful desires, which they fear will get out of control. In order to prevent this they learn to control every area of life and avoid close contact with the opposite sex or any situation that could conceivably trigger their lustful desires. Naturally this restricts their freedom. One young man I counseled would not allow himself to go to the beach because he believed the women there dressed "so indecently." Because he had not resolved his lustful thoughts he had to carefully limit his lifestyle to avoid any contact that might stir up the feelings. Consequently his concept of the type of person he should be took on a highly rigid and restrictive flavor. This person had a major conflict because his conscious ideals said he should not even be tempted (let alone give in!), but his unconscious was filled with sexual lust.

Similarly a person with feelings of bitterness or resentment may repress these feelings by developing a careful, controlled lifestyle. By becoming rigid and controlled, and perhaps nonfeeling, this type of person attempts to ward off feelings that are inconsistent with his or her personal ideals. Any number of other negative or sinful wishes may stimulate similar restrictions of conscience. Rather than facing our sinful tendencies, we try to push them from awareness and mold ourselves into the type of person who could not possibly (we hope!) fall prey to them. Unfortunately this repression both fails to resolve the problem and creates new ones. We are forced to develop a rigid, neurotic, and inhibiting conscience in order to ward off our forbidden desires. Although the biblical concept of a weak conscience is not necessarily the same thing as the inhibiting conscience it certainly has some close similarities (see 1 Cor. 8:7-12).

THE PUNITIVE CONSCIENCE

The punitive conscience is closely related to the restrictive, inhibiting one. Many people with rigid and inhibiting consciences also suffer from large measures of self-punitiveness. In much the same way, rigid and inhibiting ideals can grow either out of the person's own unacceptable wishes and goals or the unrealistic or inappropriate expectations of parents and others, so punitive guilt feelings can grow from either our own internal psychic processes or from the corrective attitudes of others. In this case the two most influential factors in the development of a punitive conscience are (1) the child's own feelings of resentment and hostility and, (2) punitive or rejecting parental attempts at correction.

In chapter 18 we saw how the anger and frustration that children experience when their wishes or needs are not fulfilled lead to punitive guilt emotions. The child becomes angry at his or her parents and consequently (through the mechanism of projection) assumes that his parents are equally angry at him. As he identifies with his parents' corrective attitudes, he takes them into his developing conscience not as the parents are in reality but as he perceives them. Because of this distortion, the harshness of the guilt emotions growing out of the punitive conscience is as much a result of the child's anger and frustration as it is of the parents' punitive treatment.

This internalization of projectively distorted anger is one source of the punitive conscience. The other factor is the actual degree of parental punitiveness. If parents lovingly and sensitively discipline their children, the children are likely to develop healthy, love-based corrective attitudes. But if parents correct in anger, subtly reject the children, or undermine their self-esteem, children are likely to develop a punitive, condemning conscience. One patient told me how her mother once drew a circle on the refrigerator door and told her she was going to put a black mark in it every time the daughter misbehaved. "If the circle ever gets filled," she said, "God won't love you anymore!"

The severest, or most punitive, conscience develops from the combination of actual parental punitiveness and projected hostility. In these cases the child's own projected anger is added to the parents' punitiveness to form severe and punitive attitudes of self-condemnation and rejection.

THE SOCIOPATHIC ABSENCE OF GUILT

Now we come to the person who appears to have an underdeveloped conscience, or sense of guilt. In contrast to those suffering punitive guilt or excessive inhibitions, these individuals engage in all sorts of sinful or antisocial activities with no apparent sense of guilt or regret. These individuals are typically described as having no guilt or as being without a conscience. Actually people whose moral functioning allows them to repeatedly engage in sinful or antisocial behavior are no more homogeneous than those with consciences that more effectively (or too effectively) inhibit. There are at least three distinct personality patterns that engage in so-called sociopathic or psychopathic activities. Unfortunately the current *Diagnostic and Statistical Manual of Mental Disorders*[1] does not clearly distinguish between the first two of these personalities. The previous manual[2] more helpfully differentiated between two types of sociopaths.

The first, *the dyssocial personality,* only appears to be lacking guilt or remorse. The reason he engages in antisocial acts is not the lack of guilt or constructive sorrow but his inadequate antisocial or sinful *ideals.* Quite often these individuals have been reared in a community (or by parents) where theft, violence, or some other type of criminal or sinful activity is entirely socially acceptable. A child may be taught to steal, for example, or a member of the Mafia may be taught to murder. They experience little or no guilt or constructive sorrow not because they lack feelings of love or loyalty (as in the case of the true antisocial or psychopathic personality), but rather, because they have the wrong standards.

In fact, individuals reared in subcultures or families with antisocial or unbiblical values may experience a great deal of guilt (or shame) when violating their subcultural standards. They may feel guilty or ashamed because they do *not* steal, or because they do *not* commit murder or some other crime. Their problem, in other words, is not the lack of guilt (or even constructive sorrow) but rather that their guilt is over the wrong things. Their problem is not a lack of proper corrective attitudes but wrong ideals. To a significant degree their environmental training seems to have dulled or repressed the law of God written on the heart.

The *psychopathic personality* truly does have an absence of both psychological guilt and constructive sorrow. This person has neither the loving controls of constructive sorrow nor the punitive, restrictive controls of psychological guilt. Although this person's ideals and standards may not be adequate, his fundamental disturbance is not his values or standards (as in the dyssocial personality) but rather the lack of any effective corrective attitudes (either guilt emotions or constructive sorrow). Fundamentally, the

[1]American Psychiatric Association, *Diagnostic and Statistical Manual of Mental Disorders,* 3rd ed. (Washington: APA, 1980).

[2]American Psychiatric Association, *Diagnostic and Statistical Manual of Mental Disorders* (Washington: APA, 1952).

disorder of the psychopathic conscience is the inability to love or be loved. The true psychopath cares little if at all for other people or their rights. Instead he uses or manipulates people for his own ends. People are not individuals to be respected. They are objects to be used. I believe this person most closely fits the biblical concept of a "seared conscience," and is referred to in Proverbs 30:20, "This is the way of an adulterous woman: She eats and wipes her mouth, and says, 'I have done no wrong.' "

Tracing down the causes of this type of conscience, we usually find a child who for some reason did not establish a loving relationship with his parents. Sometimes this failure comes because one or both parents were cruel and rejecting. Children who are severely beaten or mistreated, for example, may simply learn to shut off their positive emotions. Steeling themselves against the periodical rage or rejection of their parents by "not caring" they become superficially "hard," or "tough." They learn to fight for survival whatever the cost. Rather than passively receiving their parents' anger and internalizing those punitive corrective attitudes in the form of guilt and depression, these people deny their need for love, build a sturdy wall around themselves and ward off their needs to love and be loved. Maslow describes them this way:

> There are people who according to the best data available, have been starved for love in the earliest months of their lives and have simply lost forever the desire and the ability to give and to receive affection.[3]

This steeling of oneself against life and intimacy makes it practically impossible to develop either psychological guilt or constructive sorrow. Constructive sorrow can not develop since it is based on a love for others, which the psychopathic personality doesn't have. If he treats others well it is because he knows it is best for him to do so, not because it is best for others or because he cares.

Even psychological guilt fails to develop in the psychopath because of a lack of love. Without the desire to be loved by one's parents one has no motivation for taking in the parents' corrective attitudes. Since the budding psychopathic personality does not truly feel loved he has no reason to identify with his or her parents'

[3]A. Maslow, *Motivation and Personality* (New York: Harper, 1954), pp. 98-99.

values. Consequently, he develops his own idiosyncratic ego ideal whose primary ingredient is to do whatever he likes and to use people for whatever he wants as long as he does not get caught. Bandura and Walters for example, found that "... the fathers of the aggressive (antisocial) boys were typically hostile to and rejecting of, their sons, expressed little warmth for them, and had spent little time in affectionate interaction with them during the boys' childhood."[4]

Other individuals who seemingly lack both guilt and constructive sorrow are actually not sociopathic or psychopathic personalities. Since these individuals are frequently viewed (at least by lay persons) as psychopathic, I have labeled them "pseudo-psychopathic" personalities. Some of these personality types are actually psychotic instead of psychopathic. Although their actions may be blatantly psychopathic, their psychological structure is characterized not so much by the absence of guilt as by the perceptual distortions and thought disorders of the psychotic. Some mass murderers, especially those engaged in bizarre crimes and sadistic or cultic rituals are actually suffering from paranoid delusions or schizophrenic thought disorders. Their bizarre thought processes have allowed them to so distort reality that they have found ways of justifying even murder and torture. In instances like this, the presence or absence of guilt is secondary to psychotic processes and the lack of appropriate ideals or corrective attitudes is based on a broader dysfunction of the total personality that results in an inability to accurately judge either reality or the rights and needs of others.

A less obvious form of pseudopsychopathic conscience is found in individuals who periodically engage in sinful or antisocial ac-

---

[4] A. Bandura and R. H. Walters, *Adolescent Aggression* (New York: Ronald, 1959), p. 354. J. Knight writes, "A chief difficulty in the formation of conscience lies in the incapacity to effect a lasting identification and internalization of values of significant persons. One can assume that this is the result of the early loss of stable relationships with the parents, as well as the fact that the parents themselves offer most unsatisfactory figures for identification. Such situations as moving from one foster home to another, exposure to inconsistencies in discipline, and receiving serious physical maltreatment from a parent furnish the matrix for structural defects in the child's conscience" (J. Knight, *Conscience and Guilt* [New York: Appleton-Century-Crofts, 1969], pp. 131-32).

tions but who do not engage in bizarre or blatently criminal actions. These individuals may lie, drink excessively, use drugs, engage in a variety of adolescent-like rebellious activities and occasionally commit a real crime. The dynamic behind these actions (especially in the latter case) is not too *little* but too *much* guilt. These individuals have often been raised by parents who exerted a great deal of pressure and relied excessively on guilt motivation, punishment, and conditional acceptance. After living for years with pressure and guilt they entered late adolescence or early adulthood with strict and punitive consciences. At some point they either came under the influence of an alternative philosophy or began rebelling against their parental upbringing. In attempting to throw off the strictures of their childhood they rebelled against their guilt feelings by engaging in previously forbidden actions. Their apparent lack of guilt is actually only a conscious lack of guilt accompanied by antisocial or sinful behavior designed to proclaim their freedom from the punitive consciences they have had for years. Underneath they are still under sway of strong guilt feelings.[5]

SUMMARY

In this appendix I have attempted to pull together our understanding of the processes influencing the development of conscience in order to explain why people have different types of conscience. We can summarize the likely causes of the various malfunctions of conscience in the table in Figure 15.

[5]Donnelly, for example, postulates "that there is a sizable group of psychopaths who, rather than having a weak superego, have, indeed, a very strong one based upon identification with one parent with whom he maintains a very dependent and hostile relationship but from which he never secures gratification of his intense dependency needs" ("Aspects of the Psychodynamics of the Psychopath," *American Journal of Psychiatry*, vol. 120, no. 12, 1964, pp. 1149-54).

Figure 15

TYPE OF CONSCIENCE	CAUSES
Neurotic Inhibiting Conscience	1. Attempt to repress one's own sinful wishes because of one's exalted image of oneself that results in also repressing positive growth potential and spontaneity. 2. Unrealistic, rigid, or inappropriate expectations of parents or significant others.
Punitive Conscience	1. Child's own frustration and hostility is projected onto parents and reinternalized in the form of punitive guilt emotions. 2. Parents' actual punitiveness and rejecting attitudes are internalized in the form of punitive guilt emotions.
Sociopathic Conscience (Dyssocial Personality)	1. Internalized antisocial sinful goals, standards or aspirations. 2. Sinful, selfish desires.
Psychopathic Conscience	1. Lack of any enduring love relationships, which made it impossible to internalize positive ideals or develop either guilt emotions or constructive sorrow. 2. Frequently associated with a lack of parental controls and a great deal of resentment to parents and society. 3. Selfish desire to have one's own way.
Pseudopsychopathic Conscience	1. Psychotic personality structure with severe distortions of reality and an inability to love that lead to bizarre ideals and an absence of both constructive sorrow and psychological guilt. 2. Excessive punitive guilt, which is repressed and denied through sinful or antisocial behavior.

Reference List

Adams, J. *The Christian Counselor's Manual.* Grand Rapids: Baker, 1973.

Adams, J. *Competent to Counsel.* Nutley, N.J.: Presbyterian and Reformed, 1972 (1970).

Adams, J. *What about Nouthetic Counseling?* Grand Rapids: Baker, 1977.

Allen, R. & Spilka, B. "Committed and Consensual Religion: A Specification of Religion and Prejudice Relationships." *Journal for the Scientific Study of Religion,* 6, 1967, pp. 191-206.

Allison, C. F. *Guilt, Anger and God.* New York: Seabury, 1972.

Allport, G. *Becoming: Basic Considerations for a Psychology of Personality.* New Haven: Yale University Press, 1960.

American Psychiatric Association. *Diagnostic and Statistical Manual of Mental Disorders.* Washington: APA, 1952.

American Psychiatric Association. *Diagnostic and Statistical Manual of Mental Disorders,* third edition. Washington: APA, 1980.

Angyal, A. *Neurosis and Treatment: A Holistic Theory.* New York: John Wiley & Sons, 1965.

Ashbrook, J. "Paul Tillich Converses with Psychotherapists." *Journal of Religion and Health* 11(1), 1972, pp. 40-72.

Ausubel, D. *Ego Development and the Personality Disorders: A Developmental Approach to Psychopathology.* New York: Grune & Stratton, 1965.

Ausubel, D. *Ego Psychology and Mental Disorder: A Developmental Approach to Psychopathology,* D. Kirk, ed. New York: Grune & Stratton, 1977.

Bainton, R. *Here I Stand: A Life of Martin Luther.* New York: Mentor Books, 1955.

Baird, T. *Conscience.* Kilmarnock, Scotland: John Ritchie, n.d.

Bandura, A. *Social Learning Theory.* Englewood Cliffs, N.J.: Prentice Hall, 1977.

Bandura, A. & Walters, R. H. *Adolescent Aggression.* New York: Ronald, 1959.

Bandura, A. & Walters, R. H. *Social Learning and Personality Development.* New York: Holt, Rinehart, and Winston, 1963.

Barabas, S. "Conscience," in *Zondervan Pictorial Bible Dictionary,* M. Tenney, ed. Grand Rapids: Zondervan, 1963.

Barclay, W. *The Letters to Timothy, Titus and Philemon.* Philadelphia: Westminster, 1960.

Barnes, A. *Notes on the Acts of the Apostles.* Philadelphia: Westminster, 1960.

Barrett, C. *A Commentary on the Epistle to the Romans.* New York: Harper, 1958.

Bavinck, H. *Gereform Eerde Dogmatiek,* III. Kampen: J. H. Kok, 1898.

Becker, E. *The Denial of Death.* New York: The Free Press, 1973.

Belgum, D. *Guilt: Where Religion and Psychology Meet.* Minneapolis: Augsburg, 1970.

Bergin, A. "Psychotherapy and Religious Values." *Journal of Consulting and Clinical Psychology* 48, 1980, pp. 95-105.

Berkhof, L. *Systematic Theology.* Grand Rapids: Eerdmans, 1964.

Berkouwer, G. *Man: The Image of God.* Grand Rapids: Eerdmans, 1962.

Berkouwer, G. *Studies in Dogmatics: Sin.* Grand Rapids: Eerdmans, 1971.

Binswanger, L. *Being in the World: Selected Papers of Ludwig Binswanger.* J. Needleman, trans. New York: Harper and Row, 1968.

Bobgan, M. & Bobgan, D. *The Psychological Way/the Spiritual Way.* Minneapolis: Bethany Fellowship, 1979.

Bonhoeffer, D. *Creation and Fall.* New York: Macmillan, 1959.

Bonhoeffer, D. *Ethics.* New York: Macmillan, 1965.

Boss, M. *Psychoanalysis and Daseinsanalysis.* New York: Basic Books, 1963.

Brenner, C. *An Elementary Textbook of Psychoanalysis.* New York: International Universities Press, 1974.

Brenner, C. *An Elementary Textbook of Psychoanalysis.* Garden City: Anchor Press, 1965.

Bromiley, G. *The International Standard Bible Encyclopedia.* Grand Rapids: Eerdmans, 1978.

Brown, C. "Conscience," in C. Brown, ed. *The New International Dictionary of New Testament Theology,* Vol. 1. Grand Rapids: Zondervan, 1975.

Buber, M. *The Knowledge of Man.* London: George Allen & Unwin, 1965.

Calvin, J. *Commentaries on the Book of Genesis.* Vol. 1. Grand Rapids: Baker, 1979.

Calvin, J. *Institutes of the Christian Religion.* Vols. I and II. Grand Rapids: Eerdmans, 1953.

Carkhuff, R. & Truax, C. *Toward Effective Counseling and Psychotherapy.* New York: Aldine, 1967.

Carnell, E. *An Introduction to Christian Apologetics.* Grand Rapids: Eerdmans, 1948.

Carter, J. "Toward a Biblical Model of Counseling." *Journal of Psychology and Theology* 8(1), 1980, 45-52.

Carter, J. & Narramore, B. *Integration of Psychology and Theology: An Introduction.* Grand Rapids: Zondervan, 1979.

CBN Spiritual Life Division, *Counseling Handbook for Telephone and Personnel Ministry.* Virginia Beach: Christian Broadcasting Network, n.d.

Chesen, E. *Religion May be Hazardous to Your Health.* New York: Pater H. Wyden, 1972.

Cohu, J. *Vital Problems of Religion.* Edinburgh: T. & T. Clark, 1914.

Congdon, R. "The Doctrine of Conscience," *Bibliotheca Sacra,* 102, 1945, pp. 226-32 and 470-89.

Counts, W. & Narramore, B. *Freedom from Guilt.* Santa Ana: Harvest House, 1974.

Counts, W. *Called to be Free.* Old Tappan: Fleming H. Revell, 1980.

Crabb, L. *Effective Biblical Counseling.* Grand Rapids: Zondervan, 1977.

Cranfield, C. "A Critical and Exegetical Commentary on the Epistles to the Romans," in *The International Critical Commentary.* Edinburgh: T. & T. Clark, 1975.

Delitzsch, F. *Biblical Psychology.* Grand Rapids: Baker, 1977.

Dodd, C. H. *The Epistle of Paul to the Romans.* London: Holden and Stroughton, 1932.

Donnelly, J. "Aspects of the Psychodynamics of the Psychopath." *American Journal of Psychiatry* 120(12), 1964, pp. 1149-54.

Drakeford, J. *Integrity Therapy.* Nashville: Broadman, 1967.

Ellis, A. AAP Tape Library, Vol. 1. Ellis, A. "The Case against Religion." New York: Institute for Rational Living, n.d.

Ellis, A. AAP Tape Library, Vol. 1, "Loretta." New York: Institute for Rational Living, n.d.

Ellis, A. *Humanistic Psychotherapy.* New York: McGraw-Hill, 1974.

Ellis, A. *Reason and Emotion in Psychotherapy.* New York: Lyle Stuart, 1962.

Ellis, A. & Griegen, R. *Handbook of Rational Emotive Therapy.* New York: Springer, 1977.

Erdman, C. *The Pastoral Epistles of Paul.* Philadelphia: Westminster, 1925.

Erikson, E. *Young Man Luther: A Study in Psychoanalysis and History.* New York: W. W. Norton, 1962.

Fenichel, O. *The Psychoanalytic Theory of Neurosis.* New York: W. W. Norton, 1945.

Fiedler, F. "The Concept of an Ideal Therapeutic Relationship." *Journal of Consulting Psychology,* 14, 1950, pp. 239-45.

Fleck, R.; Ballard, S.; Reilly, J. "Development of Religious Concepts and Maturity: A Three-stage Model," *Journal of Psychology and Theology,* 3(3), 1975, pp. 156-63.

Frank, J. "The Present Status of Outcome Studies." *Journal of Consulting and Clinical Psychology,* 47(2), 1979, pp. 310-16.

Freud, A. *The Ego and the Mechanisms of Defense.* New York: International Universities Press, 1966.

Freud, S. "Civilization and its Discontents." *The Standard Edition of the Complete Psychological Works of Sigmund Freud.* J. Strachery, trans. London: Hogarth, 1961. Vol. XXI, pp. 9-145.

Freud, S. *The Ego and the Id.* New York: W. W. Norton, 1962.

Freud, S. "The Future of an Illusion." *The Standard Edition of the Complete Works of Sigmund Freud.* J. Strachery, trans. London: Hogarth, 1961. Vol. XXI, pp. 1-162.

Freud, S. "Moses and Monotheism." *The Standard Edition of the Complete Psychological Works of Sigmund Freud.* J. Strachery, trans. London: Hogarth, 1961. Vol. XXI, pp. 3-137.

Freud, S. *New Introductory Lectures on Psychoanalysis.* J. Strachery, trans. New York: W. W. Norton, 1965.

Freud, S. *Standard Edition of the Complete Works of Sigmund Freud,* J. Strachery, trans. London: Hogarth Press, 1961, Vol. 18, p. 252.

Freud, S. "Totem and Taboo." *The Standard Edition of the Complete Psychological Works of Sigmund Freud.* J. Strachery, trans. London: Hogarth, 1961. Vol. XXI, pp. 1-162.

Fromm, E. *Anatomy of Human Destructiveness.* New York: Holt, Rinehart, and Winston, 1973.

Fromm, E. *Escape from Freedom.* New York: Rinehart, 1941.

Fromm, E. *The Heart of Man.* New York: Harper & Row, 1964.

Fromm, E. *Man for Himself: An Inquiry into the Psychology of Ethics.* New York: Rinehart, 1947.

Fromm, E. *Marχ's Concept of Man.* New York: Frederic Ingar, 1961.

Fromm, E. *Psychoanalysis and Religion.* New Haven: Yale University Press, 1956.

Fromm, E. *Socialist Humanism: An International Symposium.* Garden City: Doubleday, 1965.

Fromm, E. *You Shall be as Gods.* New York: Holt, Rinehart, and Winston, 1966.

Geis, H. *Guilt Feelings and Inferiority Feelings: An Experimental Comparison.* Ann Arbor: University Microfilms, 1965.

Glasser, W. *Reality Therapy.* New York: Harper & Row, 1965.

Godet, F. *Commentary on Romans.* Grand Rapids: Kregel, 1977.

Gordon, M. "Regeneration," in *The New Bible Dictionary.* J. D. Douglas, ed. Grand Rapids: Eerdmans, 1962.

Greenson, R. *The Theory and Practice of Psychoanalysis.* New York: International Universities Press, 1967.

Guntrip, H. *Personality Structure and Human Interaction.* New York: International Universities Press, 1961.

Haigh, G. "Existential Guilt: Neurotic and Real." *Review of Existential Psychology and Psychiatry* 1, 1961, pp. 120-30.

Hallesby, E. *Conscience.* London: Inter-Varsity, 1962.

Hammes, J. *Humanistic Psychology: A Christian Interpretation.* New York: Greene, 1971.

Harris, B. "ΣΥΝΕΙΔΗΣΙΣ (Conscience) in the Pauline Writings." *Westminster Theological Journal* 24 (May 1962): 173-86.

Henry, C. *Christian Personal Ethics.* Grand Rapids: Eerdmans, 1957.

Hession, R. *The Calvary Road.* Fort Washington: Christian Literature Crusade, 1964.

Hodge, C. *Commentary on the Epistle to the Romans.* Grand Rapids: Eerdmans, 1950.

Hodge, C. *Commentary on the First Epistle to the Corinthians.* Grand Rapids: Eerdmans, 1976 (reprint).

Hoffman, J. *Ethical Confrontation in Counseling*. Chicago: The University of Chicago Press, 1979.

Horney, K. *Neurosis and Human Growth*. New York: W. W. Norton, 1950.

Hulme, W. *Counseling and Theology*. Philadelphia: Fortress 1967.

Hulme, W. *The Dynamics of Sanctification*. Minneapolis, Augsburg, 1966.

Jacobson, E. *The Self and the Object World*. New York: International Universities Press, 1964.

Jamieson, R.; Fausset, A.; & Brown, D. *Commentary on the Whole Bible*. Grand Rapids: Zondervan, 1961.

Johnson, R.; Ackerman, M.; and Frank, H. "Resistance to Temptation, Guilt Following Yielding and Psychopathology." *Journal of Consulting and Clinical Psychology* 32(2), 1965, pp. 169-75.

Jones, R. *A Factorial Measure of Ellis' Irrational Belief Systems with Personality and Maladjustment Correlated*. Wichita: Test Systems Inc., 1968.

Jourard, S. *Personal Adjustment*. New York: Macmillan, 1963.

Jourard, S. *Personality Theories: A Comparative Analysis*. Homewerd, Ill.: Dorsey, 1972.

Justice, W. *Guilt: The Source and the Solution*. Wheaton: Tyndale, 1981.

Kernberg, O. *Object-relations Theory and Clinical Psychoanalysis*. New York: Jason Arenson, 1976.

Knight, J. *Conscience and Guilt*. New York: Appleton-Century-Crofts, 1969.

Kohlberg, L. "Development of Moral Character and Moral Ideology." In M. L. Hoffman and L. W. Hoffman, eds. *Review of Child Development Research*. Vol. I. New York: Russell Sage Foundation, 1964, pp. 383-427.

Kohlberg, L. "Moral Stages and Moralization: The Cognitive Developmental Approach." In T. Lichone, *Moral Development and Moral Behavior*. New York: Holt, 1976.

Kohlberg, L. "Stage and Sequence: The Cognitive Developmental Approach to Socialization." In D. A. Goslin, ed. *Handbook of Socialization Theory and Research*. Chicago: Rand McNally, 1968, pp. 347-480.

Kohlberg, L. "Stages of Moral Development as a Basis for Education." In C. M. Beck, et al., eds. *Moral Education: Interdisciplinary*

Approaches. Toronto: University of Toronto Press, 1971.

Kuyper, A. E. *Voto,* III. Quoted in G. Berkouwer, *Man: The Image of God.* Grand Rapids: Eerdmans, 1962.

Lange, J. *Lange's Commentary on the Holy Scriptures,* Vol. 5. Grand Rapids: Zondervan, 1960.

Lehmann, P. *Ethics in a Christian Context.* New York: Harper & Row, 1963.

Lenski, R. *The Interpretation of St. Paul's Epistle to the Romans.* Minneapolis: Augsburg, 1961.

Lewis, H. *Shame and Guilt in Neurosis.* New York: International Universities Press, 1971.

Lloyd-Jones, M. *Romans: The Law: Its Functions and Limits.* Grand Rapids: Zondervan, 1974.

London, P. *Modes and Morals of Psychotherapy.* New York: Holt, Rinehart, and Winston, 1964.

Luther, M. *Commentary on Romans.* T. Mueller, trans. Grand Rapids: Kregel, 1976.

Lynd, H. *On Shame and the Search for Identity.* New York: Harcourt, Brace & World, 1958.

Maddi, S. *Personality Theories: A Comparative Analysis.* Homewerd, Illinois: Dorsey, 1972.

Maslow, A. *Motivation and Personality.* New York: Harper & Brothers, 1954.

Maslow, A. *Toward a Psychology of Being.* Princeton: D. Van Nostrand, 1962.

Maurer, C. "συνειδησις," in *Theological Dictionary of the New Testament,* Vol. 17, Gerhard Friedrich, ed. Geoffrey Bromiley, trans. Grand Rapids: Eerdmans, 1971.

McDonald, P. & McDonald, D. *Guilt Free.* New York: Grosset & Dunlap, 1977.

McGregor, G. H. "Conscience," *The Interpreter's Bible,* Vol. 2, G. H. Buttrick, et al., eds. New York: Abingdon-Cokesbury, 1951, p. 297.

McKenzie, J. *Guilt: Its Meaning and Significance.* New York: Abingdon, 1962.

McNulty, F. & Wakin, E. *Should You Ever Feel Guilty?* New York: Paulist Press, 1978.

Meehl, P., ed. *What, Then is Man?* St. Louis: Concordia, 1958.

Mosher, D. Sex, Guilt, and Premarital Sexual Experiences of College Students. *Journal of Consulting and Clinical Psychology* 36(1) (Feb. 1971): 7-32.

Mowrer, O. H. *The Crisis in Psychiatry and Religion*. New York: D. Van Nostrand Company, 1961.

Narramore, B. *You're Someone Special*. Grand Rapids: Zondervan, 1978.

Nelson, E., ed. *Conscience: Theological and Psychological Perspectives*. New York: Newman, 1973.

Oates, W. *Confessions of a Workaholic*, 1971.

Oden, T. *Agenda for Theology*. New York: Harper & Row, 1979.

Oden, T. *Kerygma and Counseling*. Philadelphia: Westminster, 1966.

Oden, T. *The Structure of Awareness*. Nashville: Abingdon, 1969.

Osborne, H. "Συνείδησις." *Journal of Theological Studies* 32 (April 1932).

Pattison, E. M. "Ego Morality: An Emerging Psychotherapeutic Concept." *Psychoanalytic Review* 55(2), 1968, pp. 187-222.

Pattison, M. "On the Failure to Forgive or to be Forgiven." *American Journal of Psychotherapy* 19, 1965, pp. 106-15.

Pierce, C. *Conscience in the New Testament*. London: SCM, 1955.

Piers, G. & Singer, M. *Shame and Guilt: A Psychoanalytic and Cultural Study*. New York: Norton, 1971.

Ramm, B. *The Christian View of Science and Scripture*. Grand Rapids: Eerdmans, 1954.

Rehioinkel, A. "Conscience." *Baker's Dictionary of Theology*. E. F. Harrison, ed. Grand Rapids: Baker, 1960.

Robinson, H. *The Christian Doctrine of Man*. Edinburgh: T. & T. Clark, 1958.

Rogers, C. *Client Centered Therapy*. Boston: Houghton Mifflin, 1965.

Schaeffer, F. *Death in the City*. Downers Grove: InterVarsity, 1969.

Schafer, R. *Aspects of Internalization*. New York: International Universities Press, 1968.

Schafer, R. "The Loving and Beloved Superego in Freud's Structural Theory." *The Psychoanalytic Study of the Child* 15, 1960, pp. 163-88.

The Seattle *Times*, "Guilty? Spray Away." December 27, 1980.

Segal, H. *Introduction to the Work of Melanie Klein*. New York: Basic Books, 1973.

Spitz, R. *The First Year of Life*. New York: International Universities Press, 1965.

Stein, E. *Guilt: Theory and Therapy*. Philadelphia: Westminster, 1968.

Stott, J. *Basic Christianity*. Grand Rapids: Eerdmans, 1971.

Strong, A. *Systematic Theology*. Old Tappan: Revell, 1907.

Strupp, H. *Psychotherapists in Action.* New York: Grune & Stratton, 1960.

Thieliche, H. *Theological Ethics.* W. Lazareth, ed. TDNT. Philadelphia: Fortress, 1966.

Thrall, M. *The First and Second Letters of Paul to the Corinthians.* Cambridge: Cambridge University Press, 1965.

Thrall, M. "The Pauline Use of ΣΥΝΕΙΔΗΣΙΣ," *New Testament Studies* 14, 1967-68, pp. 118-25.

Tournier, P. *Guilt and Grace.* New York: Harper & Row, 1962.

Truax, C. "Reinforcement and Nonreinforcement in Rogerian Psychotherapy." *Journal of Abnormal Psychology* 71(1), 1966, pp. 1-9.

Truax, C. & Carkhuff, R. *Toward Effective Counseling and Psychotherapy.* New York: Aldine, 1967.

Vitz, P. *Secular and Christian Moral Education: A Critique and a Proposal.* Unpublished manuscript.

Von Rad, G. *Genesis: A Commentary.* Philadelphia: Westminster, 1972.

Wagner, M. *The Sensation of Being Somebody.* Grand Rapids: Zondervan, 1976.

Wakin, E. & McNulty, F. *Should You Ever Feel Guilty?* New York: Paulist Press, 1978.

Walker, W. L. "Fear." *The International Standard Bible Encyclopedia.* James Orr, ed. Grand Rapids: Eerdmans, 1956, Vol. 2, p. 1102.

Winnicott, D. *Through Pediatrics to Psychoanalysis.* New York: Basic Books, 1975.

Wolberg, L. *The Technique of Psychotherapy.* 3rd edition. New York: Grune & Stratton, 1977.

Wuest, K. *Hebrews in the Greek New Testament.* Grand Rapids: Eerdmans, 1947.

General Index

Ackerman, M., 189
Adam and Eve, 29, 32, 57-66, 181
Adams, J., 26, 116, 121-23, 265-66
Allison, C., 17, 22, 39, 139
Allport, G., 105
Ambivalence, 239, 243-56
Anger, 37-39, 44-45, 71-72
Angyal, A., 250
Anxiety, 48-56, 60-65, 67-75. *See also* Fear.
Atonement
    Christ's, 201-2, 221-25. *See also* Justification.
    self, 146-47, 162, 221-23, 289-90
Ausubel, D., 27, 29, 111-12, 228
Authoritarian conscience. *See* Conscience, authoritarian.
Autonomy, 35, 58-60, 110-14, 172, 222

Baird, T., 190
Ballard, S., 60
Bandura, A., 135
Barabas, S., 184
Barclay, W., 208
Barnes, A., 208
Barrett, C., 197
Barth, K., 272
Bavinck, H., 192
Becker, E., 22
Bergin, A., 269-70
Berkhof, L., 151
Berkouwer, A., 192, 198

Binswanger, L., 100
Bonhoeffer, D., 62, 192, 221
Boss, M., 100, 106
Brenner, C., 26, 30, 50, 88
Bromiley, G., 158
Brown, C., 150, 186

Calvin, J., 61, 205, 221
Carkhuff, R., 257
Carnell, E., 25
Carter, J., 24, 97, 171-76
Chesen, E., 137
Cohu, J., 94
Compulsive personality. *See* Obsessive compulsive personality.
Condemnation, 15-16, 46, 142-44, 197, 199-202, 218, 223
Confession, 20, 28, 292
Congdon, R., 215
Conscience
    authoritarian, 102-3
    clear, 207-10, 214
    defiled. *See* seared.
    definition of, 186-90
    functions of, 195-217
    good. *See* clear.
    humanistic, 103-5
    inhibiting, 312-14
    in the New Testament, 216
    in the Old Testament, 185-86
    and law, 198-206